A Short Guide
to College Writing

Sylvan Barnet was born in Brooklyn, New York, and educated at Erasmus Hall High School, New York University (BA), and Harvard University (MA, PhD). For a while he was a semiprofessional magician, but when he found that he could fool all of the people all of the time the work became boring, and so he became a college professor. He taught composition and English literature at Tufts University for thirty years, published scholarly articles on Shakespeare, and is the author and coauthor of several books about the art of writing.

Pat Bellanca was born in East Hanover, New Jersey; she holds degrees in English from Wellesley College (BA) and Rutgers University (MA, PhD). She teaches in the Expository Writing Program at Harvard College and is Director of Writing Programs at the Harvard Extension School, the university's open-enrollment evening division. Her research interests include composition studies and Gothic fiction, fields that are not unrelated.

Marcia Stubbs was born in Newark, New Jersey, where she was drum majorette of Weequahic High School's band, and she was educated at Stanford University and the University of Michigan. She has taught at Tufts University, Harvard University, and Wellesley College, where she has directed the Writing Program. In addition to annotations on students' compositions, she has written poems and verse translations, and she is the coauthor of several books on writing.

A Short Guide to College Writing

THIRD EDITION

Sylvan Barnet
Tufts University

Pat Bellanca
Harvard University

Marcia Stubbs
Wellesley College

PENGUIN ACADEMICS

PEARSON
Longman

New York   San Francisco   Boston
London   Toronto   Sydney   Tokyo   Singapore   Madrid
Mexico City   Munich   Paris   Cape Town   Hong Kong   Montreal

Senior Vice President and Publisher: Joseph Opiela
Senior Sponsoring Editor: Virginia L. Blanford
Senior Marketing Manager: Sandra McGuire
Production Manager: Savoula Amanatidis
Project Coordination, Text Design, and Electronic Page Makeup:
    GGS Book Services
Cover Designer: John Callahan
Cover Image: Courtesy of Getty Images
Manufacturing Manager: Mary Fischer
Printer and Binder: R.R. Donnelley & Sons Company, Harrisonburg
Cover Printer: Phoenix Color Corporation

For permission to use copyrighted material, grateful acknowledgment is made
to the copyright holders on page 346, which are hereby made part of this
copyright page.

Library of Congress Cataloging-in-Publication Data
Barnet, Sylvan.
    A short guide to college writing / Sylvan Barnet, Pat Bellanca, Marcia
Stubbs. —3rd ed.
        p. cm.—(Penguin academics)
    Includes index.
    ISBN 0-321-45742-0
    1. English language—Rhetoric—Handbooks, manuals, etc. 2. Report
writing—Handbooks, manuals, etc. I. Bellanca, Pat. II. Stubbs, Marcia.
III. Title.

PE1408.B4315 2007
808'.042—dc22   2006025763

Please visit us at http://www.ablongman.com.

ISBN–13: 978-0-321-45742-4
ISBN–10:   0-321-45742-0

    4 5 6 7 8 9 10—DOH—10 09

Contents

PART THREE A WRITER'S HANDBOOK 241

Preface

A Short Guide to College Writing, Third Edition, offers students practical advice on writing successful college essays from the beginning of the process to the end. Students can turn to this book for matters large and small—about choosing a topic, developing a thesis, constructing a paragraph, documenting a source, and using a semicolon. The instructor can suggest chapters or passages that the student should consult in generating ideas, revising a draft, editing a revision, or preparing final copy. As in earlier editions of this book, we emphasize critical thinking, which is to say that we emphasize analysis, argument, and research because skill in these matters is central to college writing— whether the student is writing a brief essay for a required first-year composition course, a longer essay for an art history course, or even a term paper for a political science seminar.

When students write essays, most of what they write sets forth a thesis and its support, which is to say that their writing advances a point of view, explains ideas, and lets readers see how the writers arrived at them. Because they want to be believed, writers must present their ideas and evidence persuasively and cite and document their sources accurately. In this third edition of *A Short Guide to College Writing*, we provide even more help in these critical areas. We have emphasized throughout the link between critical thinking and strong writing, and we have stressed the reader's role as a collaborator in the writing process. We have added a brief discussion of visual rhetoric, focused on the analysis of advertisements, to Chapter 7, "Analyzing Texts." Chapter 8, "Persuading Readers," now includes essays by Alan Dershowitz and Philip Heymann on torture that represent opposing positions in an ongoing debate. A new chapter, "Writing Essay Examinations" (Chapter 11), offers practical advice on an important form of college writing, a form about which students generally receive little information or instruction. We have added more checklists and bulleted lists, and more Rules for Writers—a feature that instructors have told us that they find useful.

A Short Guide to College Writing, Third Edition, offers practical and accessible advice on all matters that concern student writers. The book will be useful not only to students in first-year composition courses but also to those in writing-intensive and writing-across-the-curriculum courses—courses that focus on a particular academic topic. We therefore omit writing assignments and extended readings. Where there is too much, the saying goes, something is missing. This book, we hope, offers just enough.

Acknowledgments

We thank the following reviewers for valuable suggestions that we have incorporated into this revision of the book: Karin Becker, Fort Lewis College; Dr. Linda Cullum, Kutztown University; Dr. Lynnell Edwards, University of Louisville; Catherine A. Henze, University of Wisconsin–Green Bay; Arden Jensen, Lee University; Kari Miller, Georgia Perimeter College; Arnold Wood, Jr., Florida Community College at Jacksonville, South.

We thank the following reviewers of the first and second editions for their suggestions: Alan Baragona, Virginia Military Institute; Kerry L. Ceszyk, University of Wyoming; Bruce Closser, Andrews University; Shawn Fullmer, Fort Lewis College; Gloria Gitlin, Baylor University; Lisa Justine Hernandez, St. Edwards University; Cheryl Hindrichs, The Ohio State University; J. Paul Johnson, Winona State University; Mary M. Juzwik, University of Wisconsin, Madison; Erika Kreger, San Jose State University; Joan Livingstone-Weber, Western Illinois University; Craig N. Owens, Indiana University; Amy Pawl, Washington University; Chere L. Peguesse, Valdosta State University; Roxanne Pisiak, SUNY–Morrisville; Rachana Sachdev, Susquehanna University; Mary Sauer, IUPUI, Indianapolis; Julianne Seenan, Bellevue Community College; and Von Underwood, Cameron University.

We are grateful to our colleagues at Person Longman—Senior Sponsoring Editor Virginia L. Blanford, Assistant Editor Rebecca Gilpin, Senior Managing Editor Patti Brecht, Production Manager Savoula Amanatidis, and Marketing Manager Sandra McGuire—and to Senior

Production Editor Doug Bell and Copy Editor Stephanie Magean at GGS Book Services for their collaboration on this edition.

Finally, we thank the following friends and colleagues for their advice and support: Marilyn Brown, Patricia A. Cahill, Jody Clineff, Michael Curley, Nancy Sommers, Kerry Walk, and Wini Wood.

SYLVAN BARNET
PAT BELLANCA
MARCIA STUBBS

A Short Guide
to College Writing

PART ONE

THE WRITING PROCESS

The Balloon of the Mind

Hands, do what you're bid:

Bring the balloon of the mind

That bellies and drags in the wind

Into its narrow shed.

—*William Butler Yeats*

CHAPTER ONE

DEVELOPING IDEAS

> All there is to writing is having ideas. To
> learn to write is to learn to have ideas.
>
> —*Robert Frost*

Starting

How to Write: Writing as a Physical Act

"One takes a piece of paper," William Carlos Williams wrote, "anything,
the flat of a shingle, slate, cardboard and with anything handy to the
purpose begins to put down the words after the desired expression in
mind." Good advice, from a writer who produced novels, plays, articles,
book reviews, an autobiography, a voluminous correspondence, and
more than twenty-five books of poetry, while raising a family, enjoying a
wide circle of friends, and practicing medicine in Rutherford, New
Jersey. Not the last word on writing (we have approximately 30,000 of
our own to add), but where we would like to begin: "One takes a piece
of paper . . . and . . . begins to put down the words. . . ."

Some Ideas About Ideas: Strategies for Invention

When asked to write an essay for a college course, students often have
one of two complaints: "I have nothing to say," or "I have the ideas but
I don't know how to express them." When we face a blank page, words
and ideas may elude us. We must actively seek them out. Since classical
times the term "invention," from the Latin *invenere* ("to come upon," or
"to find"), has been used to describe the active search for ideas.

Invention includes such activities as asking and answering questions, listing, clustering, and freewriting. In the following pages we'll briefly describe several invention strategies. All of these strategies have one step in common: starting to write by writing.

Asking Questions and Answering Them   One of the first things journalists learn to do in getting a story is to ask six questions:

- Who?
- What?
- When?
- Where?
- Why?
- How?

The questions that journalists ask are appropriate to their task: to report who did what to whom, and so on. Learning to write academic essays is largely learning to ask—and to answer—questions appropriate to academic disciplines.

Asking questions can be a useful strategy early in the writing process, especially for students who feel they don't have much to say about the material they've been asked to write about. That material, most often, will be a text of some kind: a written text (perhaps a treaty, or a judicial opinion, or a speech, or a poem), or some other object of interpretation (a film, painting, music video, even food on a plate). The first step in developing ideas about a text is to look closely at it. Asking questions and answering them is one way to focus your attention; it's also a way to begin finding things to say. Unexpected answers often emerge as soon as you raise a question.

In analyzing a visual text, for example, an art history student might ask and answer certain basic questions:

- When, where, and by whom was the work made?
- Where would the work originally have been seen? (Almost certainly *not* in a museum.)
- What purpose did the work serve?
- In what condition has the work survived?
- For whom was the work made?
- From what materials was it made?

Dorothea Lange, *Migrant Mother, Nipomo, California*, 1936. Gelatin-silver print. © Corbis.

Then, depending on the work, the student might pose more detailed questions. If, say, the work is a photograph (for example, Dorothea Lange's *Migrant Mother*, shown above), the following questions might be appropriate:

- What is the focus of the composition?
- What is the apparent distance between the viewer and the subjects?
- What is the mother's facial expression?
- How are the figures arranged?
- What's surprising or strange about the image?
- How might the subject have felt about being photographed?

A student in a sociology seminar writing a review of research on a topic would ask other kinds of questions about each study under review:

- What major question is posed in this study?
- What is its chief method of investigation?
- What mode of observation was employed, and is the mode limited in some way?
- How is the sample of observations defined, and is the sample representative?

A student in a literature class writing an analysis or exposition of a poem (for example, the Yeats poem on p. 1) would ask yet other kinds of questions:

- What is the poem about?
- What does the balloon represent?
- What is the speaker's tone?
- What does his tone reveal about his attitude toward the poem's subject?
- What makes this attitude complicated, tricky to pin down?

Students in all disciplines—art history, social science, and literature are given here only as examples—learn what questions matter by listening to lectures, participating in class discussions, and reading assigned books and articles. The questions differ from discipline to discipline, but the process—of asking and answering the questions that matter—is common to all of them.

Listing   Like asking questions and answering them, **listing** is a way to generate ideas; it can also help you pin down ideas that seem formless or vague. Listing is an especially useful strategy when you are making a comparison—of two figures in a photograph, for example, or two characters in a story, or two positions on an issue. Start writing by listing the similarities, and then list the differences. Or, start writing both lists at once, making brief entries, as they occur to you, in parallel columns.

Listing can help you generate and develop ideas; it can also help you to find a **topic** to write about. For instance, if for a course in ethics you are writing an essay on whether torture is ever acceptable— let's say to get information that will prevent a bomb from destroying a building and killing hundreds of persons—you might find yourself drawing up lists of pros and cons, in which you in effect argue with yourself.

Jot down a point, and then play the devil's advocate by jotting down the best arguments that can be made against it. You may then see the need to find better arguments for your position, or you may even come to shift sides.

Here are the first points one student listed in preparation for writing an essay about the use of torture.

Pro

1. Given a ticking bomb, surely everyone would agree that to save thousands of lives--to prevent another 9/11 for example--it would be acceptable to torture a person who knew of the plan and could reveal it in time to avert disaster.

2. The circumstances would have to be extreme, and the procedure would have to be authorized at a high level, by high-ranking judges or cabinet officers. Certain people would have to be held responsible; they couldn't just say that "circumstances required" or "we were only obeying orders." Because they would know that they would be held accountable, we can assume (a) they would authorize torture infrequently and (b) it would be as a last resort.

3. The issue--specifically, whether torture is an acceptable response to terrorism-- is immensely important,

Con

1. But *would* everyone agree? Someone might argue that there are things we do not do, under any circum- stances, and one of them is torture. Torture is something that we expect in dic- tatorships, NOT in a democracy.

2. Well, how extreme is extreme? Suppose only *one* life might be taken--a politician's, for example? Would it be OK to torture the person who--in our view--had the necessary information? And would Supreme Court judges, or cabinet members, accept responsibility for authorizing tor- ture? Maybe this whole business about a tick- ing bomb is a fantasy. Are there any cases when a person was apprehended with infor- mation that would have saved lives?

3. The "ticking bomb" isn't relevant here. In these cases no one was apprehended before the incident. And there are

and, given the disaster of 9/11, suicide bombings in Israel, and bombings in Madrid and London--it is not merely hypothetical; it is very real.

plenty of false reports about imminent danger. (After all certain officials believed that Iraq possessed weapons of mass destruction, but that wasn't true.) What if the authorities mistakenly tortured an innocent person? Is this how things are done in the land of freedom?

4. Wouldn't anyone today think it would have been perfectly acceptable to have assassinated Hitler in order to save countless lives that he later took?

4. The business about Hitler is off the point. We are talking about using torture to prevent future deaths, not about killing a guilty man.

In this case, the list provides more than a topic; the student who wrote the list above is now several steps closer to a draft of an essay she may actually be able to write.

Clustering   Although it takes a different visual form, **clustering** is similar to listing. Sometimes ideas don't seem to line up vertically one after another. Instead, they seem to form a cluster, with one idea or word or phrase related to a group of several others. It may be useful then to start by putting a key phrase or statement (usually a tentative thesis) in a circle in the center of the page, and then to jot down other phrases and sentences as they occur.

The example shown here concerns the issue of whether states ought to support gambling by sponsoring lotteries. It was sent to us, with the permission of the student, by a professor who teaches in Maryland, where the state has authorized a lottery. (The student has numbered the sequence of thoughts, and drawn arrows, which are helpful to us as readers but which normally are not part of the procedure.)

If you start writing by putting down phrases that occur to you in a map or cluster, it may help you to visualize the relationship between ideas. The visualization may also prompt still other ideas and connections between them.

Freewriting   One reason students have trouble getting words down on paper is that they mistakenly believe they must draft, revise, and edit their work simultaneously. In fact, however, these processes are separate, and the attempt to do them all at once can be paralyzing. **Freewriting** can help students who feel that they have ideas, but don't know how to get them on paper, because the strategy enables them to forget the rules for a while and just start writing.

To begin the process of freewriting, all you need to do is put your hands on a keyboard or pick up a pen or pencil and *start writing*. Forget about crafting the perfect introductory paragraph; don't worry about grammar or spelling or punctuation. If you can't think of the right word, write something close to it, or leave a blank space and move on. If you find yourself going in a direction you hadn't anticipated, keep writing anyway. Maybe there's something worth thinking about down the road— you won't know until you get there. If, for example, you're writing about why you disagree with one argument in the passage, a point on which you agree with the author may occur to you. Fine. Write it down now, while you're thinking of it. You can organize your points of agreement and disagreement later. Even if what you're thinking is something along the lines of "I hate this poem" (or photograph or whatever), put the thought down on paper and keep going. Why do you hate the poem? Is it confusing? Why? Does it appear to say two different things? What are they? Even an apparently unpromising line of thought can produce ideas. But if you reach what appears to be a dead end, simply move on, or start again someplace else. You are writing to discover what you think, and it's a good idea to work as quickly as you can. (Take Satchel Paige's advice: Don't look back; something might be gaining on you.)

Focusing

Critical Thinking: Subject, Topic, Thesis
So far, we've discussed several strategies for discovering and generating ideas. But to write a successful college essay, it's not enough simply to choose a **subject** and to generate ideas about it; you must also give those ideas focus, narrowing your area of interest to a **topic** within the

subject, a process you may already have begun as you followed one or more of the above invention strategies. And you must state your idea about that topic in the form of a **thesis,** an argument, a *point.*

To do all this, you must think critically about the ideas you have generated. You probably have already begun to refine your ideas as you followed one or more of the invention strategies above. Note, for example, that as our student listed reasons for torturing suspects, she was able also to generate an opposing list of arguments against torture. **Critical thinking** does not mean being negative. Rather, *critical* (deriving from the Greek word meaning "to separate," "to discern," "to choose") here means *analyzing, separating into parts.* Most important, critical thinking means adopting a skeptical view. When we think critically, we are skeptical not only of others' ideas but also of our own. Critical thinking thus entails three types of questioning:

- Questioning our own assumptions
- Questioning our own evidence and conclusions
- Questioning the implications of what we have read, heard, thought, or written

Finding a Topic Any assignment requires you to narrow the subject so that you can treat it thoroughly in the allotted space and time. Therefore you write not on political primaries (a subject), but on a specific proposal to abolish them (a topic); not on penguins (a subject), but on the male penguin's role in hatching (a topic). A good general rule in finding a topic is to follow your inclinations: Focus on something about the subject that interests you.

Suppose that for a religion course, your assignment is to read the Book of Ruth in the Hebrew Bible and to write an essay of 500 to 1000 words on it. If you start with a topic like "The Book of Ruth: A Charming Tale," you're in trouble. The topic is much too vague. In writing about it you'll find yourself hopping around from one place in the book to another, and in desperation saying things like "The Book of Ruth is probably one of the most charming tales in all literature," when you haven't read all literature, and couldn't define *charm* precisely, if your life depended on it.

What to do? Focus on something that interested you, or surprised you, or confused you about the book. (If you read the book with pencil in hand, taking some notes, underlining some passages, putting question marks at others, you'll have some good clues to start with.) The book is named after Ruth, but perhaps you find Naomi the more interesting character. If so, you might jot down: "Although the Book of Ruth is named after Ruth, I find the character of Naomi more interesting."

Stuck again? Ask yourself questions; **think critically.** *Why* do you find her more interesting? To answer that question, reread the book, focusing your attention on all the passages in which Naomi acts or speaks or is spoken of by others. Ruth's actions, you may find, are always clearly motivated by her love for Naomi. But Naomi's actions are more complex, more puzzling. If you're puzzled, trust your feeling—*there is something puzzling there. What* motivated Naomi? Convert your question to "Naomi's Motivation" and you have a *topic.*

"Naomi's Motivation" is a topic in literary criticism, but if your special interest is, for example, economics, or sociology, or law, your topic might be one of these:

Economic Motivation in the Book of Ruth

Attitudes Toward Intermarriage in the Book of Ruth

The Status of Women in the Book of Ruth

Any one of these topics might be managed in 500 to 1000 words. But remember, you were assigned to write on the Book of Ruth. Suppress the impulse to put everything you know about economics or intermarriage or the-status-of-women-through-the-ages in between two thin slices, an opening sentence and a concluding sentence, on the Book of Ruth.

Let's take another example. Suppose that in a course on modern revolutionary movements you're assigned a research essay on any subject covered by the readings or lectures. You're interested in Mexican history, and after a preliminary search you decide to focus on the Revolution of 1910 or some events leading up to it. Depending on what is available in your library, or what you find in an Internet search, you might narrow your topic to one of these:

Mexican Bandits: The First Twentieth-Century Revolutionists

The Exploits of Joaquin Murieta and Tiburcio Vasquez: Romantic Legend and Fact

In short, it is not enough to have a subject (the Book of Ruth, revolutions); you must concentrate your vision on a topic, a significant part of the field, just as a landscape painter or photographer selects a portion of the landscape and then focuses on it. Your interests are your most trustworthy guides to the portion of the landscape on which to focus. Thinking critically about your focus will enable you to refine it as you develop your **thesis** about it—as you make your topic your *own.*

Developing a Thesis   As you think about your topic and information relating to it, try to formulate a **tentative thesis.** This *tentative* thesis is a working hypothesis, a proposition to be proved, disproved, or revised in light of information you discover.

> ### A RULE FOR WRITERS
>
> A thesis ought to be a statement about which intelligent people *might disagree.*

Readers won't bother to finish reading an essay if its thesis is an obvious truth, such as:

> George Washington owned slaves.
>
> More men than women attend major league baseball games.

There's no particular reason to argue a point that everyone would agree on. The two theses just specified can of course be supported with evidence: the number of slaves Washington owned, or the number of men and women who attend major league games. Nevertheless, the theses themselves remain unarguable and uninteresting. They need to be developed, most likely after additional reading and thinking, into more debatable statements:

> Although Washington owned slaves, some evidence indicates that he believed slavery was an evil institution.
>
> The number of women who attend major league games has in the past decade slightly increased, probably because. . . .

Your "working thesis," which usually can be stated in a sentence or two, will help you to maintain your focus, to keep in mind the points that you must support with evidence: quotations, facts, statistics, reasons, descriptions, and illustrative anecdotes. But be prepared to modify your working thesis, perhaps more than once, and perhaps substantially. Your first draft might, for example, contain this tentative thesis:

```
Naomi's character is more interesting than Ruth's
because her behavior is more complicated.
```

That tentative thesis might be revised at a later stage:

```
Although Naomi's actions suggest her concern for her
daughter-in-law, they also reveal self-interest.
```

Note that both the working thesis and the revised thesis are *arguable*. One can imagine a reader *disagreeing* with either statement. "No," such a reader might say, "Naomi's behavior is *not* more complicated than Ruth's." Or: "I disagree—Naomi *is* concerned about her daughter-in-law; she's not self-interested at all." Once you begin amassing evidence to support your arguments, you may find to your surprise that the evidence supports a different thesis. Your best ideas on your topic may turn out to be radically different from the ideas with which you began. As we pointed out earlier, writing is not simply a way to express ideas you already have; it is also a way to discover new ones.

Another example: An early draft of an essay about Charlotte Perkins Gilman's late nineteenth-century story "The Yellow Wallpaper," about a woman who goes mad, might present the thesis that the story is about "the oppression of women." But a classroom discussion of the story and a very small amount of library or Internet research would soon reveal that many, many readers have reached the conclusion that the story is in some way about the oppression of women. Because almost everyone would agree with this point, it is no longer arguable. A stronger thesis, developed through careful attention to the text, might specify the nature of the "oppression" and its particular results. One might note that the narrator has just had a baby and that the husband (perhaps as a consequence) treats his wife as if she were a child. The thesis might then say: "The inherent conflict between the needs of the narrator's child and the expectations of her husband precipitates her eventual decline into madness." This point is more arguable and therefore more interesting than the idea that the story is about the oppression of women; one can imagine readers who might disagree with it by attributing the narrator's madness to other causes.

Although essays based on substantial analysis or research almost always include an explicit thesis sentence in the finished essay, short essays based on personal experience often do not. An essay recounting a writer's experience of racism, for example, or conveying the particular atmosphere of a neighborhood, is likely to have a central idea or focus, a **thesis idea,** rather than a **thesis sentence.** But whether stated or implied, the thesis idea must be developed (explained, supported, or proved) by evidence presented in the body of the essay. The kind of evidence will vary, of course, not only with your topic but also with your audience and purpose.

Developing Ideas

What constitutes evidence, and where does it come from? Writers explain, support, and develop their ideas with material derived from the reading, thinking, note-taking, questioning, and remembering that are part of the writing process from beginning to end. Materials for developing an essay on Naomi's motivation will be passages from the Book of Ruth, quotations that the writer introduces and explains. Materials for developing an essay on Dorothea Lange's photograph will include a detailed description of the figures, a discussion of their relation to each other, and perhaps some information about the photographer herself. In all of these instances, in fact, imagining a reader helps a writer develop ideas.

Thinking About Audience and Purpose:
The Reader as Collaborator

Thinking about your audience, about what you want your readers to understand and believe, is central to the revision process, which we discuss in Chapter 2. But thinking about audience and purpose can be helpful at earlier stages of writing too, when you are trying to develop an idea and to work up evidence to support it. If you are uncertain how to begin, or if, on the other hand, you are overwhelmed by the materials you have unearthed and don't know how to sort them out, try asking yourself these questions:

- Who are my readers?
- What do they need to know?
- What do I want them to believe?
- Why should they care about what I have to say?

When you ask, "Who is my reader?" the obvious answer—the teacher who assigned the essay—is, paradoxically, the least helpful. To learn to write well, you'll have to force that fact out of your mind, pretend it isn't true, or you're likely to feel defeated from the beginning. Write instead for an interested intelligent person who understands your material less well than you: a classmate, a roommate.

A RULE FOR WRITERS

When you write, you are the teacher. It's probably easier to assume the role of the teacher if you imagine your reader to be someone in your class—that is, someone intelligent and reasonably well informed who shares some of your interests but who does not happen to be you, and who therefore does not see the material in precisely the way you do. That reader can't know your thoughts unless you organize them and explain them clearly and thoroughly.

Writing academic essays usually requires examining and evaluating texts and other evidence beyond your personal experience or previous knowledge. Nevertheless, you still must trust your own ideas. Trusting your own ideas does not, of course, mean being satisfied with the first thought that pops into your head. Rather, it means respecting your ideas enough to examine them thoughtfully; it means testing, refining, and sometimes changing them. But it is always your reading of a text, your conduct of an experiment, your understanding of an issue that your essay attempts to communicate. If it does so, your reader will care—because you've brought new ideas, new insights, to the topic at hand.

Writing the Draft

If you have used one or more of the invention strategies we discuss above, and if you've begun to develop a focus on a topic within your larger subject, you should at this point have some sense of what your essay will be about. Now is the time to start writing the draft. How to begin?

1. Sit down and start writing. If you have the ideas but don't know how to express them, start writing anyway. Resist the temptation to check your e-mail, to make a cup of soup, to call your mother. Now is *not* the time to do your laundry or to make your bed. Sit down and start putting one word after another.

2. Start with something easy. Start anywhere. Start with what comes to mind first. For example, you might start by summarizing the passage you're responding to or by sketching any one of your ideas about it. *Don't think you must start with an introductory paragraph;* you can write an introduction later, once your ideas have become better defined. It doesn't matter where you begin, only that you do begin. Start anywhere, and keep going.

3. Try freewriting. Just write. Pick up a pen, grab a pencil, or put your hands on the keyboard; think about the material you've chosen to write about, and write what you're thinking. Don't worry about spelling or punctuation or grammar; don't censor yourself. No one but you will see what you've written. Your goal here is simply to put words on paper; you can evaluate them later.

4. Plan to stop writing. Give yourself a time limit. If you tend to procrastinate, try keeping your first sessions short. Promise yourself that you'll stop working after, say, twenty minutes, and *keep that promise.* If at the start you limit your writing sessions, you accomplish two things. You reduce anxiety: The thought of working at your desk for twenty minutes is not nearly as daunting as the thought of writing four or five pages. And after twenty minutes you'll have *something* down on paper. You can gradually increase the length of the sessions—to an hour, or three, or whatever is reasonable, given the assignment and your schedule.

5. Revise later. After a few false starts and probably more than one session, your ideas will begin to take form on the page. But at this early stage, don't expect them to appear in final form, beautifully organized and in polished sentences. Ideas rarely exist that way in one's mind. In fact, until we put them into words, ideas are usually only rough impressions or images, not clear thoughts at all. (As E. M. Forster wrote, "How do I know what I think until I see what I say?") Once you do get some ideas down on paper, you can begin to see which ones must be developed or deleted, where connections need to be made, where examples need to be added. At this stage, you may be close to having a first draft. Whether or not you like what you've written, take a rest from it. Do something else: Make your bed, or if you like, just climb into it.

CHAPTER TWO

DRAFTING AND REVISING

> I have never thought of myself as a good
> writer. Anyone who wants reassurance of
> that should read one of my first drafts. But
> I'm one of the world's great revisers.
>
> —*James Michener*

Reading Drafts

In Chapter 1, we focused on how to have ideas and how to get them down on paper. From the start of a project, the writer is almost simultaneously both inventing ideas and refining them. But we also advised that, particularly at the start, it's best to suspend critical judgment until you have begun to capture your thoughts, however roughly expressed, on paper. In this chapter, we will focus on ways to improve and refine rough drafts. We want to begin by making what may seem like an obvious point: To improve the draft you have written, *you must first read it*. Moreover, you must try to read it objectively and critically.

Imagining Your Audience and Asking Questions
To read your draft objectively, to make sure that you have said what you intended to say, put it aside for a day, or at least for a couple of hours. Then read it through, as if you were not the writer, but someone reading it for the first time.

> **A RULE FOR WRITERS**
>
> Be sure to read at least one hard copy draft of your essay; don't plan to do all of your revising on the computer screen. The change in form will give you a fresh perspective—the reader's perspective—on what you have written.

As you read, try to imagine the questions such a reader might ask you about what you have written. Then, read your draft again, asking yourself the following questions:

1. Does the draft present an idea? Does it have a focus or make a unified point?
2. Is the idea or are the ideas clearly supported? Is there convincing evidence? Are there sufficient specific details?
3. Is the material effectively organized?

There are many other questions you might ask as you think critically about what you've written, and we'll suggest some before we're done. But let's start with these.

1. Does the draft present an idea? Does it have a focus or make a unified point? Let's first consider the rare case: If on reading your draft objectively, you find that it doesn't present an idea, a point to develop, then there's probably no reason to tinker with it. It may be better to start again, using the invention techniques we discussed earlier. (Rereading the assignment is probably a good idea too.)

Almost surely, however, you will find some interesting material in your draft, but you won't yet be sure what it adds up to. The chances are that some extraneous material is getting in your way—some false starts, needless repetition, or interesting but irrelevant information. Some pruning is probably in order.

Picasso said that in painting a picture he advanced by a series of destructions. A story about a sculptor makes a similar point. When asked how he had made such a lifelike image of an elephant from a block of wood, the sculptor answered, "Well, I just knocked off everything that didn't look like elephant." Often, revising a draft begins with similar "destructions." Having identified your main point, don't be afraid to hack away competing material until you can see that point clearly in its bold outline. Of course, you must have a lot of stuff on paper to begin with. (At the start, nothing succeeds like excess.) But often you must remove some of it before you can see that you have in fact roughly formulated the main point you want to make, and even produced some evidence to support it.

2. Is the idea or are the ideas clearly supported? Is there convincing evidence? Are there sufficient specific details? Writers are always reluctant to delete. Students with an assignment to write 500 or 1000 words by a deadline are, understandably, among the most reluctant. But, almost certainly, once you have settled on the focus of your essay, you will be adding material as well as deleting it. It isn't enough simply to state a point; you must also prove or demonstrate it.

If you argue, for example, that smoking should be banned in all public places, including parks and outdoor cafes, you must offer reasons for your position and also meet possible objections with counterarguments. If you are arguing that in Plato's *Apology*, Socrates' definition of truth goes beyond mere correspondence to fact, you will need to summarize relevant passages of the *Apology* and introduce quotations illuminating Socrates' definition. Almost all drafts need the addition of specific details and examples to support and clarify generalizations.

3. Is the material effectively organized? As you prune away the irrelevancies and add the specific details and examples that will clarify and strengthen your point, as your draft begins more and more to "look like an elephant," ask yourself if the parts of your draft are arranged in the best order.

- If you have given two examples, or stated three reasons, with which one is it best to begin?
- Are paragraphs presented in a reasonable sequence?
- Will the relationship of one point to the next be clear to your reader?
- Does the evidence in each paragraph support the point of that paragraph? (The same evidence may be more appropriate to a different paragraph.)
- Does your opening paragraph provide the reader with a focus? Or, if the paragraph performs some other important function, such as getting the reader's attention, does the essay provide the reader with a focus soon enough?

In general, when working on the organization of drafts, follow two rules:

- Put together what belongs together.
- Put yourself in the position of your reader; make it as easy as possible for the reader to follow you.

A RULE FOR WRITERS

Whether or not you write an outline before drafting your essay, you should consider outlining your final draft to see (1) if it is organized, and (2) if the organization will be evident to the reader.

Peer Review: The Benefits of Having a Real Audience

Occasionally a writing assignment will specify the reader you should address. More often, your reader must be imagined. As we note in Chapter 1, you should imagine an intelligent reader who knows the material less well than you do, someone who has not thought about your topic or considered the specific evidence you intend to examine.

In many writing classes, students routinely break up into small groups to read and discuss each other's work. **Peer review,** as this practice is commonly called, is useful in several ways.

Peer review gives the writer a real audience, readers who can point to what puzzles or pleases them, who ask questions and make suggestions, who may often disagree (with the writer or with each other), and who frequently, though not willfully, misread. Though writers don't necessarily like everything they hear, reading and discussing their work with others almost always gives them a fresh perspective on their work. (Having your intentions misread, because your writing isn't clear enough, can be particularly stimulating.)

Moreover, when students write drafts that will be commented on, they are doing what professional writers do. Like journalists, scholars, engineers, lawyers—anyone whose work is ordinarily reviewed many times, by friends and spouses, by colleagues, and by editors, before the work is published—students who write drafts for peer review know they will have a chance to discuss their writing with their colleagues (other students) before submitting a final version for evaluation. Writers accustomed to writing for a real audience are able, to some extent, to internalize the demands of a real audience. Even as they work on early drafts, they are sensitive to what needs to be added, or deleted, or clarified. Students who discuss their work with other students derive similar benefits. They are likely to write and revise with more confidence, and more energy.

The writer whose work is being reviewed is not the sole beneficiary. When students regularly serve as readers for each other, they become better readers of their own work, and consequently better revisers. *Learning to write is in large measure learning to read.*

Peer review in the classroom takes many forms; we'll look in a moment at an example as we trace a student's essay that is revised largely as a result of peer review. But even if peer review is not part of your writing class, you may want to work with a friend or another student in the class, reading each other's drafts.

When you work on your essay with your classmates or your friends, good manners and academic practice require that you thank them for their help, that you **document** their contributions. You can offer a sentence or two of general thanks at the end of the essay—something like this:

> I'd like to thank the members of my peer revision group, Rebecca Sharp and Isabella Thorpe, for helping me to clarify the main idea of my essay and for suggesting ways to edit my sentences.

Or you can thank your peer reviewers for their specific contributions by inserting a footnote or endnote at the end of the sentence that contains an idea or words you wish to acknowledge, and then writing a sentence like this:

> Kevin Doughten drew my attention to the narrator's play on words here; I wish to thank him for helping me develop this point.

A RULE FOR WRITERS

Be sure to document the contributions of your peer readers and editors.

From Assignment to Essay: A Case History

On September 12, Suki Hudson was given the following assignment:

> Write an essay (roughly 500 words) defining racism or narrating an experience in which you were either the victim or the perpetrator of a racist incident. Your essay should offer a thesis supported by evidence from your experience. Bring a first draft with two copies to class on September 16 for peer review. Revised essay due September 26.

Suki kept no record of her first thoughts and jottings on the topic, but what follows is an early attempt to get something down on paper. Because it was far from the finished essay she would write, not yet even a first draft, we label it a Zero Draft:

Zero Draft. Sept. 13

It was a warm sunny day in the playground. My three-
year-old brother and other children were playing gaily
until one of the boys' mothers interrupted. She called
her son, whispered something, and when he went back to
the playground he excluded my brother from playing
together. I didn't know what to call the incident,
but my heart ached as I watched my little brother
enviously looked at the other kids. I immediately left
the playground with him, and the playground has never
been the same since that day.

At that point, having reached the end of the anecdote, Suki stopped. What she had written was not yet an essay, and it was far short of the suggested 500 words, but it was a start, which is all she had hoped to accomplish on this first try.

Later she read what she had written, and asked a friend to read it and see if he had any suggestions. It was a frustrating conversation. The friend didn't understand why Suki thought this was a "racist incident." Why did Suki leave the playground? Why hadn't she just asked the boy's mother for an explanation? The questions took her by surprise; she felt annoyed, then miserable. So she changed the subject.

But "the subject" didn't go away. Still later, she wrote the following account of the conversation in her journal:

Sept. 13

I asked J to read my paper and he thought I was
being paranoid. Why didn't I just ask the boy's
mother what was the matter? But I could not have
even thought of going up to the woman to question her
motives. It was beyond my control if she wanted to
be ignorant and cruel to a different race. (Or was
it really my ignorance to walk away from a simple
explanation?)

The following day, looking over what she had written, it occurred to her to try adding the journal entry to the anecdote. Maybe in a concluding paragraph she could explain why what happened in the playground was obviously a racist incident.

Here is the conclusion:

Sept. 14

Most people in modern society don't recognize the more subtle cases of racism. People feel if they are not assaulting physically they are not violating the law, and as long as they are living according to the law, racism is not committed. However, the law or the constitution does not protect the human heart from getting hurt, and without a doubt the most critical racist action could be committed by close friends or their loved ones.

But having written that last line Suki was struck by something odd about it. The woman in the playground was not a loved one, nor was she a close friend. Still, it was true that racist acts can be committed by friends, and even if the acts are undramatic, they should be recognized as racist acts. At this point, she thought that she had a thesis for her essay, but she also realized that she had begun to recall a different experience. Starting again, she wrote the following account:

In Korea, I had a very close friend whose father was Chinese. Although her mother was a Korean woman, they were treated as foreign people in town, and they were singled out on many occasions. Her father died when she was little but everyone in town knew she was a half Chinese. Her mother ran a Chinese restaurant, and they lived very quietly. My family knew her mother well and I was close friends with the girl and for many years I was the only friend she ever had. However, as I entered junior high school my new group of friends didn't approve of her background, and I drifted away from her. She was a very quiet, shy person and although I stopped calling or visiting her, she always remembered me on holidays to send presents. After graduating from junior high school she went to Taiwan to live with her grand-parents, whom she had never met. I gathered she could

```
not stand the isolation any longer at her age. Many
years later I realized how cruel I have been to her,
and I tried to locate her without success.
```

The following day Suki combined the two drafts (hoping to come closer to the 500 words), added a new concluding paragraph, and (rather disgusted with the whole assignment) typed up her first draft to hand in the next day. She photocopied it, as instructed, for peer review in class.

Peer review in the classroom takes many forms. Ordinarily, the instructor distributes some questions to be answered by both the writer

Questions for Peer Review   Writing 125R

Read each draft once, quickly. Then read it again, with the following questions in mind:

1. What is the essay's topic? Is it one of the assigned topics, or a variation from it? Does the draft show promise of fulfilling the assignment?

2. Looking at the essay as a whole, what thesis (main idea) is stated or implied? If stated, where is it stated? If implied, try to state it in your own words.

3. Looking at each paragraph separately:
   • What is the basic point (the topic sentence or idea)? How does the paragraph relate to the essay's main idea or to the previous paragraph?
   • Is each sentence clearly related to the previous sentence?
   • Is the paragraph adequately developed? Are there sufficient specific details or examples?
   • Is the transition from one paragraph to the next clear?

4. Look again at the introductory paragraph. Does it focus your attention on the main point of the essay? If not, does it effectively serve some other purpose? Does the opening sentence interest you in the essay? Do you want to keep reading?

5. Is the conclusion clear? Is the last sentence satisfying?

6. Does the essay have a title? Is it interesting? Informative?

7. What is the greatest strength of the essay? What is its main weakness?

8. What is the most important piece of advice you would offer on this essay?

and the readers. Typically the writer is asked to speak first, explaining how far along he or she is in writing the essay, and what help readers might give. The writer might also be asked, "What are you most pleased with in your writing so far?"

Readers are then asked to respond. Instructions may vary, depending on the particular assignment, but the questions distributed in Suki's class, on previous page, are fairly typical.

First Draft   What follows is first the draft Suki gave the two members of her group, and then a summary of the group's discussion. Before reading her draft aloud (the procedure the instructor recommended for this session), Suki explained how she had happened to narrate two experiences and asked which narrative she should keep, or if she could keep both.

First Draft

S. Hudson

Sept. 16

1   It was a warm sunny day in the playground. My three-year-old brother and other children were playing gaily until one of the boys' mothers interrupted. She called her son to whisper something and when he went back to the playground he excluded my brother from playing together. I didn't know what to call the incident, but my heart ached as I watched my little brother enviously looked at other kids. I immediately left the playground with him, and the playground has never been the same since that day.

2   A friend of mine said I was being paranoid. It would have been appropriate to ask the boy's mother what was the matter, or if she had anything to do with the kids excluding my brother from playing. But I could not have even thought of going up to the woman to question her motives. It was beyond my control if she wanted to be ignorant and cruel to a different race, or perhaps my ignorance to walk away from a simple explanation.

3   Most people in modern society recognize only the dramatic instances of racism, and on a daily basis

people don't recognize the more subtle cases of racism. People feel if they are not assaulting physically they are not violating the law, and as long as they are living according to the law, the racism is not committed. However, the law or the constitution does not protect the human heart from getting hurt, and without a doubt the most critical racist action could be committed by close friends or their loved ones.

4   In Korea, I had a very close friend whose father was Chinese. Although her mother was a Korean woman they were treated as foreign people in town, and they were singled out on many occasions. Her father died when she was little, but everyone in town knew she was a half Chinese. Her mother ran a Chinese restaurant, and they lived very quietly. My family knew her mother well and I was close friends with the girl and for many years I was the only friend she ever had. However, as I entered junior high school my new group of friends didn't approve of her background and I drifted away from her. She was a very quiet, shy person, and although I stopped calling or visiting her, she always remembered me on holidays to send presents. After graduating from junior high school she went to Taiwan to live with her grandparents whom she had never met. I gathered she could not stand the isolation any longer at her age. Many years later, I realized how cruel I have been to her, and I tried to locate her without success.

5   She was a victim in a homogeneous society, and had to experience the pain she did not deserve. It is part of human nature to resent the unknown, and sometimes people become racist to cover their fears or ignorance.

Summary of Peer Group Discussion

1. The group immediately understood why the friend (in the second paragraph) had difficulty understanding that the first incident was racist. It might well have been racist, but, they pointed out, Suki had said nothing about the racial mix at the playground. It does become clear by the fourth paragraph that the writer and her brother are

Korean, but we don't get this information early enough, and we know nothing of the race of the woman who whispers to her son. Suki had neglected to say—because it was so perfectly obvious to her—that she and her brother were Korean; the mother, the other child, in fact all others in the playground, were Caucasian.

A RULE FOR WRITERS

Keep your readers in mind as you revise.

2. Suki's readers confirmed her uneasiness about the third paragraph. They found it confusing for several reasons: (a) Suki had written "people don't recognize the more subtle cases of racism." Did she mean that the mother didn't recognize her action as racist, or that Suki didn't? (b) In the first paragraph Suki had written "I didn't know what to call the incident." But then the second paragraph is contradictory. There she seems to accuse the mother of being "cruel to a different race." (c) And the last sentence of the third paragraph, they agreed, in which Suki writes of racist acts "committed by close friends," did not tie in at all with the first part of the essay, although it did serve to introduce the second anecdote.

3. Her group was enthusiastic, though, about Suki's telling of the two stories and advised her to keep both. Both were accounts of more or less subtle acts of racism. One student thought that they should appear in chronological order: first the Korean story and then the more recent story, set in the playground. But both readers were sure that she could find some way to put them together.

4. They were less sure what the essay's thesis was, or whether it even had one. One student proposed this:

Subtle racist acts can be as destructive as dramatic instances (implied in paragraph 3).

The other proposed combining two points:

It is part of human nature to resent the unknown

and

. . . sometimes people become racist to cover their fears or ignorance (from the final paragraph).

All three members of Suki's group (Suki included) thought that the ideas in the essay were supported by the narratives. But the draft didn't yet hang together: Suki would have to work on the way the separate parts connected.

5. One member of the group then pointed out that the second paragraph could be deleted. The friend mentioned in it (who called Suki "paranoid") had been important to Suki's thinking about her first draft, but served no useful purpose in the draft they were looking at, and other details in that paragraph were murky.

6. On the other hand, the first paragraph probably needed additional details about the setting, the people involved, what each did. How does a three-year-old know he's been excluded from a play group? What happened? What did the other children do? What did he do? And, as the group had seen at once, some details were needed to establish the racist nature of the incident. They also reminded Suki that her essay needed a title.

7. Finally, some small details of grammar. Suki's English is excellent, although English is her second language. But the other two in her group, being native speakers of English, were able to catch the slightly odd syntax in

```
she always remembered me on holidays to send presents
```

and the error in

```
my heart ached as I watched my little brother envi-
ously looked at other kids.
```

Suki asked if the past tense was right in

```
I realized how cruel I have been to her
```

and the others supplied

```
I realized how cruel I had been to her
```

(though they could not explain the difference).

Final Version   Several days later, Suki consulted her notes and resumed work on her draft, and by September 25, the night before it was due, she was able to print the final version, which follows here.

Suki Hudson

Ms. Cahill

Writing 125R

September 20, 2006

Two Sides of a Story

1   It was a warm sunny day in the playground. My three-year-old brother and two other small boys were playing together in the sandbox. My brother was very happy, digging in the sand with a shovel one of the other boys had brought, when one of the mothers sitting on a bench across from me called to her son. She bent over and whispered something to him, and he went right over to my brother and pulled the shovel out of his hand. He pushed my brother aside and moved to the other side of the sandbox. The other boy followed him, and they continued to play. My heart ached as I watched my little brother enviously looking at the other kids. I didn't fully understand what had happened. I looked across at the mother, but she turned her head away. Then I picked up my brother and immediately left the playground with him.

2   I thought the woman was extremely rude and cruel, but I didn't think then that she was behaving in a racist way. We had only recently come here from Korea, and although I had been told that there was much racism in America, I thought that meant that it was hard for some people, like blacks, to find jobs or go to good schools. In some places there were street gangs and violence. But I didn't understand that there could be subtle acts of racism too. I was aware, though, in the playground that my brother and I were the only Koreans, the only nonwhites. When the woman turned her face away from me it felt like a sharp slap, but I was ignorant about her motives. I only guessed that she told her child not to play with my brother, and I knew that the playground was never the same since that day.

3   That incident was several months ago. When I started to think about it again recently, I thought also of another time when I was ignorant of racism.

4   In Korea, I had a very close friend whose father was Chinese. Although her mother was a Korean woman they were treated as foreign people in town, and they were singled out on many occasions. Her father died when she was little, but everyone in town knew she was half Chinese. Her mother ran a Chinese restaurant, and they lived very quietly. My family knew her mother well and I was close friends with the girl, and for many years I was the only friend she ever had. However, as I entered junior high school my new group of friends didn't approve of her background and I drifted away from her. She was a very quiet, shy person, and although I stopped calling or visiting her, she always remembered to send me presents on holidays. After graduating from junior high school, she went to Taiwan to live with her grandparents, whom she had never met. I gathered she could not stand the isolation any longer at her age. Many years later, I realized how cruel I had been to her, and I tried to locate her without success.

5   She was a victim in a homogeneous society, and had to experience pain she did not deserve. There was no law to protect her from that, just as there was no law to protect my little brother. Perhaps the woman in the playground did not realize how cruel she was being. She probably didn't think of herself as a racist, and maybe she acted the way I did in Korea, without thinking why. It isn't only the dramatic acts that are racist, and maybe it isn't only cruel people who commit racist acts. It is part of human nature to fear the unknown, and sometimes people become racist to cover their fears, or ignorance.

Acknowledgments

I would like to thank Ann Weston and Tory Chang for helping me to develop my main point and to organize and edit my essay.

CHECKLIST FOR DRAFTING AND REVISING

- ☐ Have I reread my draft? (See p. 18.)
- ☐ Have I imagined my audience? (See pp. 18–19.)
- ☐ What is my main idea? (See pp. 19–20.)
- ☐ Is it a good one? (See pp. 19–20.)
- ☐ How and where is the idea supported? (See p. 20.)
- ☐ Do I offer specific details? (See p. 20.)
- ☐ How is the material organized? (See p. 20.)
- ☐ Is the organization effective? (See p. 20.)
- ☐ Has the essay been read by peers or friends? (See pp. 21–22.)
- ☐ Have I acknowledged help from my readers? (See p. 22.)

CHAPTER THREE

SHAPING PARAGRAPHS

Paragraph Form and Substance

It is commonly said that a good paragraph is

- *unified* (it makes one point, or it indicates where one unit of a topic begins and ends);
- *organized* (the point or unit is developed according to some pattern); and
- *coherent* (the pattern of development, sentence by sentence, is clear to the reader).

In this chapter, we will say these things too. But first we feel obliged to issue this warning: You can learn to write a unified, organized, coherent paragraph that no one in his or her right mind would choose to read. Here is an example:

```
        Charles Darwin's great accomplishments in the
field of natural science resulted from many factors.
While innate qualities and characteristics played a
large part in leading him to his discoveries, various
environmental circumstances and events were decisive
factors as well. Darwin himself considered his voyage
on the Beagle the most decisive event of his life,
precisely because this was to him an educational
experience similar to if not more valuable than that
of college, in that it determined his whole career
and taught him of the world as well.
```

Notice that the paragraph is unified, organized, and coherent. It has a **topic sentence** (the first sentence, which briefly states the main idea of the paragraph). It uses **transitional devices** ("while," "as well," "Darwin himself") and, as is often helpful, it **repeats key words.** But notice also that it is wordy, vague, and inflated ("in the field of," "many factors," "qualities and characteristics," "circumstances and events," "precisely because," "educational experience," "similar to if not more valuable than"). It is, in short, thin and boring. To whom does it teach what?

Consider, by contrast, these paragraphs from another essay on Darwin:

> Charles Darwin's youth was unmarked by signs of genius. Born in 1809 into the well-to-do Darwin and Wedgwood clans (his mother was a Wedgwood, and Darwin himself was to marry another), he led a secure and carefree childhood, happy with his family, indifferent to books, responsive to nature. The son and grandson of impressively successful physicians, he eventually tried medical training himself, but found the studies dull and surgery (before anesthesia) too ghastly even to watch. So, for want of anything better, he followed the advice of his awesome father (6′ 2″, 336 pounds, domineering in temperament) and studied for the ministry, taking his B.A. at Christ's College, Cambridge, in 1831.
>
> Then a remarkable turn of events saved Darwin from a country parsonage. His science teacher at Cambridge, John Stevens Henslow, arranged for Darwin the invitation to be naturalist on H.M.S. *Beagle* during a long voyage of exploration. Despite his father's initial reluctance, Darwin got the position, and at the end of 1831 left England for a five-year voyage around the globe that turned out to be not only a crucial experience for Darwin himself, but a passage of consequence for the whole world.
>
> *—Philip Appleman*

Notice how full of life these paragraphs are, compared to the paragraph that begins by asserting that "Charles Darwin's great accomplishments in the field of natural science resulted from many factors." These far more interesting paragraphs are filled with specific details, facts, and names that combine to convey ideas. We finish reading them with a sense of having learned something worth knowing, from someone fully engaged not only with the topic, but also with conveying it to someone else.

The one indispensable quality of a good paragraph is **substance.** A paragraph may

- define a term,
- describe a person or a place,
- make a comparison,
- analyze a point,
- summarize an opinion,
- draw a conclusion.

It may do almost anything provided that it holds the readers' attention by telling them something they want or need to know, or are reminded of with pleasure.

But even a substantial paragraph does not guarantee that you'll hold the attention of your readers, because readers, like writers, are often lazy and impatient. If readers find that they must work too hard to understand you, if they are confused by what you write, they can and will stop reading. The art of writing is in large part the art of keeping your readers' goodwill while you teach them what you want them to learn. Now, experienced writers can usually tell what makes a satisfactory unit, and their paragraphs do not always exactly follow the principles we are going to suggest. But we think that if you follow these principles you will develop a sense of paragraphing. Or, to put it another way, you will improve your sense of how to develop an idea.

The Shape of a Paragraph

The shape of a paragraph—the way in which its idea is set forth—will largely depend not only on the content but also on the position of the paragraph in the essay.

- The **content** of a paragraph explaining something may move from cause to effect, or from effect to cause; the content of a paragraph arguing a point may move from evidence to conclusion, or from conclusion to evidence.

- The **position** of the paragraph, its place in the essay as a whole, will also determine its shape. An opening paragraph will in one way or another lead into the topic. (Its main point may therefore come at the end.) A middle paragraph should follow easily from the preceding paragraph, and it should also lead into the next paragraph—so a middle paragraph might begin with a transitional sentence (a sentence that begins with a "Furthermore" or a "Nevertheless") and announce its main point in the second sentence. Or even in its last sentence.

We will discuss such matters in detail in the following pages. But here we can say that when you revise a draft, you want to make certain not only that each paragraph is clear in itself but also that it fits neatly into your essay.

Paragraph Unity: Topic Sentences, Topic Ideas

The idea developed in each paragraph often appears, briefly stated, as a topic sentence. Topic sentences are most useful, and are therefore especially common, in paragraphs that offer arguments; they are much less useful, and therefore less common, in narrative and descriptive paragraphs.

The topic sentence usually is the first sentence in the paragraph—or the second, if the first sentence is transitional—because writers usually want their readers to know from the start where the paragraph is going. Sometimes, though, you may not wish to forecast what is to come; you may prefer to put your topic sentence at the end of the paragraph, summarizing the points that earlier sentences have made, or drawing a generalization based on the earlier details. Even if you do not include a topic sentence anywhere in the paragraph, the paragraph should have a **topic idea,** an idea that holds the sentences together.

Examples of Topic Sentences at Beginning and at End, and of Topic Ideas

1. The following paragraph, from an essay in which a professor of physiology compares Darwin and Freud, begins with a topic sentence.

> To begin with, Darwin and Freud were both multifaceted geniuses with many talents in common. Both were great observers, attuned to perceiving in familiar phenomena a significance that had escaped almost everyone else. Searching with insatiable curiosity for underlying explanations, both did far more than discover new facts or solve circumscribed problems, such as the structure of DNA: they synthesized knowledge from a wide range of fields and created new conceptual frameworks, large parts of which are still accepted today. Both were

prolific writers and forceful communicators who eventually converted many or most of their contemporaries to their positions.

—Jared Diamond

The first sentence announces the topic the rest of the paragraph will develop, the talents Darwin and Freud had in common. Each sentence that follows this topic sentence develops or amplifies it by considering one of the talents the two men shared. The second sentence concerns their powers of observation. The third sentence concerns their curiosity about "underlying explanations" and their ability to create "new conceptual frameworks." Note also the logical order of subtopics in the paragraph: The discussion moves from *observation*, to *analysis* and *synthesis*, to *communication*.

2. The next paragraph has its topic sentence at the end:

If we try to recall Boris Karloff's face as the monster in the film of *Frankenstein* (1931), most of us probably think of the seams holding the pieces together, and if we cannot recall other details we assume that the face evokes horror. But when we actually look at a picture of the face rather than recall a memory of it, we are perhaps chiefly impressed by the high, steep forehead (a feature often associated with intelligence), by the darkness surrounding the eyes (often associated with physical or spiritual weariness), and by the gaunt cheeks and the thin lips slightly turned down at the corners (associated with deprivation or restraint). The monster's face is of course in some ways shocking, but probably our chief impression as we look at it is that this is not the face of one who causes suffering but of one who himself is heroically undergoing suffering.

—Sylvia Rodriguez

When the topic sentence is at the end, the paragraph usually develops from the particular to the general, the topic sentence serving to generalize or summarize the information that precedes it. Such a topic sentence can be especially effective in presenting an argument: The reader hears, considers, and accepts the evidence before the writer explicitly states the argument, and if the writer has effectively presented the evidence, the reader willingly accepts the conclusion.

3. The next paragraph has no topic sentence:

A few years ago when you mentioned Walt Disney at a respectable party—or anyway this is how it was in California, where I was then— the standard response was a headshake and a groan. Intellectuals spoke of how he butchered the classics—from *Pinocchio* to *Winnie the Pooh*, how his wildlife pictures were sadistic and coy, how the World's Fair sculptures of hippopotamuses were a national if not international disgrace. A few crazies disagreed, and since crazies are always the people to watch, it began to be admitted that the early Pluto movies had a considerable measure of *je ne sais quoi*, that the background animation in *Snow White* was "quite extraordinary," that *Fantasia* did indeed have *one* great sequence (then it became two; now everyone says three, though there's fierce disagreement on exactly which three).

—John Gardner

The topic idea here is, roughly, "Intellectuals used to scorn Disney, but recently they have been praising him." Such a sentence could easily begin the paragraph, but it is not necessary because even without it the reader has no difficulty following the discussion. The first two sentences talk about Disney's earlier reputation; then the sentence about the "crazies" introduces the contrary view and the rest of the paragraph illustrates the growing popularity of this contrary view. The paragraph develops its point so clearly and consistently (it is essentially a narrative, in chronological order) that the reader, unlike the reader of a complex analytic paragraph, does not need the help of a topic sentence either at the beginning, to prepare for what follows, or at the end, to pull the whole together.

Unity in Paragraphs

Although we emphasize **unity** in paragraphs, don't assume that every development or refinement or alteration of your thought requires a new paragraph. Such an assumption would lead to an essay consisting entirely of one-sentence paragraphs. A good paragraph may, for instance,

- ask a question *and* answer it, or
- describe an effect *and* then explain the cause, or
- set forth details *and* then offer a generalization.

Indeed, if the question or the effect or the details can be set forth in a sentence or two, and the answer or the cause or the generalization can be set forth in a sentence or two, the two halves of the topic should be pulled together into a single paragraph. Only if, for example, the question is long and complex and the answer equally long or longer, will you need two or more paragraphs.

Let's consider three paragraphs from an essay on ballooning. In the essay from which the following paragraphs are taken, the writer has already explained that ballooning was born in late eighteenth-century France and that almost from its start there were two types of balloons, gas and hot air. Notice that in the paragraphs printed below:

- the first is on gas,
- the second is chiefly on hot air (but it helpfully makes comparisons with gas),
- and the third is on the length of flights of both gas and hot-air balloons.

In other words, each paragraph is about one thing—gas balloons, hot-air balloons, length of flight—but each paragraph also builds on what the reader has learned in the previous paragraphs. That the third paragraph is about the flights of gas *and* of hot-air balloons does not mean that it lacks unity; it is a unified discussion of flight lengths.

Gas balloons swim around in air like a sleeping fish in water, because they weigh about the same as the fluid they're in. A good, big, trans-Atlantic balloon will have 2,000 pounds of vehicle, including gas bag and pilot, taking up about 30 cubic feet (as big as a refrigerator), plus 300 pounds of a "nothing" stuff called helium, which fills 30,000 cubic feet (as big as three houses). Air to fill this 30,000 cubic feet would also weigh 2,300 pounds, so the balloon system averages the same as air, floating in it as part of the wind.

Hot-air balloons use the same size bag filled with hot air instead of helium, kept hot by a boot-sized blowtorch riding just over the pilot's head. Hot air is light, but not as light as helium, so you can't carry as much equipment in a hot-air balloon. You also can't fly as long or as far. Helium will carry a balloon for days (three and a half days is the record), until a lot of gas has leaked out. But a hot-air balloon cools down in minutes, like a house as soon as its heat source runs out of fuel; and today's best fuel (heat-for-weight), propane, lasts only several hours.

A good hot-air flight goes a hundred miles, yet the gas record is 1,897 miles, set by a German in 1914 with the junk (by today's standards) they had then. Unmanned scientific gas balloons have flown half a million miles, staying up more than a year. Japan bombed Oregon in World War II with balloons. Two hot-air balloonists, Tracy Barnes and

Malcolm Forbes, have made what they called transcontinental flights, but each was the sum of dozens of end-to-end hops, trailed by pick-up trucks, like throwing a frisbee from Hollywood to Atlantic City.

—*David Royce*

Because Royce's paragraphs are unified, the reader is able to proceed from point to point without stumbling and without confusion. By contrast, the following paragraph, from a book on athletic coaching, lacks unity, and the effect is disconcerting.

> Leadership qualities are a prerequisite for achievement in coaching. A leader is one who is respected for what he says and does, and who is admired by his team. The coach gains respect by giving respect, and by possessing knowledge and skills associated with the sport. There are many "successful" coaches who are domineering, forceful leaders, gaining power more through fear and even hate than through respect. These military-type men are primarily from the old school of thought, and many younger coaches are achieving their goals through more humanistic approaches.

Something is wrong here. The first half of the paragraph tells us that "a leader is one who is respected for what he says and does," but the second half of the paragraph contradicts that assertion, telling us that "many" leaders hold their position "more through fear and even hate than through respect." The trouble is *not* that the writer is talking about two kinds of leaders; a moment ago we saw that a writer can in one paragraph talk about two kinds of balloons. The trouble here is that we need a unifying idea if these two points are to be given in one paragraph. The idea might be: There are two kinds of leaders, those who are respected and those who are feared. This idea might be developed along these lines:

> Leadership qualities are a prerequisite for achievement in coaching, but these qualities can be of two radically different kinds. One kind of leader is respected and admired by his team for what he says and does. The coach gains respect by giving respect, and by possessing knowledge and skills associated with the sport. The other kind of coach is a domineering, forceful leader, gaining power more through fear than through respect. These military-type men are primarily from the old school of thought, whereas most of the younger coaches achieve their goals through the more humane approaches of the first type.

Organization in Paragraphs

A paragraph needs more than a unified point; it needs a reasonable **organization** or sequence. Exactly how the parts of a paragraph will fit together depends on what the paragraph is doing.

- If it is *describing* a place, it may move from a general view to the significant details—or from immediately striking details to some less obvious but perhaps more important ones. It may move from near to far, or from far to near, or from the past to the present.

- If it is *explaining*, it may move from cause to effect, or from effect to cause, or from past to present; or it may offer an example.

- If it is *arguing*, it may move from evidence to conclusion, or from a conclusion to supporting evidence; or it may offer one piece of evidence—for instance, an anecdote that illustrates the argument.

- If it is *narrating*, it will likely move chronologically.

- If a paragraph is *classifying* (dividing a subject into its parts), it may begin by enumerating the parts and go on to study each, perhaps in climactic order. Here is an example from a student essay on masks:

> The chief reasons people wear masks are these: to have fun, to protect themselves, to disguise themselves, and to achieve a new identity. At Halloween, children wear masks for fun; they may, of course, also think they are disguising themselves, but chiefly their motive is to experience the joy of saying "boo" to someone. As for protection, soldiers wore masks in ancient times against swords and battle-axes, in more recent times against poison gas. Masked bank robbers illustrate the third reason, disguise, and though of course this disguise is a sort of protection, a robber's reason for wearing a mask is fairly distinct from a soldier's. All of these reasons so far are easily understood, but we may have more trouble grasping the reason that people use masks in order to achieve a new identity. In some religious rituals, masks may be worn to frighten away evil spirits, or they may be disguises so that the evil spirits will not know who the wearer is. But most religious

> masks are worn with the idea that the wearer
> achieves a new identity, a union with supernatural
> powers, and thus in effect the wearer becomes--
> really becomes, not merely pretends to be--a new
> person.

Notice that the first sentence offers four reasons for wearing masks. The rest of the paragraph amplifies these reasons, one by one, and in the order indicated in the first sentence. Since the writer regards the last reason as the most interesting and the most difficult to grasp, she discusses it at the greatest length, giving it about as much space as she gives to the first three reasons altogether.

The way in which a paragraph is organized, then, will depend on the writer's purpose. Almost always, one purpose is to make something clear to a reader, which means that the writer must present information in an orderly way. Writers use several common methods to organize a paragraph and to keep things clear:

1. General to particular (topic sentence usually at the beginning)
2. Particular to general (topic sentence usually at the end)
3. Enumeration of parts or details or reasons (probably in climactic order)
4. Question and answer
5. Cause and effect
6. Comparison and contrast
7. Analogy
8. Chronology
9. Spatial order (e.g., near to far, or right to left)

The only rule that can cover all paragraphs is this: Readers must never feel that they are wandering in a maze as they follow the writer to the end of the paragraph.

Coherence in Paragraphs

In addition to having a unified point and a reasonable organization, a good paragraph is **coherent**—that is, the connections between ideas in the paragraph are clear. Coherence can often be achieved by inserting the right transitional words or by taking care to repeat key words.

Transitions

Richard Wagner, commenting on his work as a composer of operas, said, "The art of composition is the art of transition," for his art moved from note to note, measure to measure, scene to scene. **Transitions** establish connections between ideas; they alert readers to what will follow. Here are some of the most common transitional words and phrases, categorized by their function:

1. **Amplification or likeness:** similarly, likewise, and, also, again, second, third, in addition, furthermore, moreover, finally

2. **Emphasis:** chiefly, equally, indeed, even more important

3. **Contrast or concession:** but, on the contrary, on the other hand, by contrast, of course, however, still, doubtless, no doubt, nevertheless, granted that, conversely, although, admittedly

4. **Example:** for example, for instance, as an example, specifically, consider as an illustration, that is, such as, like

5. **Consequence or cause and effect:** thus, so, then, it follows, as a result, therefore, hence

6. **Restatement:** in short, that is, in effect, in other words

7. **Place:** in the foreground, further back, in the distance

8. **Time:** afterward, next, then, as soon as, later, until, when, finally, last, at last

9. **Conclusion:** finally, therefore, thus, to sum up

Consider the following paragraph:

Folklorists are just beginning to look at Africa. A great quantity of folklore materials has been gathered from African countries in the past century and published by missionaries, travelers, administrators, linguists, and anthropologists incidentally to their main pursuits. No fieldworker has devoted himself exclusively or even largely to the recording and analysis of folklore materials, according to a committee of the African Studies Association reporting in 1966 on the state of research in the African arts. Yet Africa is the continent supreme for traditional cultures that nurture folklore. Why this neglect?

—*Richard M. Dorson*

The reader gets the point, but the second sentence seems to contradict the first: The first sentence tells us that folklorists are just beginning to look at Africa, but the next tells us that lots of folklore has been collected. An "although" between these sentences would clarify the author's point, especially if the third sentence were hooked on to the second, thus:

> Folklorists are just beginning to look at Africa. Although a great quantity of folklore materials has been gathered from African countries in the past century by missionaries, travelers, administrators, linguists, and anthropologists incidentally to their main pursuits, no fieldworker has devoted himself . . .

But this revision gives us an uncomfortably long second sentence. Further revision would help. The real point of the original passage, though it is smothered, is that *although* many people have incidentally collected folklore materials in Africa, *professional* folklorists have not been active there. The contrast ought to be sharpened:

> Folklorists are just beginning to look at Africa. True, missionaries, travelers, administrators, linguists, and anthropologists have collected a quantity of folklore materials incidentally to their main pursuits, but folklorists have lagged behind. No fieldworker . . .

In this revision the words that clarify are the small but important words "true" and "but." The original paragraph is like a jigsaw puzzle that's missing some tiny but necessary pieces.

Repetition

Coherence is also achieved through the **repetition** of key words. When you repeat words or phrases, or when you provide clear substitutes, such as pronouns and demonstrative adjectives, you are helping the reader to keep step with your developing thoughts. Grammatical constructions too can be repeated, the repetitions or parallels linking the sentences or ideas.

In the following example, notice how the repetitions provide continuity.

> In the movement from the miraculous prose of Toni Morrison to the screen, the story of *Beloved* has lost some of its breadth, complexity, and imaginative range. But its central messages—historical and human— have been sustained and, in some ways, enhanced by the gifts of the innovative Jonathan Demme and his associates and by the talent and commitment of the actors. We see in the film the wounds of slavery, inflicted and then self-inflicted through resistance—or, rather, we see the memories of

these wounds as they still disturb the free. We see the resources of an African-American community for defining those wounds, for quarreling about them, and for healing them. The story of trauma and recovery is distinctive, but it is told so as to invite others in, into the haunted house at 124 Bluestone and into Baby Sugg's clearing in the woods.

—*Natalie Zemon Davis*

Notice not only the exact repetitions ("wounds," "we see," "them") but also the slight variations, such as "inflicted," and "self-inflicted"; and the parallel construction of the last phrases of the last sentence ("into the haunted house [. . .] into Baby Sugg's clearing"), which brings a sense of closure to the paragraph.

Linking Paragraphs Together

Since each paragraph in an essay generally develops a single idea, a single, new aspect of the main point of the essay, as one paragraph follows another, readers should feel they are getting somewhere, smoothly and without stumbling. As you move from one paragraph to the next, from one step in the development of your main idea to the next, you probably can keep your readers with you if you link the beginning of each new paragraph to the end of the paragraph that precedes it. Often a transitional word or phrase (such as those listed on p. 43) will suffice; sometimes repeating key terms will help connect a sequence of paragraphs together and make your essay, as many writers put it, "flow."

Consider the movement of ideas in the following essay written in response to an assignment that asked students to analyze a family photograph.

Cheryl Lee

Writing 125

Ms. Medina

April 1, 2006

The Story Behind the Gestures

1   At the close of my graduation ceremony, my entire family gathered together to immortalize the special moment on film. No one escaped the flash of my mother's

camera because she was determined to document every minute of the occasion at every possible angle. My mother made sure that she took pictures of me with my hat on, with my hat off, holding the bouquet, sitting, standing, and in countless other positions. By the time this family picture was taken, my smile was intact, frozen on my face. This is not to say that my smile was anything less than genuine, for it truly was a smile of thankfulness and joy. It is just that after posing for so many pictures, what initially began as a spontaneous reaction became a frozen expression.

2   The viewer should, however, consider not so much the frozen expressions of those in the photograph, but rather the fact that the picture is posed. A posed picture supposedly shows only what the people in the picture want the viewer to see--in this case, their happiness. But ironically the photograph reveals much more about its subjects than the viewer first imagines. The photograph speaks of relationships and personalities. It speaks about the more intimate details that first seem invisible but that become undeniable through the study of gestures.

3   In the photograph, the most prominent and symbolic of gestures is the use and position of the arms. Both my father and mother place an arm around me and in turn around each other. Their encircling arms, however, do more than just show affection; they unify the three figures into a close huddle that leads the viewer's eye directly to them as opposed to the background or the periphery. The slightly bended arms that rest at their sides act as arrows that not only reinforce the three figures as the focal point but also exclude the fourth figure, my brother, from sharing the spotlight. Unlike the other members of the family whose arms and hands are intertwined, Edwin stands with both hands down in front of him, latching onto no one. The lack of physical contact between the huddled figures and Edwin is again emphasized as he positions himself away from the viewer's eye as he stands in the periphery.

4   Edwin's position in the photograph is indicative of him as a person, for he always seems to isolate

himself from the spotlight, from being the center of attention. Thus, it is his decision to escape public scrutiny, not the force of my parents' arms that drives him to the side. His quiet, humble nature directs him away from even being the focal point of a picture and leads him towards establishing his own individuality and independence in privacy. His long hair and his "hand-me-down" clothes are all an expression of his simply being himself. The reason behind his physical independence is the emotional independence that he already possesses at the age of sixteen. He stands alone because he can stand alone.

5   While Edwin stands apart from the other three figures, I stand enclosed and protected. The lock of arms as well as the bouquet restrain me; they dissuade me from breaking away in favor of independence. Although my mother wants me to achieve the same kind of independence that Edwin has achieved, she works to delay the time when I actually will move away to the periphery. Perhaps my being the only daughter, the only other female in the family, has something to do with my mother's desire to keep me close and dependent as long as possible. Her arm reaches out with bouquet in hand as if to shield me from the world's unpleasantness. Even though my father also holds onto me with an encircling arm, it is my mother's firm grip that alone persuades me to stay within the boundary of their protective arms.

6   Her grip, which proves more powerful than my father's hold, restrains not only me but also my father. In the picture, he falls victim to the same outstretched hand, the same touch of the bouquet. Yet this time, my mother's bouquet does more than just restrain; it seems to push my father back "into line" or into his so-called place. The picture illustrates this exertion of influence well, for my mother in real life does indeed assume the role of the dominant figure. Although my father remains the head of the household in title, it is my mother around whom the household revolves; she oversees the insignificant details as well as the major ones. But my father

doesn't mind at all. Like me, he also enjoys the
protection her restraining arm offers. It is because
of our mutual dependence on my mother that my
father and I seem to draw closer. This dependence
in turn strengthens both of our relationships with my
mother.

7   At the time the picture was taken, I seriously
doubt that my mother realized the significance of her
position in the picture or the import of her gestures.
All of us in fact seem too blinded by the festivity of
the occasion to realize that this photograph would show
more than just a happy family at a daughter's graduation. The family photograph would inevitably become a
telling portrait of each member of the family. It
would, in a sense, leave us vulnerable to the specula-
tive eyes of the viewer, who in carefully examining the
photograph would recognize the secrets hidden in each
frozen expression.

Cheryl Lee, *The Story Behind the Gestures: A Family Photograph.*
Reprinted by permission of the author, Cheryl Lee Rim.

A few observations on these paragraphs may be useful. First, notice that each paragraph in the sequence examines a different aspect of the photograph and introduces a new point into the discussion.

- Paragraph 1 gives background information (the photograph was taken at Lee's graduation).

- Paragraph 2 states the writer's point—that studying the gestures of her family members enables us to understand the "personalities and relationships."

Each succeeding paragraph treats one of these gestures, or one of the personalities or relationships:

- Paragraph 3 considers the "encircling arms" of Lee's parents.

- Paragraph 4 focuses on the writer's brother Edwin.

- Paragraph 5 focuses on Lee's relationship to her mother.

- Paragraph 6 focuses on her mother and father.

Second, notice how Lee makes the essay cohere. Although she uses some transitional words ("however" at the beginning of the second paragraph; "while" at the beginning of the fifth paragraph), she establishes coherence in this essay primarily by repeating the key terms of her discussion. The first sentence of each new paragraph picks up a word or phrase from the last sentence of the paragraph preceding it. The phrase "frozen expressions" links the end of the first paragraph to the beginning of the second; "gesture" links the second paragraph to the third; "position" links the third to the fourth; "stand" links the fourth to the fifth; and so on. These links are hardly noticeable on a first reading, but because Lee uses transitions and repetition effectively, the writing flows, and the reader never stumbles.

Paragraph Length

Although a paragraph can contain any number of sentences, two is probably too few, and ten might be too many. It is not a matter, however, of counting sentences; paragraphs are coherent blocks, substantial units of your essay, and the spaces between them are brief resting-places allowing the reader to take in what you have said. One double-spaced, word-processed page of writing (approximately 250 words) is about as much as the reader can take before requiring a slight break. On the other hand, a single page with half a dozen paragraphs is probably faulty because the reader is too often interrupted with needless pauses and because the page has too few *developed* ideas: An assertion is made, and then another, and another. These assertions are unconvincing because they are not supported with detail.

The Use and Abuse of Short Paragraphs

A short paragraph can be effective when it summarizes a highly detailed previous paragraph or group of paragraphs, or when it serves as a transition between two complicated paragraphs, but unless you are sure that the reader needs a break, avoid thin paragraphs. A paragraph that is nothing but a transition can usually be altered into a transitional phrase or clause or sentence that starts the next paragraph. But of course there are times when a short paragraph is exactly right. Notice the effect of the two-sentence paragraph between two longer paragraphs:

> After I returned to prison, I took a long look at myself and, for the first time in my life, admitted that I was wrong, that I had gone astray—astray not so much from the white man's law as from being human, civilized—for I could not approve the act of rape. Even though I had some insight into my own motivations, I did not feel justified. I lost my self-respect. My pride as a man dissolved and my whole fragile moral structure seemed to collapse, completely shattered.
>
> That is why I started to write. To save myself.
>
> I realized that no one could save me but myself. The prison authorities were both uninterested and unable to help me. I had to seek out the truth and unravel the snarled web of my motivations. I had to find out who I am and what I want to be, what type of man I should be, and what I could do to become the best of which I was capable. I understood that what had happened to me had also happened to countless other blacks and it would happen to many, many more.
>
> —*Eldridge Cleaver*

If the content of the second paragraph were less momentous, it would hardly merit a paragraph. Here the brevity contributes to the enormous impact; those two simple sentences, set off by themselves, seem equal in weight, so to speak, to the longer paragraphs that precede and follow. They are the hinges on which the door turns.

When used for emphasis, short paragraphs can be effective.

Often, though, short paragraphs (like the one directly above) leave readers feeling unsatisfied, even annoyed. Consider these two consecutive paragraphs from a draft of a student's essay on Leonardo da Vinci's *Mona Lisa:*

> Leonardo's <u>Mona Lisa</u>, painted about 1502, has caused many people to wonder about the lady's expression. Different viewers see different things.
>
> The explanation of the puzzle is chiefly in the mysterious expression that Leonardo conveys. The mouth and the eyes are especially important.

Sometimes you can improve a sequence of short paragraphs merely by joining one paragraph to the next. But unsatisfactory short paragraphs usually cannot be repaired so simply: The source of the problem is usually not that sentences have been needlessly separated from each other, but that generalizations have not been supported by details, or that claims have not been supported by evidence. Here is the student's revision, strengthening the two thin paragraphs of the draft.

> Leonardo's <u>Mona Lisa</u>, painted about 1502, has caused many people to wonder about the lady's expression. Doubtless she is remarkably lifelike but exactly what experience of life, what mood, does she reveal? Is she sad, or gently mocking, or uncertain or self-satisfied, or lost in daydreams? Why are we never satisfied when we try to name her emotion?
>
> Part of the uncertainty may of course be due to the subject as a whole. What can we make out of the combination of this smiling woman and that utterly unpopulated landscape? But surely a large part of the explanation lies in the way that Leonardo painted the face's two most expressive features, the eyes and the mouth. He slightly obscured the corners of these, so that we cannot precisely characterize them: although on one viewing we may see them one way, on another viewing we may see them slightly differently. If today we think she looks detached, tomorrow we may think she looks slightly threatening.

Leonardo da Vinci,
Mona Lisa.
© Alinari/Art Resource.

This revision is not simply a padded version of the earlier paragraphs; it is a necessary clarification of them, for without the details the generalizations mean almost nothing to a reader.

Introductory Paragraphs

As the poet Byron said, at the beginning of a long part of a long poem, "Nothing so difficult as a beginning." Almost all writers find that the first paragraphs in their drafts are false starts. As we suggest in Chapter 1, we think you shouldn't worry too much about the opening paragraph of your draft; you'll almost surely want to revise your opening later anyway.

When writing a first draft, you merely need something to break the ice. But in your finished paper the opening cannot be mere throat-clearing. The opening should be interesting. Here are some common *un*interesting openings to avoid:

- A dictionary definition ("Webster says . . . ").

- A restatement of your title. The title is (let's assume) "Anarchism and the Marx Brothers," and the first sentence says, "This essay will study the anarchic acts of the Marx Brothers." True, the sentence announces the topic of the essay, but it gives no information about the topic beyond what the title already offers, and it provides no information about you either—that is, no sense of your response to the topic, such as might be present in, say, "The Marx Brothers are funny, but one often has the feeling that under the fun the violence has serious implications."

• A broad generalization, such as "Ever since the beginning of time, human beings have been violent." Again, such a sentence may be fine if it helps you to start drafting, but it should not remain in your final version: It's dull—and it tells your readers almost nothing about the essay they're about to read. (Our example, after all, could begin anything from an analysis of *The Matrix* to a term paper on Darfur.) To put it another way, the ever-since-the-beginning-of-time opening lacks substance—and if your opening lacks substance, it will not matter what you say next. You've already lost your reader's attention.

What is left? What *is* a good way for an introductory paragraph to begin?

• It will be at least moderately interesting if it provides **information**.

• It will be pleasing if the information provides **focus**—that is, if it lets the reader know exactly what your topic is and what you will say about it.

• And it will capture a reader's attention if it articulates a **problem** and suggests why the essay is worth reading.

When you write, *you* are the teacher; it won't do to begin with a vague statement:

```
George Orwell says he shot the elephant because . . .
```

We need some information, identifying the text you are writing about:

```
    George Orwell, in "Shooting an Elephant," says
he shot the elephant because . . .
```

Even better is,

```
In "Shooting an Elephant," George Orwell sets
forth his reflections on his service as a policeman
in Burma. He suggests that he once shot an elephant
```

```
because . . . but his final paragraph suggests that we
must look for additional reasons.
```

Why is this opening better? Because it begins to suggest why the essay is worth reading. It points to a contradiction in the Orwell piece, a problem worth examining: Orwell says one thing, but that thing may not be entirely true.

Compare, for example, the opening sentences from three essays written by students on Anne Moody's *Coming of Age in Mississippi*. The book is the autobiography of an African American woman, covering her early years with her sharecropper parents, her schooling, and finally her work in the civil rights movement.

```
The environment that surrounds a person from an early
age tends to be a major factor in determining their
character.
```

This is an all-purpose sentence that serves no specific purpose well; it could conceivably begin an essay on almost any topic: a study of the moral development of children, an analysis of the film *Brokeback Mountain*, a biography of Napoleon. Notice also the faulty reference of the pronoun (the plural "their" refers to the singular "a person"), the weaseling of "tends to be a major factor," and the vagueness of "early age" and "environment" and "character." These all warn us that the writer will waste our time.

```
It is unfortunate but true that racial or color prej-
udice shows itself early in the life of a child.
```

Less pretentious than the first example, but it labors the obvious, sounds preachy, and still doesn't say much about the topic at hand.

```
Anne Moody's autobiography, Coming of Age in
Mississippi, vividly illustrates how she discovered
her identity as an African American.
```

Surely this is the best of the three openings. Informative and focused, it identifies the book's theme and method, and it offers an evaluation. The essayist has been considerate of her readers: If we are interested in women's autobiographies or life in the South, we will read on. If we aren't, we are grateful to her for letting us off the bus at the first stop.

Let's look now not simply at an opening sentence but at an entire first paragraph, the opening paragraph of an analytic essay. Notice how the student provides necessary information about the book she is discussing (the diary of a man whose son has a serious brain disorder) and also focuses the reader's attention on the essay's topic (the quality that distinguishes this diary from others).

> Josh Greenfeld's diary, <u>A Place for Noah</u>, records the attempts of a smart, thoughtful man to reconcile himself to his son's autism, a severe mental and physical disorder. Most diaries function as havens for secret thoughts, and Greenfeld's diary does frequently supply a voice to his darkest fears about who will ultimately care for Noah. It provides, too, an intimate glimpse of a family striving to remain a coherent unit despite their tragedy. But beyond affording such urgent and personal revelations, <u>A Place for Noah</u>, in chronicling the isolation of the Greenfelds, reveals how inadequate and ineffectual our medical and educational systems are in responding to families victimized by catastrophic illness.

This example is engaging, in part because it indicates why a reader might be interested in reading the essay it begins: Greenfeld's book is more than just a diary; it also explores the consequences of a problem—catastrophic illness—that can affect anyone.

Of course you can provide interest and focus by other means, among them the following:

- A quotation
- An anecdote or other short narrative
- An interesting fact (a statistic, for instance, showing the reader that you know something about your topic)
- A definition of an important term—but not merely one derived from a dictionary
- A question—but an interesting one, such as "Why do we call some words obscene?"
- A glance at the opposition
- An assertion that a problem exists

Many excellent opening paragraphs do not use any of these devices, and you need not use any of them if they feel forced. But in your reading you may observe that these devices are used widely. Here is an example of the second device, **an anecdote,** that makes an effective, indeed an unnerving, introduction to an essay on aging.

> There is an old American folk tale about a wooden bowl. It seems that Grandmother, with her trembling hands, was guilty of occasionally breaking a dish. Her daughter angrily gave her a wooden bowl, and told her that she must eat out of it from now on. The young granddaughter, observing this, asked her mother why Grandmother must eat from a wooden bowl when the rest of the family was given china plates. "Because she is old!" answered her mother. The child thought for a moment and then told her mother, "You must save the wooden bowl when Grandma dies." Her mother asked why, and the child replied, "For when you are old."
>
> —*Sharon R. Curtin*

The third strategy, **an interesting detail,** shows the reader that you know something about your topic and that you are worth reading. We have already seen (p. 34) a rather quiet example of this device, in a paragraph about Charles Darwin, which begins "Charles Darwin's youth was unmarked by signs of genius." Here is a more obvious example, from a student essay on blue jeans:

> That blue jeans or denims are not found only in Texas is not surprising if we recall that jeans are named for Genoa (Gene), where the cloth was first made, and that denim is cloth de Nîmes, that is, from Nîmes, a city in France.

(Such information is to be had by spending about thirty seconds with a dictionary.)

The fourth strategy, **a definition,** is fairly common in analytic essays; the essayist first clears the ground by specifying the topic. Here is the beginning of a student's essay on bilingual education.

> Let's begin by defining "bilingual education." As commonly used today, the term does not mean teaching students a language other than English. Almost everyone would agree that foreign-language instruction should be available, and that it is desirable for Americans to be

fluent not only in English but also in some other language. Nor does "bilingual education" mean offering courses in English as a second language to students whose native language is, for example, Chinese, or Spanish or Navajo or Aleut. Again, almost everyone would agree that such instruction should be offered where economically possible. Rather, it means offering instruction in such courses as mathematics, history, and science <u>in the student's native language</u>, while also offering courses in English as a second language. Programs vary in details, but the idea is that the non-native speaker should be spared the trauma of total immersion in English until he or she has completed several years of studying English as a second language. During this period, instruction in other subjects is given in the student's native language.

—Tina Bakka

The fifth strategy, **a question,** is briefly illustrated by the opening paragraph of an essay about whether it is sometimes permissible for doctors to lie to their patients.

Should doctors ever lie to benefit their patients—to speed recovery or to conceal the approach of death? In medicine as in law, government, and other lines of work, the requirements of honesty often seem dwarfed by greater needs: the need to shelter from brutal news or to uphold a promise of secrecy; to expose corruption or to promote the public interest.

—*Sissela Bok*

The sixth strategy, **a glance at the opposition,** is especially effective if the opposing view is well established, but while you state it, you should manage to convey your distrust of it. Here is an example:

One often hears, correctly, that there is a world food crisis, and one almost as often hears that not enough food is produced to feed the world's entire population. The wealthier countries, it is said, jeopardize their own chances for survival when they attempt to subsidize all of the poorer countries in which the masses are starving. Often the lifeboat analogy is offered: There is room in the boat for only X people, and to take in *X*+1 is to overload the boat and to invite the destruction of all. But is it true that the world cannot and does not produce enough food to save the whole population from starving?

—*V. Nagarajan*

The seventh strategy, **an assertion that a problem exists,** is common in essays that make proposals. The following example is the first paragraph of a grant proposal written by biomedical engineers seeking government funding for their research project, a new method for treating liver cancer. Notice that the paragraph does not offer the authors' proposal; it simply points out that there is an unsolved problem, and the reader infers that the proposal will offer the solution.

Liver cancer, especially metastatic colorectal cancer, is a significant and increasing health concern. In the United States, half of the 157,000 new cases of colorectal cancer will develop metastases in the liver. These metastases will lead to over 17,000 deaths annually. And while not as significant a health risk as colorectal metastasis, hepatocellular carcinoma is being diagnosed with increasing frequency. The current standard of practice for treating liver cancer is surgical resection, but only 10% of patients are eligible for this procedure. (Circumstances limiting eligibility include the tumor location, the number of lobes affected by the cancer, the patient's general poor health, and cirrhosis.) Moreover, fewer than 20% of those patients who undergo resection survive for three years without recurrence. Transplantation is an alternative to resection, but this technique is not appropriate for metastatic disease or for larger cancers, and the shortage of liver grafts limits the usefulness of this technique. Systemic chemotherapy has been shown to have a therapeutic effect on metastases, but it has also been shown to have no effect on long-term survival rates.

—*Michael Curley and Patrick Hamilton*

Clearly, there is no one way to write an opening paragraph, but we want to add that you cannot go wrong in beginning your essay—especially if it's an analytic essay written for a course in the humanities—with a paragraph that includes **a statement of your thesis.** A common version of this kind of paragraph follows this pattern:

- It offers some background (if you're writing about a novel, for example, you'll give the author and title as well as relevant information about the novel's plot).

- It suggests the problem the essay will address (in the paragraph below, the problem is implied: In *Frankenstein* similar characters meet very different fates; how can we account for the difference?).

- It ends with a sentence that states the main point, or thesis, of the essay.

> In Frankenstein, Mary Shelley frames the novel
> with narratives of two similar characters who meet
> markedly different fates. Frankenstein, the medical
> researcher, and Walton, the explorer, are both
> passionately determined to push forward the bound-
> aries of human knowledge. But while Walton's ambition
> to explore unknown regions of the earth is directed
> by reason and purpose, Frankenstein's ambition to
> create life is unfocussed and misguided. This differ-
> ence in the nature of their ambitions determines
> their fates. Walton's controlled ambition leads him
> to abandon his goal in order to save the lives of
> his crew members. When we last see him, he is heading
> toward home and safety. Frankenstein's unchecked
> ambition leads to his own death and the self-
> destruction of his creature.

Concluding Paragraphs

Concluding paragraphs, like opening paragraphs, are especially difficult if only because they are so conspicuous. Fortunately, you are not
always obliged to write one. Descriptive essays, for example, may end
merely with a final paragraph, not with a paragraph that draws a conclusion. In an expository essay explaining a process or mechanism, you
may simply stop when you have finished.

But if you do have to write a concluding paragraph, say something
interesting. It is not of the slightest interest to say "Thus we see . . ."
and then echo your title and first paragraph. There is some justification
for a summary at the end of a long essay because the reader may have
half forgotten some of the ideas presented thirty pages earlier, but an
essay that can easily be held in the mind needs something more. A good
concluding paragraph rounds out the previous discussion. Such a paragraph may offer a few sentences that summarize (it should not begin
with the dull phrase, "in summary"); but it will probably also draw an

inference that has not previously been expressed. To draw such an inference is not to introduce an entirely new idea—the end of an essay is hardly the place for that. Rather it is to see the previous material in a fresh perspective, to take the discussion perhaps one step further.

Because all writers have to find out what they think about any given topic, and have to find the strategies appropriate for presenting these thoughts to a particular audience, we hesitate to offer a do-it-yourself kit for final paragraphs, but the following simple devices often work:

- End with a quotation, especially a quotation that amplifies or varies a quotation used in the opening paragraph.

- End with some idea or detail from the beginning of the essay and thus bring it full circle.

- End with a new (but related) point, one that takes your discussion a step further.

- End with an allusion, say to a historical or mythological figure or event, putting your topic in a larger framework.

- End with a glance at the readers—not with a demand that they mount the barricades, but with a suggestion that the next move is theirs.

If you adopt any of these devices, do so quietly; the aim is not to write a grand finale, but to complete or round out a discussion.

All essayists must find their own ways of ending each essay; the five strategies we have suggested are common, but they are not for you if you don't find them useful. And so, rather than ending this section with rules about how to end essays, we suggest how not to end them: Don't merely summarize, don't say "in conclusion," don't introduce a totally new point, and don't apologize.

CHECKLIST FOR REVISING PARAGRAPHS

☐ Does the paragraph *say* anything? Does it have substance? (See pp. 34–35.)

☐ Does the paragraph have a topic sentence? If so, is it in the best place? If the paragraph doesn't have a topic sentence, might one improve the paragraph? Or does the paragraph have a clear topic idea? (See pp. 36–38.)

☐ If the paragraph is an opening paragraph, is it interesting enough to attract and to hold a reader's attention? (See pp. 52–59.) If it is a later paragraph, does it easily evolve out of the previous paragraph and lead into the next paragraph? (See pp. 45–49.)

☐ Does the paragraph contain some principle of development—for instance, from cause to effect or from general to particular? What is the purpose of the paragraph? Does the paragraph fulfill the purpose? (See pp. 41–42.)

☐ Does each sentence clearly follow from the preceding sentence? Have you provided transitional words or cues to guide your reader? Would it be useful to repeat certain key words, for clarity? (See pp. 42–45.)

☐ Is the closing paragraph effective, or is it an unnecessary restatement of the obvious? (See pp. 59–60.)

CHAPTER FOUR

REVISING FOR CONCISENESS

Excess is the common substitute for energy.
—*Marianne Moore*

Writers who want to keep the attention and confidence of their audience revise for conciseness. The general rule is to say everything relevant in as few words as possible. The conclusion of the Supreme Court's decision in *Brown v. the Board of Education of Topeka*, for example—"Separate educational facilities are inherently unequal"—says it all in six words.

The writers of the following sentences bore us because they don't make every word count.

```
There are two pine trees which grow behind this house.

On his left shoulder is a small figure standing. He is
about the size of the doctor's head.

The judge is seated behind the bench and he is wearing
a judicial robe.
```

Compare those three sentences with these revisions:

```
Two pine trees grow behind this house.

On his left shoulder stands a small figure, about the
size of the doctor's head.

The judge, wearing a robe, sits behind the bench.
```

The time to begin revising for conciseness is when you think you have an acceptable draft in hand—something that pretty much covers your topic and comes reasonably close to saying what you believe about it. As you go over your draft, study each sentence to see what can be deleted without loss of meaning. Read each paragraph, preferably aloud, to see if each sentence supports the topic sentence or idea and clarifies the point you are making. Leave in the concrete details and examples that support your ideas, but cut out all the deadwood that chokes them:

- Extra words
- Empty or pretentious phrases
- Weak qualifiers
- Redundancies
- Negative constructions
- Wordy uses of the verb *to be*
- Other extra verbs and verb phrases

Instant Prose

Here are some examples of Instant Prose from students' essays:

> Frequently a chapter title in a book reveals to the
> reader the main point that the author desires to
> bring out during the course of the chapter.

We could try revising this, cutting the twenty-seven words down to seven:

> A chapter's title often reveals its thesis.

But why bother? Unless the title is an exception, is the point worth making?

> The two poems are basically similar in many ways, yet
> they have their significant differences.

True, all poems are both similar to and different from other poems. Start over with your next sentence, perhaps something like:

> The two poems, superficially similar in rough
> paraphrase, are strikingly different in diction.

> Although the essay is simple in plot, the theme encompasses many vital concepts of emotional makeup.
>
> Following a transcendental vein, the nostalgia in the poem takes on a spiritual quality.
>
> Cassell only presents a particular situation concerning the issue, and with clear descriptions and a certain style sets up an interesting article.

These examples fall into the category of Unadulterated Instant Prose. Not even the writers of these sentences now know what they mean.

Writing Instant Prose is an acquired habit, like smoking cigarettes; fortunately it's easier to kick. It often begins in high school, sometimes earlier, when the victim is assigned a ten-page paper, or is told that a paragraph *must* contain at least three sentences, or that a thesis is stated in the introduction to an essay, elaborated in the body, and repeated in the conclusion. If the instructions appear arbitrary, and the student is bored or intimidated by them, the response is likely to be meaningless and mechanical.

Such students have forgotten the true purpose of writing—the discovery and communication of ideas, attitudes, and judgments. They concentrate instead on the word count: stuffing sentences, padding paragraphs, repeating points, and adding flourishes. Rewarded by a satisfactory grade, they repeat the performance, and in time, through practice, develop some fluency in spilling out words without thought or commitment, and almost without effort. Such students may enter college feeling somehow inauthentic, perhaps even aware that they don't really mean what they write—a sure symptom of habitual use of, or addiction to, Instant Prose.

How to Avoid Instant Prose

1. Trust yourself. Writing Instant Prose is not only a habit; it's also a form of alienation. If you habitually resort to Instant Prose, you probably don't think of what you write as your own but as something you produce on demand for someone else, most likely that unreasonable authority, the teacher, whose mysterious whims and insatiable appetite for words must somehow be satisfied. Breaking the habit begins with recognizing it. It means learning to respect your ideas and experiences, and determining that when you write, you'll write what you mean. This involves taking some risks, of course; habits offer some security or they would have no grip on us. Moreover, we all have moments when we doubt that our ideas are worth taking seriously. Keep writing honestly anyway. The self-doubts will pass; accomplishing something—writing one clear sentence—can help make them pass.

2. Learn to recognize Instant Prose Additives in your writing and in what you read. And you *will* find them in what you read—in textbooks and in academic journals, notoriously. Here's an example from a recent book on contemporary theater:

> One of the principal and most persistent sources of error that tends to bedevil a considerable proportion of contemporary literary analysis is the assumption that the writer's creative process is a wholly conscious and purposive type of activity.

Notice all the extra stuff in the sentence: "principal and most persistent," "tends to bedevil," "considerable proportion," "type of activity." Cleared of deadwood the sentence might read:

> The assumption that the writer's creative process is wholly conscious bedevils much contemporary criticism.

3. Acquire two things: a new habit, Revising for Conciseness; and what Isaac Singer calls "the writer's best friend," a wastebasket.

Extra Words and Empty Words

Delete extra words; replace vague, empty, or pretentious words and phrases with specific and direct language. Notice how, in the examples provided, the following words crop up: *significant, situation, involving, effect.* These words have legitimate uses but are often no more than Instant Prose Additives. Delete them whenever you can. Similar words to watch out for: *aspect, basically, facet, factor, fundamental, manner, nature, type, ultimate, utilization, viable, virtually, vital.* If they make your writing sound good, don't hesitate—cross them out at once.

Wordy

However, it must be remembered that Ruth's marriage could have positive effects on Naomi's situation.

Concise

Ruth's marriage, however, will also provide security for Naomi.

In the revision, the unnecessary "it must be remembered that" has been struck out. For the vague words "positive effects" and "situation," specific words have been substituted. The revision, though briefer, says more.

Wordy

In high school, where I had the opportunity for three years of working with the student government, I realized how significantly a person's enthusiasm could be destroyed merely by the attitudes of his superiors.

Concise

In high school, during three years on the student council, I saw students' enthusiasm destroyed by insecure teachers and cynical administrators.

Again, the revised sentence gives more information in fewer words. How?

Wordy

It creates a better motivation of learning when students can design their own programs involving education. This way students' interests can be focused on.

Concise

Motivation improves when students design their own programs, focused on their own interests.

Weak Intensifiers

Words like *very*, *quite*, *rather*, *completely*, *definitely*, and *so* can usually be struck from a sentence without loss. Paradoxically, sentences are often more emphatic without intensifiers. Try reading the following sentences both with and without the bracketed words:

At that time I was [very] idealistic.

We found the proposal [quite] feasible.

The scene was [extremely] typical.

The death scene is [truly] grotesque.

Always avoid using intensifiers with *unique*. Either something is unique—the only one of its kind—or it is not. It can't be very, quite, so, pretty, or fairly unique.

Circumlocutions

Roundabout or long-winded ways of saying things weaken your prose and tire your reader. Notice how each circumlocution in the first column is matched by a concise expression in the second.

I came to the realization that	I realized that
She is of the opinion that	She thinks that
The quotation is supportive of	The quotation supports
Concerning the matter of	About
During the course of	During
For the period of a week	For a week
In the event that	If
In the process of	During, while
Regardless of the fact that	Although
Due to the fact that	Because
For the simple reason that	Because
The fact that	That
Inasmuch as	Since
If the case was such that	If
It is often the case that	Often
In all cases	Always
I made contact with	I called, saw, phoned, wrote
At that point in time	Then
At this point in time	Now

Now revise this sentence:

These movies have a large degree of popularity for the simple reason that they give the viewers insight in many cases.

Wordy Beginnings
Vague words and phrases sometimes clog the beginnings of sentences. They're like elaborate windups before the pitch.

Wordy

By analyzing carefully the last lines in this stanza, you find the connections between the loose ends of the poem.

Concise

The last lines of the stanza connect the loose ends of the poem.

Wordy

What the cartoonist is illustrating and trying to get across is the greed of the oil producers.

Concise

The cartoon illustrates the greed of the oil producers.

Wordy

In opposition to the situation of the younger son is that of the elder who remained in his father's house, working hard and handling his inheritance wisely.

Concise

The elder son, by contrast, remained in his father's house, worked hard, and handled his inheritance wisely.

Notice that when the deadwood is cleared from the beginning of the sentence, the subject appears early, and the main verb appears close to it:

The last lines . . . connect. . .

The cartoon illustrates. . .

The elder son . . . remained. . .

Locating the right noun for the subject, and the right verb for the predicate, is the key to revising sentences with wordy beginnings.

Empty Conclusions

Often a sentence that begins well has an empty conclusion. The words go on but the sentence seems to stand still; if it's not revised, it requires another sentence to explain it.

Empty

"Those Winter Sundays" is composed so that a reader can feel what the poet was saying. [How is it composed? What is he saying?]

Informative

"Those Winter Sundays" describes the speaker's anger as a child, and his remorse as an adult.

Empty

In both Orwell's and Baldwin's essays the feeling of white supremacy is very important. [Why is white supremacy important?]

Informative

Both Orwell and Baldwin trace the insidious consequences of white supremacy.

Wordy Uses of the Verbs To Be, To Have, *and* To Make

Notice that in the preceding unrevised sentences a form of the verb *to be* introduces the empty conclusion: "*was* saying," "*is* very important." In each revision, the right verb added and generated substance. In the following sentences, substitutions for the verb *to be* both invigorate and shorten otherwise substantial sentences. (The wordy expressions are italicized, and so are the revisions.)

Wordy

The scene *is taking place* at night, in front of the capitol building.

Concise

The scene *takes place* at night, in front of the capitol building.

Wordy

In this shoeshining and early rising *there are indications* of church attendance.

Concise

The early rising and shoeshining *indicate* church attendance.

Wordy

The words "flashing," "rushing," "plunging," and "tossing" *are suggestive of* excitement.

Concise

The words "flashing," "rushing," "plunging," and "tossing" *suggest* excitement.

A RULE FOR WRITERS

Whenever you can, replace a form of the verb *to be* with a stronger verb.

To Be	**Strong Verb**
and a participle (*is taking*)	*takes*
and a noun (*are indications*)	*indicate*
and an adjective (*are suggestive*)	*suggest*

In the following example, substitutions for the verbs *to have* and *to make* shorten and enliven the sentence.

Wordy

The Friar *has knowledge* that Juliet is alive.

Concise

The Friar *knows* that Juliet is alive.

Wordy

The stanzas *make a vivid contrast* between Heaven and Hell.

Concise

The stanzas *vividly contrast* Heaven and Hell.

Like all rules, this one has exceptions. We don't list them here; you'll discover them by listening to your sentences.

Redundancy

Redundancy refers to unnecessary repetition in the expression of ideas. "Future plans," after all, are only plans, and "to glide smoothly" or "to scurry rapidly" is only to glide or to scurry. Unlike repetition, which often provides emphasis or coherence (for example, "government of the people, by the people, for the people"), redundancy can always be eliminated.

Redundant

Any student could randomly sit anywhere. (If the students could sit anywhere, the seating was random.)

Concise

Students could sit anywhere.

Students chose their seats at random.

Redundant

In the orthodox Cuban culture, the surface of the female role seemed degrading. [Perhaps this sentence means what it says. More probably "surface" and "seemed" are redundant.]

Concise

In the orthodox Cuban culture, the female role seemed degrading.

In the orthodox Cuban culture, the female role was superficially degrading.

Redundant

In "Araby" the boy feels alienated emotionally from his family.

Concise

In "Araby" the boy feels alienated from his family.

What words can be crossed out of the following phrases?

throughout the entire article

her attitude of indifference

a conservative type suit

his own personal opinion

elements common to both of them

emotions and feelings

shared together

alleged suspect

Many phrases in common use are redundant. For example, there is no need to write "blare noisily," since the meaning of the adverb "noisily" is conveyed in the verb "blare." Watch for phrases like these when you revise:

round in shape	resulting effect
tall in stature	prove conclusively
must necessarily	connected together
basic fundamentals	very unique
true fact	very universal
free gift	the reason why is because

Negative Constructions

Negative constructions are often wordy and sometimes pretentious.

Wordy

Housing for married students is *not unworthy of* consideration.

Concise

Housing for married students is worth considering.

Better

The trustees should earmark funds for married students' housing. [Probably what the author meant.]

"See what I mean? You're never sure just where you stand with them."
© The New Yorker Collection 1971. Al Rossi from Cartoonbank.com. All Rights Reserved.

A (GOLDEN) RULE FOR WRITERS

Write for others as you would have them write for you (not "Write for others in a manner not unreasonably dissimilar to the manner in which you would have them write for you").

Extra Sentences, Extra Clauses: Subordination

Sentences are sometimes wordy because ideas are given more elaborate grammatical constructions than they need. When revising, try to reduce these constructions. Two sentences, for example, may be reduced to one, or a clause may be reduced to a phrase.

Wordy

The Book of Ruth was probably written in the fifth century B.C. It was a time when women were considered the property of men.

Concise

The Book of Ruth was probably written in the fifth century B.C., when women were considered the property of men.

Wordy

The first group was the largest. This group was seated in the center of the dining hall.

Concise

The first group, the largest, was seated in the center of the dining hall.

Who, Which, That

Watch for clauses beginning with *who, which,* and *that.*

Wordy

George Orwell is the pen name of Eric Blair, *who was* an English writer.

Concise

George Orwell is the pen name of Eric Blair, an English writer.

Wordy

They are seated at a table *which* is covered with a patched and tattered cloth.

Concise

They are seated at a table covered with a patched and tattered cloth.

Wordy

There is one feature *that is* grossly out of proportion.

Concise

One feature is grossly out of proportion.

For further discussion of *which* clauses, see "A Writer's Glossary" in Chapter 13 (p. 292).

It Is, This Is, There Are

Watch for sentences and clauses beginning with *it is, this is, there are* (again, wordy uses of the verb *to be*). These expressions often lead to a *which* or a *that,* but even when they don't they may be wordy.

Wordy

This is a quotation from Black Elk's autobiography *which* discloses his prophetic powers.

Concise

This quotation from Black Elk's autobiography discloses his prophetic powers.

Wordy

It is frequently considered *that Hamlet* is Shakespeare's most puzzling play.

Concise

Hamlet is frequently considered Shakespeare's most puzzling play.

Wordy

In Notman's photograph of Buffalo Bill and Sitting Bull *there are* definite contrasts between the two figures.

Concise

Notman's photograph of Buffalo Bill and Sitting Bull contrasts the two figures.

Some Concluding Remarks About Conciseness

We spoke earlier about how students succumb to Instant Prose and acquire other wordy habits—by writing what they think the teacher has asked for. We haven't forgotten that instructors assign papers of a certain length in college too. But the length given is not an arbitrary limit that must be reached—the instructor who asks for a ten-page paper is probably trying to tell you that it's likely to take you ten pages to develop your ideas on the topic at hand. Such, apparently, was the intention of William Randolph Hearst, the newspaper publisher, who cabled an astronomer, "Is there life on Mars? Cable reply 1000 words." The astronomer's reply was, "Nobody knows," repeated 500 times.

What do you do when you've been asked to produce a ten-page paper and after diligent writing and revising you find you've said everything relevant to your topic in seven and a half pages? Our advice is, hand it in. We can't remember ever counting the words or pages of a substantial, interesting essay; we assume that our colleagues elsewhere are equally reasonable and equally overworked. If we're wrong, tell us about it—in writing, and in the fewest possible words.

CHECKLIST FOR REVISING FOR CONCISENESS

☐ Does every word count? Can any words or phrases be cut without loss of meaning?

☐ Are there any empty or pretentious words such as *situation, factor, virtually, significant,* and *utilize?* (See pp. 65–66.)

☐ Do intensifiers such as *very, truly,* and *rather* weaken your sentences? (See p. 66.)

☐ Are there any roundabout or long-winded locutions? Do you say, for example, *at that point in time* when you mean *then,* or *for the simple reason that* when you mean *because?* (See pp. 66–67.)

☐ Do sentences get off to a fast start? Can you cut any sentences that open with "it is . . . that"? (See pp. 67–68, 73–74.)

☐ Can you replace forms of the verbs *to be, to have,* and *to make* with precise and active verbs? (See pp. 69–70.)

☐ Are there any redundancies or negative constructions? (See pp. 70–72.)

☐ Can any sentences be combined using subordination? (See pp. 72–73.)

CHAPTER FIVE

REVISING FOR CLARITY

> Here's to plain speaking and clear
> understanding.
> —*Sidney Greenstreet, in* The Maltese Falcon

Clarity

First, read the following two passages:

We have seen new realities created by the advance of physics. But this chain of creation can be traced back far beyond the starting point of physics. One of the most primitive concepts is that of an object. The concepts of a tree, a horse, any material body, are creations gained on the basis of experience, though the impressions from which they arise are primitive in comparison with the world of physical phenomena. A cat teasing a mouse also creates, by thought, its own primitive reality. The fact that the cat reacts in a similar way toward any mouse it meets shows that it forms concepts and theories which are its guide through its own world of sense impressions.

—*Albert Einstein and Leopold Infeld*

Skills constitute the manipulative techniques of human goal attainment and control in relation to the physical world, so far as artifacts or machines especially designed as tools do not yet supplement them. Truly human skills are guided by organized and codified *knowledge* of both the things to be manipulated and the human capacities that are used to manipulate them. Such knowledge is an aspect of cultural-level symbolic processes, and, like other aspects to be discussed presently, requires the capacities of the human central nervous system, particularly the brain. This organic system is clearly essential to all of the symbolic processes; as we well know, the human brain is far superior to the brain of any other species.

—*Talcott Parsons*

Why is the first passage easier to understand than the second?

Both passages discuss the relationship between the brain and the physical world it attempts to understand. The first passage, by Einstein and Infeld, is, if anything, more complex both in what it asserts and in what it suggests than the second, by Parsons. Both passages explain that the brain organizes sense impressions. But Einstein and Infeld further explain that the history of physics can be understood as an extension of the simplest sort of organization, such as we all make in distinguishing a tree from a horse, or such as even a cat makes in teasing a mouse. Parsons only promises that "other aspects" will "be discussed presently." How many of us are eager for those next pages?

Good writing is clear, not because it presents simple ideas but because it presents ideas in the simplest form the subject permits. A clear analysis doesn't falsely reduce a complex problem to a simple one; it breaks it down into its simple, comprehensible parts and discusses them, one by one. A clear paragraph explains one of these parts coherently, and in language as simple and as particular as the reader's understanding requires and the context allows. Where Parsons writes of "organized and codified *knowledge* of . . . the things to be manipulated," Einstein and Infeld write simply of the concept of an object. And even "object," a simple but general word, is further clarified by the specific, familiar examples, "tree" and "horse." Parsons writes of "the manipulative techniques of . . . goal attainment and control in relation to the physical world, so far as artifacts or machines especially designed as tools do not yet supplement them." Einstein and Infeld show us a cat teasing a mouse.

A RULE FOR WRITERS

Present ideas in the simplest form the subject permits.

Notice also the clear organization of Einstein and Infeld's paragraph. The first sentence, clearly transitional, refers to the advance of physics traced in the preceding pages. The next sentence, introduced by "But," reverses our direction: We are now going to look not at an advance, but at primitive beginnings. And the following sentences, to the end of the paragraph, fulfill that promise. We move back to primitive human concepts, clarified by examples, and finally to the still more primitive example of the cat. Parson's paragraph is also organized, but the route is much more difficult to follow.

Why do people write obscurely? It's difficult to write clearly.[1] Authorities may be obscure not because they want to tax you with unnecessary problems, but because they don't know how to avoid them. If you have ever tried to install a computer upgrade by following the "easy instructions," you know that the simplest kind of expository writing, giving instructions, can foil the writers most eager for your goodwill (that is, those who want you to use their products). Few instructions, unfortunately, are as unambiguous as "Go to jail. Go directly to jail. Do not pass Go. Do not collect $200."

You can, though, learn to write clearly, by learning to recognize common sources of obscurity in writing and by consciously revising your own work. We offer, to begin with, three general rules:

- Use the simplest, most exact, most specific language your subject allows.
- Put together what belongs together, in the essay, in the paragraph, and in the sentence.
- Keep your reader in mind, particularly when you revise.

Now for more specific advice, and examples—the cats and mice of revising for clarity.

Clarity and Exactness: Using the Right Word

Denotation

Be sure the word you choose has the right explicit meaning, or *denotation*. Did you mean *sarcastic* or *ironic? Fatalistic* or *pessimistic? Disinterested* or *uninterested? Biannual* or *semiannual? Enforce* or *reinforce? Use* or *usage?* If you're not sure, check the dictionary. You'll

---

[1] Our first draft of this sentence read "Writing clearly is difficult." Can you see why we changed it?

find some of the most commonly misused words discussed in "A Writer's Glossary," Chapter 13, pages 272–295. Here are examples of a few others:

Daru faces a dilemma between his humane feelings and his conceptions of justice. [Strictly speaking, a *dilemma* requires a choice between two equally unattractive alternatives. *Conflict* would be a better word here.]

However, as time dragged on, exercising seemed to lose its charisma. [What is charisma? Why is it inexact here?]

When I run, I don't allow myself to stop until I have reached my destiny. [What is the difference between *destiny* and *destination*?]

"I'm not quite clear on this, Fulton. Are you moaning about your prerequisites, your requisites, or perquisites?"

Connotation

Be sure the word you choose has the right *connotation* (association, implication). As Mark Twain said, the difference between the right word and the almost right word is the difference between lightning and the lightning bug.

> Boston politics has always upheld the reputation of being especially crooked. [*Upheld* inappropriately suggests that Boston has proudly maintained its reputation. *Has always had* would be appropriate here, but pale. *Deserved* would, in this context, be ironic, implying—accurately—the writer's scorn.]

> This book, unlike many other novels, lacks tedious descriptive passages. [*Lacks* implies a deficiency. How would you revise the sentence?]

> New Orleans, notorious for its good jazz and good food. . . . [Is *notorious* the right word here, or *famous?*]

> Sunday, Feb. 9. Another lingering day at Wellesley. [In this entry from a student's journal, *lingering* strikes us as right. What does *lingering* imply about Sundays at Wellesley that *long* would not?]

Because words have connotations, most writing—even when it pretends to be objective—conveys attitudes as well as facts. Consider, for example, this passage by Jessica Mitford, describing part of the procedure used for embalming:

> A long, hollow needle attached to a tube . . . is jabbed into the abdomen, poked around the entrails and chest cavity, the contents of which are pumped out. . . .

Here, as almost always, the writer's *purpose* in large measure determines the choice of words. Probably the sentence accurately describes part of the procedure, but it also, of course, records Mitford's contempt for the procedure. Suppose she wanted to be more respectful—suppose, for example, she were an undertaker writing an explanatory pamphlet. Instead of the needle being "jabbed" it would be "inserted," and instead of being "poked around the entrails" it would be "guided around the viscera," and the contents would not be "pumped out" but would be "drained." Mitford's words would be the wrong words for an undertaker explaining embalming to apprentices or to the general public, but, given her purpose, they are exactly the right ones because they clearly convey her attitude.

Notice, too, that many words have social, political, or sexist overtones. What is implied by the distinction? Consider the differences in *connotation* in each of the following series:

underdeveloped nations, developing nations, emerging nations

preference, bias, prejudice

upbringing, conditioning, brainwashing

intelligence gathering, espionage, spying

antiabortion, pro-life; pro-abortion, pro-choice

Avoiding Sexist Language

Traditionally, the pronouns *he* and *his* have been used as generic pronouns when both men and women are implied: "A historian must consider the context of *his* source." But contemporary writers avoid the generic use of male pronouns, because such usage is sexist (our example excludes women historians from the discussion), and because it can be misleading and unclear (the example may suggest that there are no women historians, or that women historians do something different from the men). They commonly turn to three remedies in their writing:

- Using both male and female pronouns: "A historian must consider the context of *his* or *her* source."
- Substituting the plural form: "*Historians* must consider the context of *their* source."
- Eliminating the pronoun: "Historians must consider a source's context."

Note: Writers and speakers sometimes attempt to correct sexist language by using a plural pronoun with a singular subject: "A *historian* must consider *their* source's context." But this approach produces ungrammatical sentences: The pronoun doesn't agree with its antecedent. (For more on agreement, see pp. 102–104.) Writers also sometimes use such constructions as "his/her," "him/her," or "s/he": "A historian must consider his/her source." While not incorrect, we think that this approach produces ugly sentences, and we recommend that you use one of the three remedies above.

A RULE FOR WRITERS

Avoid using *he* and *him* as generic pronouns to refer to both men and women.

© Bill Griffith. Reprinted with special permission of King Features Syndicate.

Likewise, avoid using "man" and "mankind" generically:

Man's need for approval. . . .

Substitute gender-neutral terms for gender-specific terms whenever possible—unless, of course, your sentence refers specifically to one gender. The sentence above could thus be revised:

Humanity's need for approval. . . .

Our need for approval. . . .

Here are more examples of gender-specific or sexist terms, with possible replacements:

Sexist Term	**Gender-Neutral Term**
chairman	chairperson, chair, head

manpower	personnel
layman	layperson
stewardess	flight attendant
freshman	first-year student
mailman	mail carrier
poetess	poet

Quotation Marks as Apologies

When you have used words with exact meanings (denotations) and appropriate associations (connotations) for your purpose, don't apologize for them by putting quotation marks around them. If the words *copped a plea, ripped off,* or *kids* suit your purpose better than *plea-bargained, stolen,* or *children,* use them. If they are inappropriate, don't put them in quotation marks; find the right words.

Being Specific

When writing descriptions, catch the richness, complexity, and uniqueness of things. Suppose, for example, you are describing a scene from your childhood, a setting you loved. There was, in particular, a certain tree . . . and you write: "Near the water there was a big tree that was rather impressive." Most of us would produce something like that sentence. Here is the sentence Ernesto Galarza wrote in *Barrio Boy*:

> On the edge of the pond, at the far side, there was an enormous walnut tree, standing like an open umbrella whose ribs extended halfway across the still water of the pool.

We probably could not have come up with the metaphor of the umbrella because we wouldn't have seen the similarity. (As Aristotle observed, the gift for making metaphors distinguishes the poet from the rest of us.) But we can all train ourselves to be accurate observers and reporters. For "the water" (general) we can specify "pond"; for "near" we can say how near, "on the edge of the pond," and add the specific location, "at the far side"; for "tree" we can give the species, "walnut tree"; and for "big" we can provide a picture, its branches "extended halfway across" the pond: It was, in fact, "enormous."

Galarza does not need to add limply, as we did, that the tree "was rather impressive." The tree he describes *is* impressive. That he accurately remembered it persuades us that he was impressed, without his having to tell us he was. For writing descriptions, a good general rule is: Show, don't tell.

Be as specific as you can be in all forms of exposition too. Take the time, when you revise, to find the exact word to replace vague phrases or clichés. In the following examples we have to guess or invent what the writer means.

Vague

The clown's part in *Othello* is very small.

Specific

The clown appears in only two scenes in *Othello*.

The clown in *Othello* speaks only thirty lines. [Notice the substitution of the verb *appears* or *speaks* for the frequently debilitating *is*. And in place of the weak intensifier *very* we have specific details to tell us how small the role is.]

Vague

He feels uncomfortable at the whole situation. [Many feelings are uncomfortable. Which one does he feel? What's the situation?]

Specific

He feels guilty for having distrusted his father.

Vague Cliché

Then she criticized students for living in an ivory tower. [Did she criticize them for being detached or for being secluded? For social irresponsibility or studiousness?]

Specific

Then she criticized students for being socially irresponsible.

Using Examples

In addition to exact words and specific details, illustrative examples make for clear writing. Einstein and Infeld, in the passage quoted on page 76, use as an example of a primitive concept a cat teasing not only its first mouse but also "any mouse it meets." Here is another passage from *Barrio Boy*; like the paragraph from Einstein and Infeld, this paragraph clarifies and develops its topic through examples:

> In Jalco people spoke in two languages—Spanish and with gestures. These signs were made with the face or hands or a combination of both. If you bent one arm and tapped the elbow with the other hand, it meant "He is stingy." When you sawed one arm across the other you were saying that someone you knew played the fiddle terribly. To say that a man was a tippler you made a set of cow's horns with the little finger and the thumb of one hand, bending the three middle fingers to the palm and pointing the thumb at your mouth. And if you wanted to indicate, without saying so for the sake of politeness, that a mutual acquaintance was daffy, you tapped three times on your forehead with your middle finger.
>
> —*Ernesto Galarza*

Now look at a student's paragraph, here printed in the left column, from an essay whose thesis is that rage can be a useful mechanism for effecting change. Then compare the left-hand paragraph with the same paragraph, revised, at the right. Note the specific ways, sentence by sentence, the student revised for clarity.

In my high school we had little say in the learning processes that were used. The subjects that we were required to take were irrelevant. One had to take them to earn enough points to graduate. Some of the teachers were sympathetic to our problem. They would tell us about when they were young, how they tried to oppose their school system. But when they were young	In my high school we had little say about our curriculum. We were required, for example, to choose either American or European History to earn enough points for graduation. We wanted, but were at first refused, the option of Black History. Some of our teachers were sympathetic with us; one told me about her fight opposing the penmanship course required in her school. Nor was the principal

it was a long time ago, for most of them. The principal would call assemblies to speak on the subject. They were entitled "The Value of an Education" or "Get a Good Education to Have a Bright Future." The titles were not inviting. They had nothing to do with our plight. Most students never came to any agreements with the principal because most of his thoughts and views seemed old and outdated.

totally indifferent--he called assemblies. I remember one talk he gave called "The Value of an Education in Today's World," and another, "Get a Good Education to Have a Bright Future." I don't recall hearing about a Black History course in either talk. Once, he invited a group of us to meet with him in his office, but we didn't reach any agreement. He solemnly showed us an American History text (not the one we used) that had a whole chapter devoted to Black History.

Jargon and Technical Language

Most dictionaries give three meanings for *jargon:*

- Technical language
- Meaningless language
- Inflated or pretentious language

The members of almost every profession or trade—indeed, almost all people who share any specialized interest—use the jargon of their field. And this is certainly true of members of academic disciplines. In fact, learning a new discipline involves learning a new vocabulary, a new set of technical terms. Art historians talk of *cubism, iconography*, and *formalism;* Freudians talk of *cathect, libido*, and the *oral phase;* film critics and theorists talk of *anamorphic lenses, optical printers*, and *silent speed.*

Properly used, technical language communicates information concisely and clearly, and it can create a comfortable bond between speakers, or between the writer and the reader.

Untitled, 1949. Willem de Kooning, American (b. 1904). Black enamel.
© 2004 The Willem de Kooning Foundation/Artists Rights Society (ARS), New York.

For example, in the following sentences, concerned with twentieth-century art from a museum publication, the writer reasonably assumes that her readers—most likely people who are interested in and knowledgeable about art—will be able to make sense of such technical terms as "biomorphic," "calligraphic," "gesture," and "Abstract Expressionism":

> In Willem de Kooning's biomorphic black enamel drawing . . . drawn for a member of the Julliard String Quartet, the artist has abandoned the idea of a central organizing form. Black calligraphic shapes whip across the surface of the paper. There is a sense of gesture, an essential feature of Abstract Expressionism.

On the other hand, jargon sometimes *is* inflated and pretentious. Consider, for example, the following sentence by an art historian writing on American Indian baskets made for whites in the early twentieth century:

> Native curios were privileged in bourgeois parlor decoration as metonymic representations of the premodern, their significations

DILBERT reprinted by permission of United Feature Syndicate, Inc.

enhanced by hand-made production and utilitarian function, two aspects of the premodern also valorized in the contemporary American Arts and Crafts Movement.

This sentence does communicate information to specialists. In fact, much academic prose sounds an awful lot like the quoted sentence. Nevertheless, we believe that such language doesn't communicate clearly and efficiently. One problem with the sentence is that the level of abstraction is very high. Unlike the term "biomorphic," which means "evoking images of biological organisms," or the term "calligraphic," which here describes figures that recall the curves and loops of handwriting, the terms "premodern," "significations," and "valorized" don't call to mind specific, concrete things. The other problem with such language is that it is inflated, or more complicated than it needs to be. Consider the following paraphrase of the sentence on baskets:

Middle-class whites valued native curios and displayed them in their parlors. Because these objects were handmade and because they had been used in daily life, they stood for a pre-industrial world, a world celebrated also in the contemporary American Arts and Crafts Movement.

In general, it's best to use plain English—or, at least, the plainest English possible. After all, in an essay you wouldn't speak of a "preliminary overall strategizing concept" when "plan" would do. Don't use abstract, inflated language simply in order to sound impressive. On the other hand, do use the specialized terms of your field if you have come to know what they mean, if they are the best way to make your point, and if you are fairly confident that your imagined reader is familiar with them. If it's your hunch that your reader does not know the terms, you'll have to define them.

Clichés

Clichés (literally, in French, molds from which type is cast) are trite expressions, mechanically reproduced. Since they are available without thought, they are great Instant Prose Additives (see p. 65). Writers who use clichés are usually surprised to be criticized: They find the phrases attractive and may even think them exact. (Phrases become clichés precisely because they have wide appeal and therefore wide use.) But clichés, by their very nature, cannot communicate the uniqueness of your thoughts. Furthermore, because they come instantly to mind, they tend to block the specific detail or exact expression that will let the reader know what precisely is in your mind. In revising, when you strike out a cliché, you force yourself to do the work of writing clearly. How many clichés can you spot in the following example?

> Finally, the long-awaited day arrived. Up bright and early. . . . She peered at me with suspicion; then a faint smile crossed her face.

Here are some other worn-out phrases to avoid:

first and foremost	time honored
the acid test	bustled to and fro
fatal flaw	short but sweet
budding genius	few and far between
slowly but surely	D-day arrived
little did I know	sigh of relief
the big moment	last but not least

In attempting to avoid clichés, however, don't go to the other extreme of wildly original, super-vivid writing—"'Well then, say something to her,' he roared, his whole countenance gnarled in rage." It's better to

"You're right as rain. It's the dawn of history, and there are no clichés as yet. I'll drink to that."

write, "he said." (Anyone who intends to write dialogue should memorize Ring Lardner's intentionally funny line, "'Shut up!' he explained.")

Metaphors and Mixed Metaphors

Ordinary speech abounds with metaphors. We speak or write of the *foot of a mountain*, the *germ of an idea*, the *root of a problem*. Metaphors so deeply embedded in the language that they no longer evoke pictures in our minds are called **dead metaphors.** Usually they offer us, as writers, no problems: We need neither seek them nor avoid them; they are simply there. (Notice, for example, "embedded" two sentences back.) Such metaphors become problems, however, when we unwittingly call them back to life, as Howard Nemerov observes: "That these metaphors may be not dead but only sleeping, or that they may arise from the grave and walk in our sentences, is something that has troubled everyone who has ever tried to write plain expository prose."

Dead metaphors are most likely to haunt us when they are embodied in clichés. Since we use clichés without attention to what they literally say or point to, we are unlikely to be aware of the dead metaphors buried in them. But when we attach one cliché to another, we may raise the metaphors from the grave. The result is likely to be a **mixed metaphor;** the effect is almost always absurd.

Water seeks its own level whichever way you want to slice it.

Traditional liberal education has run out of gas and educational soup kitchens are moving into the vacuum.

The low ebb has been reached and hopefully it's turned the corner.

Her energy, drained through a stream of red tape, led only to closed doors.

As comedian Joe E. Lewis observed, "Show me a man who builds castles in the air and I'll show you a crazy architect."

Fresh metaphors, on the other hand, imaginatively combine accurate observations. They are not prefabricated ideas; they are a means of discovering or inventing new ideas. They enlarge thought and enliven prose. Here are two examples from students' journals:

        I have some sort of sporadic restlessness in me, like the pen on a polygraph machine. It moves along in curves, then suddenly shoots up, blowing a bubble in my throat, making my chest taut, forcing me to move around. It becomes almost unbearable and then suddenly it will plunge, leaving something that feels like a smooth orange wave.

        Time is like wrapping papers. It wraps memories, decorates them with sentiment. No matter (almost) what's inside, it's remembered as a beautiful piece of past time. That's why I even miss my high school years, which were filled with tiredness, boredom, confusion.

And here is a passage from an essay in which a student analyzes the style of a story he found boring:

        Every sentence yawns, stretches, shifts from side to side, and then quietly dozes off.

Experiment with metaphors, let them surface in the early drafts of your essays and in your journals, and by all means, introduce original and accurate comparisons in your essays. But leave the mixed metaphors to politicians and comedians.

Euphemisms

Euphemisms are words substituted for other words thought to be offensive. In deodorant advertisements there are no *armpits*, only *underarms*, which may *perspire*, but not *sweat*, and even then they don't *smell*. A parent reading a report card is likely to learn not that his child got an F in conduct but that she "experiences difficulty exercising self-control: (a) verbally (b) physically." And where do old people go? To Sun City, "a retirement community for senior citizens."

We do not advise you to write or speak discourteously; we do advise you, though, to use euphemisms sparingly, when tact recommends them. It's customary in a condolence letter to avoid the word *death*, and, depending both on your own feelings and those of the bereaved, you may wish to follow that custom. But there's no reason on earth to write "Hamlet passes on." You should be aware, moreover, that some people find euphemisms themselves offensive. Margaret Kuhn, for instance, argues that the word *old* is preferable to *senior*. "Old," she says "is the right word. . . . I think we should wear our gray hair, wrinkles, and crumbling joints as badges of distinction. After all, we worked damn hard to get them."

A RULE FOR WRITERS

When revising, replace needless euphemisms with plain words.

Passive or Active Voice?

Verbs appear in either the active or passive voice. In the active voice, the subject acts on the object: "I wrote the review." ("I" is the subject.) In the passive voice, the subject receives the action: "The review was written by me." (Here, "the review" is the subject.) In general prefer the active voice. The passive voice is often vague and sentences using it are needlessly wordy.

Consider the following passage, the opening paragraph of an analytic essay on the classical aspects of a library at a women's college:

```
A person walking by Margaret Clapp Library (1908-1913)
is struck by its classical design. The symmetry of the
façade is established by the regularly spaced columns of
the Ionic order on the first story of the building and
by pilasters on the second level. In the center of the
lower tier are two bronze doors: On the left door a
relief is seen, depicting Sapientia (Wisdom), and on the
right is seen the image of Caritas (Charity). The Greco-
Roman tradition is furthered by the two bronze statues
```

on either side of the entrance. On the left is Vesta
(goddess of the hearth) and on the right Minerva (goddess of wisdom). Through the use of classical architecture and Greco-Roman images, an image is conveyed--one
which Wellesley College hopes to create in its women.

Although the paragraph is richly informative, it is sluggish, chiefly
because the writer keeps using the passive voice: "A person . . . is struck
by"; "symmetry is established by"; "a relief is seen"; "on the right is
seen"; "tradition is furthered by"; "an image is conveyed."

Converting some or all of these expressions into the active voice
greatly improves the passage:

The most striking feature of the Margaret Clapp
Library is its classical design. Regularly spaced
columns of the Ionic order on the first story, and
pilasters on the second, establish the symmetry of the
façade. In the center of the lower tier are two bronze
doors: On the left door a relief depicts Sapientia
(Wisdom), and on the right Caritas (Charity). A bronze
statue on each side of the entrance (Vesta, goddess of
the hearth, on the left, and Minerva, goddess of wisdom, on the right) furthers the Greco-Roman tradition.
Wellesley College hopes, through the use of classical
architecture and Greco-Roman sculpture, to inspire in
its students particular ideals.

There are, however, times when the passive is appropriate:

- When the doer is obvious ("Bush was elected president in 2000 and
  2004.")
- When the doer is unknown ("The picture was stolen between midnight and 1 A.M.")
- When the doer is unimportant ("Unexposed film should be kept in a
  light-proof container.")

A RULE FOR WRITERS

When revising, consider each sentence in which you have used the passive
voice. If the passive suits your meaning, retain it; if it obscures your meaning, change it. More often than not, the passive voice obscures meaning.

Passive Voice

The revolver given Daru by the gendarme *is left* in the desk drawer. [Left by whom? The passive voice here obscures the point.]

Active Voice

Daru leaves the gendarme's revolver in the desk drawer.

Passive Voice

Daru serves tea and the Arab *is offered* some. [Confusing shift from the active voice "serves" to the passive voice "is offered."]

"And remember—no more subjunctives where the correct mood is indicative."

Active Voice

Daru serves tea and *offers* the Arab some.

Finally, avoid what has been called the Academic Passive: "In this essay it has been argued that. . . . " This cumbersome form used to be common in academic writing (to convey scientific objectivity) but "I have argued" is usually preferable to such stuffiness.

The Writer's "I"

It is seldom necessary in writing an essay (even on a personal experience) to repeat "I think that" or "in my opinion." Your reader knows that what you write is your opinion. Nor is it necessary, if you've done your job well, to apologize. "After reading the story over several times I'm not really sure what it is about, but . . . " Write about something you are reasonably sure of. Occasionally, though, when there is a real problem in the text—for example, the probable date of the Book of Ruth—it is not only permissible to disclose doubts and to reveal tentative conclusions, it may be necessary to do so.

Note also that there is no reason to avoid the pronoun *I* when you are in fact writing about yourself. Attempts to avoid *I* ("this writer," "we," expressions in the passive voice such as "it has been said above" and "it was seen") are noticeably awkward and distracting. And sometimes you may want to focus on your subjective response to a topic in order to clarify a point. The following opening paragraph of a movie review provides an example:

> I take the chance of writing about Bergman's *Persona* so long after its showing because this seems to me a movie there's no hurry about. It will be with us a long time, just as it has been on my mind for a long time. Right now, when I am perhaps still under its spell, it seems to me Bergman's masterpiece, but I can't imagine ever thinking it less than one of the great movies. This of course is opinion; what I know for certain is that *Persona* is also one of the most difficult movies I will ever see; and I am afraid that in this case there is a direct connection between difficulty and value. It isn't only that *Persona* is no harder than it has to be; its peculiar haunting power, its spell, and its value come directly from the fact that it's so hard to get a firm grasp on.
>
> —*Robert Garis*

Students who have been taught not to begin sentences with *I* often produce sentences that are eerily passive even when the verbs are in the active voice. For example:

> Two reasons are important to my active participation in dance.

> The name of the program that I enrolled in is the Health Careers Summer Program.

> An eager curiosity overcame my previous feeling of fear to make me feel better.

But doesn't it make more sense to say:

> I dance for two reasons.

> I enrolled in the Health Careers Summer Program.

> My curiosity aroused, I was no longer afraid.

A RULE FOR WRITERS

Make the agent of the action the subject of the sentence.

Clarity and Coherence

Writing a coherent essay is hard work; it requires mastery of a subject and skill in presenting it; it always takes a lot of time. Writing a coherent paragraph often takes more fussing and patching than you expect, but once you have the hang of using transition and repetition to link ideas and sentences together, the work can be relatively straightforward. Writing a coherent sentence requires only that you stay awake until you get to the end of it.

We all do nod off sometimes, even over our own prose. But if you make it a practice to read over your work several times, at least once aloud, you give yourself a chance to spot the incoherent sentence before your reader does, and to revise it. Once you see that a sentence is incoherent, it's usually easy to recast it.

Cats Are Dogs

Looking at a picture of a woman, a man once said to the painter Henri Matisse, "That woman's arm is too long." "That's not a woman," Matisse replied, "it's a painting."

In some sentences a form of the verb *to be* mistakenly asserts that one thing is in a class with another. Is a picture a woman? Are cats dogs? Students did write the following sentences:

Incoherent

```
X. J. Kennedy's poem "Nothing in Heaven Functions as It
Ought" is a contrast between Heaven and Hell.
```

As soon as you ask yourself the question "Is a poem a contrast?" you have, by bringing the two words close together, isolated the problem. A poem may be a sonnet, an epic, an ode—but not a contrast. The writer was trying to say what the poem *does*, not what it *is*.

Coherent

X. J. Kennedy's poem "Nothing in Heaven Functions as It Ought" contrasts Heaven and Hell.

Incoherent

Besides, he tells himself, a matchmaker is an old Jewish custom. [Is a matchmaker a custom?]

Coherent

Besides, he tells himself, consulting a matchmaker is an old Jewish custom.

Incoherent

Ruth's devotion to Naomi is rewarded by marrying Boaz. [Does devotion marry Boaz?]

Coherent

Ruth's marriage to Boaz rewards her devotion to Naomi.

Incoherent

He demonstrates many human frailties, such as the influence of others' opinions upon one's actions. [Is influence a frailty? How might this sentence be revised?]

Items in a Series

If you were given a shopping list that mentioned apples, fruit, and pears, you would be puzzled and possibly irritated by the inclusion of "fruit." Don't puzzle or irritate your reader with a **false series** of this sort. Analyze sentences containing items in a series to be sure that the items are of the same order of generality. For example

False series

His job exposed him to the "dirty work" of the British and to the evils of imperialism. ["The 'dirty work' of the British" is a *specific* example of the more *general* "evils of imperialism." The false series makes the sentence incoherent.]

Revised

His job, by exposing him to the "dirty work" of the British, brought him to understand the evils of imperialism.

In the following sentence, which item in the series makes the sentence incoherent?

Why should one man, no matter how important, be exempt from investigation, arrest, trial, and law-enforcing tactics?

Modifiers

A modifier should appear close to the word it modifies (that is, describes or qualifies). Three kinds of faulty modifiers are common: misplaced, squinting, and dangling.

Misplaced Modifiers   A modifier that seems to modify the wrong word is called a **misplaced modifier.** Such faulty connections are often unintentionally funny. The judo parlor that advertised "For $20 learn basic methods of protecting yourself from an experienced instructor" probably attracted more amused readers than paying customers.

Misplaced

Orwell shot the elephant under pressured circumstances. [Orwell was under pressure, not the elephant. Reposition modifier.]

Revised

Orwell, under pressure, shot the elephant.

Misplaced

Orwell lost his individual right to protect the elephant as part of the imperialistic system. [The elephant was not part of the system; Orwell was.]

Revised

As part of the imperialistic system, Orwell lost his right to protect the elephant.

Misplaced

Amos Wilder has been called back to teach at the Divinity School after ten years retirement due to a colleague's illness. [Did Wilder retire for ten years because a colleague was ill? Revise the sentence.]

Sometimes other parts of sentences are misplaced:

Misplaced

We learn from the examples of our parents who we are. [The sentence appears to say we are our parents.]

Revised

We learn who we are from the examples of our parents.

Misplaced

It is up to the students to revise the scheme, not the administrators. [We all know you can't revise administrators. Revise the sentence.]

Squinting Modifiers   If a modifier is ambiguous—that is, if it can be applied equally to more than one term—it is sometimes called a **squinting modifier:** It seems to look forward as well as backward.

Squinting

Being with Jennifer more and more enrages me. [Is the writer spending more time with Jennifer, or is the writer more enraged? Probably more enraged.]

Revised

Being with Jennifer enrages me more and more.

Squinting

Writing clearly is difficult. [Is this sentence about "writing" or about "writing clearly"?]

Revised

It is clearly difficult to write.

Revised

It is difficult to write clearly.

Squinting

Students only may use this elevator. [Does "only" modify students? If so, no one else may use the elevator. Or does it modify elevator? If so, students may use no other elevator.]

Revised

Only students may use this elevator.

Students may use only this elevator.

Note: The word *only* often squints, seeming to look in two directions. In general, put *only* immediately before the word or phrase it modifies. Often it appears too early in the sentence. (See "A Writer's Glossary" in Chapter 13, p. 287.)

Dangling Modifiers   If a modifier refers to a term that appears nowhere in the sentence, you have what is called a **dangling modifier.**

Dangling

Being small, his ear scraped against the belt when his father stumbled. [The writer meant that the boy was small, not the ear. But the boy is not in the sentence.]

Revised

Because the boy was small, his ear scraped against the belt when his father stumbled.

Being small, the boy scraped his ear against the belt when his father stumbled.

Dangling

A meticulously organized person, his suitcase could be tucked under an airplane seat. [How would you revise the sentence?]

A RULE FOR WRITERS

When you revise sentences, put together what belongs together.

Reference of Pronouns

A pronoun is used in place of a noun. Because the noun usually precedes the pronoun, the noun to which the pronoun refers is called the *antecedent* (Latin: "going before"). For example:

> antecedent   pronoun
> When *Sheriff Johnson* was on a horse, *he* was a big man.

But the pronoun can also precede the noun:

> pronoun   noun
> When *he* was on a horse,   *Sheriff Johnson* was a big man.

The word *antecedent* can be used here too. In short, the antecedent is the word or group of words referred to by a pronoun.

Whenever possible, make sure that a pronoun has a clear reference. Sometimes it isn't possible: *It* is commonly used with an unspecified reference, as in "It's hot today," and "Hurry up please, it's time"; and there can be no reference for interrogative pronouns: "What's bothering you?" and "Who's on first?" But otherwise always be sure that you've made clear what noun the pronoun is standing for.

Vague Reference of Pronouns

Vague

Apparently, they fight physically and it can become rather brutal. ["It" doubtless refers to "fight," but "fight" in this sentence is the verb, not an antecedent noun.]

Clear

Their fights are apparently physical, and sometimes brutal.

Vague

I was born in Colón, the second largest city in the Republic of Panama. Despite this, Colón is still an undeveloped town. ["This" has no specific antecedent. It appears to refer to the writer's having been born in Colón.] For more on *this*, see "A Writer's Glossary," in Chapter 13, p. 292.

Clear

Although Colón, where I was born, is the second largest city in Panama, it remains undeveloped.

Shift in Pronouns   This common error is easily corrected.

In many instances the child was expected to follow the profession of your father. [Expected to follow the profession of whose father, "yours" or "his"?]

Having a tutor, you can get constant personal encouragement and advice that will help me budget my time. [If "you" have a tutor, will that help "me"?]

Ambiguous Reference of Pronouns   A pronoun normally refers to the first appropriate noun or pronoun preceding it. Same-sex pronouns and nouns, like dogs, often get into scraps.

Ambiguous

Her mother died when she was eighteen. [Who was eighteen, the mother or the daughter?]

Clear

Her mother died when Mabel was eighteen.

Her mother died at the age of eighteen. [Note the absence of ambiguity in "His mother died when he was eighteen."]

Ambiguous

Daru learns that he must take an Arab to jail against his will. [Both Daru and the Arab are male. The writer of the sentence meant that Daru learns he must act against his will.]

Clear

Daru learns that he must, against his will, take an Arab to jail.

Agreement

Noun and Pronoun Everyone knows that a singular noun requires a singular pronoun, and a plural noun requires a plural pronoun, but writers sometimes slip.

Faulty

singular   plural
A dog can easily tell if people are afraid of *them.*

Correct

singular   singular
A dog can easily tell if people are afraid of *it.*

Faulty

   singular   plural
Every student feels that Wellesley expects *them* to do their best.

Correct

   singular   singular
Every student feels that Wellesley expects *her* to do her best.

Each, everybody, nobody, no one, and *none* are especially troublesome. See the entries on these words in "A Writer's Glossary" in Chapter 13.

Subject and Verb A singular subject requires a singular verb, a plural subject a plural verb.

Faulty

> plural   singular
>
> Horror *films* bring to light a subconscious fear and *shows* a character who succeeds in coping with it.

Correct

> plural   plural
>
> *Horror films* bring to light a subconscious fear and *show* a character who succeeds in coping with it.

The student who wrote "shows" instead of "show" thought that the subject of the verb was "fear," but the subject really is "Horror films," a plural.

Faulty

> The manager, as well as the pitcher and the catcher, were fined.

Correct

> The manager, as well as the pitcher and the catcher, was fined.

If the sentence had been "The manager and the pitcher . . . ," the subject would have been plural and the required verb would be *were:*

> The manager and the pitcher were fined.

But in the sentence as it was given, "as well as" (like *in addition to, with,* and *together with*) does *not* add a subject to a subject and thereby make a plural subject. "As well as" merely indicates that what is said about the manager applies to the pitcher and the catcher.

Three Additional Points

1. A collective noun—that is, a noun that is singular in form but that denotes a collection of individuals, such as *mob, audience, jury*— normally takes a *singular* verb:

Correct

> The mob is at the gate.

Correct

> An audience of children *is* easily bored. [The subject is "an audience," *not* "children."]

Correct

> The jury is seated.

But when the emphasis is on the individuals within the group—for instance when you are calling attention to a division within the group—you can use a plural verb:

The jury disagree.

Still, because this sounds a bit odd, it is probably better to recast the sentence:

The jurors disagree.

2. Sometimes a sentence that is grammatically correct may nevertheless sound awkward:

One of its most noticeable features is the lounges.

Because the subject is "one"—*not* "features"—the verb must be singular, "is," but "is" sounds odd when it precedes the plural "lounges." The solution: **Revise the sentence.**

Among the most noticeable features are the lounges.

3. When a singular and a plural subject are joined by *or*, *either . . . or*, or *neither . . . nor*, use a verb that agrees in number with the subject closest to the verb.

Correct

Either the teacher *or the students are* mistaken.

Correct

Either the students *or the teacher is* mistaken.

The first version uses "are" because the verb is nearer to "students" (plural) than to "teacher" (singular); the second uses "is" because the verb is nearer to "teacher" than to "students."

Repetition and Variation

Sometimes repetition can help clarify or emphasize a point; sometimes repetition is simply unnecessary and dull. Here are five general rules on the subject.

1. Don't be afraid to repeat a word if it is the best word. The following paragraph repeats "joyful," "book," "moments," and "in its"; notice also "joyful" and "joy." Repetition, a device necessary for continuity and clarity, holds the paragraph together.

The Brothers Karamazov is a joyful book. Readers who know what it is about may find this an intolerably whimsical statement. It does have moments of joy, but they are only moments; the rest is greed, lust, squalor, unredeemed suffering, and sometimes terrifying darkness. But the book is joyful in another sense: in its energy and curiosity, in its formal inventiveness, in the mastery of its writing. And therefore, finally, in its vision.

—Richard Pevear

2. Use pronouns, when their reference is clear, as substitutes for nouns. Notice Pevear's use of pronouns; notice also that in the second and third sentences, he substitutes "it" for "book," and then uses "the book" again in the fourth sentence. Substitutions that neither confuse nor distract keep a paragraph from becoming dull.

3. Do not, however, confuse the substitutions we have just spoken of with the fault called Elegant Variation. A groundless fear of repetition sometimes leads students to write first, for example, of "Shakespeare" then of "the writer," then of "our author" then of "the playwright," and then of "the Bard of Avon." Such variations strike the reader as silly. They can, moreover, be confusing because they can suggest that the student is referring to different writers.

4. Don't repeat a word if it is being used in two different senses.

Confusing

My theme focuses on the theme of the book. [The first "theme" means "essay"; the second means "underlying idea" or "motif."]

Clear

My essay focuses on the theme of the book.

Confusing

Caesar's character is complex. The comic characters, however, are simple. [The first "character" means "personality"; the second means "persons" or "figures in the play."]

Clear

Caesar is complex; the comic characters, however, are simple.

5. Eliminate words repeated unnecessarily. The use of words like *surely, in all probability, it is noteworthy* may become habitual. If they don't help the reader to follow your thoughts, they are Instant Prose Additives. Cross them out.

> **A RULE FOR WRITERS**
>
> When you revise, decide if a word should be repeated, varied, or elimi-
> nated by testing sentences and paragraphs for both sound and sense.

Clarity and Sentence Structure: Parallelism

Use parallels to clarify relationships. Few of us are likely to compose
such deathless parallels as "I came, I saw, I conquered," or "of the people, by the people, for the people," but we can see to it that coordinate
expressions correspond in their grammatical form. Consider the following sentence and the revisions:

Awkward

He liked drawing and to paint.

Parallel

He liked to draw and to paint.

He liked drawing and painting.

In the first version, "drawing" (a gerund) and "to paint" (an infinitive)
are not grammatically parallel. The difference in grammatical form
blurs the writer's point that there is a similarity between the two activities; the resulting sentence is fuzzy and awkward.

In the following examples, the parallel construction is italicized.

Awkward

The dormitory rules needed revision, a smoking area was a necessity,
and a generally more active role for the school in social affairs were all
significant to her.

Parallel

She recommended that the school *revise* its dormitory rules, *provide* a
smoking area, and *organize* more social activities.

Awkward

Most Chinese parents disapprove of interracial dating or they just do not
permit it.

Parallel

Most Chinese parents *disapprove* of interracial dating, and many *forbid* it.

In parallel constructions, be sure to check the consistency of articles,
prepositions, and conjunctions. For example:

Awkward

He wrote papers on a play by Shakespeare, a novel of Dickens, and a short story by Oates.

Parallel

He wrote papers on a play by Shakespeare, a novel by Dickens, and a short story by Oates.

The shift from "by" to "of" and back to "by" serves no purpose and is merely distracting.

To sum up:

A pupil once asked Arthur Schnabel (the noted pianist) whether it was better to play in time or to play as one feels; his characteristic mordant reply was another question: "Why not feel in time?"

—*David Hamilton*

CHECKLIST FOR REVISING FOR CLARITY

☐ Is word choice precise and specific? While writing the draft, did you feel that a particular word was close to what you meant, but not quite right? If so, replace that word with the *right* word. (See pp. 78–81.)

☐ Do you offer specific examples where necessary? (See pp. 83–86.)

☐ Are technical terms used appropriately and helpfully? Can any jargon be replaced with plain English? (See pp. 86–89.)

☐ Does your prose include any dead or mixed metaphors, or clichés? (See pp. 89–91.)

☐ Have you put together what belongs together? Do modifiers appear close to, and refer clearly to, the words they modify? (See pp. 98–100.)

☐ Have you eliminated sexist language? Have you replaced such words as "mankind" and "poetess" with gender-neutral terms, and eliminated the generic "he," "him," and "his"? (See pp. 81–83.)

☐ Have you replaced passive verbs with active verbs where appropriate? (See pp. 92–95.)

☐ Do pronouns have clear references, and do they agree in number with the nouns to which they refer? (See pp. 100–104.)

☐ Does the structure of your sentence reflect the structure of your thought? Are parallel ideas in parallel constructions? (See pp. 106–107.)

CHAPTER SIX

WRITING WITH STYLE

> The friends that have it I do wrong
> When ever I remake a song,
> Should know what issue is at stake:
> It is myself that I remake.
>
> —*William Butler Yeats*

Academic Styles, Academic Audiences

When you write an essay for a course, you are learning how people working in that academic discipline express themselves. To communicate with other people in the discipline, you must adapt your voice to the conventions of the discipline and to the audience's expectations about writing within that discipline. Some disciplines (literature, for example) frown on passive verbs. But in lab reports in the sciences passive verbs are often acceptable, in part because they help focus the reader's attention on the experiment ("the vaccine was tested") rather than on the person who conducted it ("a technician tested the vaccine") and thereby help to establish authority.

To make matters even more complicated, the conventions are changing, and they vary to some degree from class to class, and instructor to instructor. For example, one literature instructor might accept an essay containing the word "we" (as in "we see here the author's fascination with landscape"); another might object to its use, arguing that the "we" falsely implies that all readers—regardless of race, class, gender, and so on—read all texts in the same way.

These differences frustrate some students. To these students, writing an essay becomes a game of figuring out What the Instructor Wants.

(For what it's worth, such students can frustrate instructors a bit too.) It may help both students and instructors to keep in mind that there isn't one *right* style—and that the differences among styles are a matter of disciplinary convention and (to some degree) theoretical approach, not arbitrary and inscrutable personal taste.

It is impossible to list here all the different conventions you'll encounter in college. You don't need to learn them all anyway. You simply need to be alert to the ways in which people talk to each other in the disciplines within which you're writing, and do your best to follow the conventions you observe. We illustrate a few of these differences below.

Here is the first paragraph of an article from an issue of the *Cambridge Journal of Economics:*

> In this paper I shall develop a framework which may be used to examine several alternative theories of the rate of interest. The four most widely accepted approaches are the Neoclassical Loanable Funds, Keynes's Liquidity Preference, Neoclassical Synthesis ISLM, and Basil Moore's Horizontalist (or endogenous money). I will use the framework developed here to present a fifth: an integration of liquidity preference theory with an endogenous money approach. I first briefly set forth the primary alternative approaches, then develop an analytical framework based on an asset or stock approach and use it to discuss several theories of the interest rate: those advanced by Keynes, by Moore, by neoclassical theory and the monetarists, by Kregel, and by Tobin. Finally, I shall use the framework to reconcile liquidity preference theory with an endogenous money approach.
>
> —*L. Randall Wray*

Note the use of the pronoun "I," the direct statement of what the writer will do ("In this paper I shall develop a framework . . . "); and the listing of the steps of his procedure ("I first briefly set forth," and so on). A literary critic would be unlikely to present his or her ideas so methodically, as the next example suggests.

Here is the first paragraph of a chapter from a study of Bram Stoker's *Dracula*, in which a literary critic analyzes the novel in its social and political context.

> "In obedience to the law as it then stood, he was buried in the centre of a *quadrivium*, or conflux of four roads (in this case four streets), with a stake driven through his heart. And over him drives for ever the uproar

of unresting London!" No, not *Dracula* (1897), but the closing lines of a much earlier nineteenth-century work, Thomas De Quincey's bleakly ironic essay "On Murder Considered as One of the Fine Arts" (1854). De Quincey is describing how in 1812 the London populace dealt with the body of one of its prize exhibits, a particularly grisly serial killer who had escaped the gallows by hanging himself in his cell in the dead of night. Yet it is difficult for us to read this gleefully chilling passage today without thinking of Bram Stoker's classic vampire novel. The quirky Christian symbolism, the mandatory staking down of the monster to keep it from roaming abroad, the sense of busily self-absorbed London unaware of its proximity to a murderous presence that haunts its most densely populated byways: together these features seem virtually to define a basic iconography for the vampire Gothic as it achieved canonical status in *Dracula*.

—*David Glover*

Note the absence of the pronoun "I" and the presence of the pronoun "we." Note also the playfulness of the style (the reference to a "gleefully chilling passage" and the "staking down of the monster"), the specificity of the language, and the variety in punctuation and sentence structure.

Here is the opening paragraph of a chemistry student's study of the enzyme calf alkaline phosphatase.

```
Enzymes, protein molecules that catalyze reactions, are
crucial for many biochemical reactions. This research
project studies the actions of the enzyme calf alkaline
phosphatase on the substrate p-nitrophenyl phosphate.
The focus of this research project is the relation of
alkaline phosphatase denaturation to temperature. Heat
denaturation has been well documented in major biology
and chemistry texts, but few textbooks mention how
extreme cold affects enzyme structure and function.
This study will examine how alkaline phosphatase
responds to both high and low temperatures.

                                      —Hilary Suzawa
```

Note the absence of personal pronouns (the "*research project* studies"), the orderly and careful presentation of information (including the brief definition of the word "enzymes" in the first sentence), and the clear statement of purpose. (You might compare this writer's first sentence with Glover's—deliberately misleading—opening.)

Defining Style

As we have suggested, style in academic writing is partly a matter of disciplinary conventions. But style also reflects the individual writer's mind, his or her values and sensibility. Style is not simply a flower here and some gilding there; it pervades the whole work. Van Gogh's style, or Walt Disney's, let us say, consists in part of features recurring throughout a single work and from one work to the next: angular or curved lines, hard or soft edges, strong or gentle contrasts, and so on. Pictures of a seated woman by Van Gogh and by Disney are utterly different, and if we have seen a few works by each, we can readily identify who did which one. Artists leave their fingerprints, so to speak, all over their work. Writers leave their voiceprints.

Although the word *style* comes from the Latin *stilus* and originally referred to a Roman writing instrument, even in Roman times *stilus* had acquired a figurative sense, referring not only to the instrument but also to the writer's choice of words and arrangement of words into sentences. But is it simply the choice and arrangement of words we comment on when we speak of a writer's style, or are we also commenting on the writer's mind? Don't we feel that a piece of writing, whether it's on Civil War photographs or on genetics and intelligence, is also about the writer? The writing, after all, sets forth the writer's views of a chosen topic. It sets forth perceptions and responses to something the writer has thought about. The writer has, from the start, from the choice of a topic, revealed that he or she found it worth thinking about. The essay, in attempting to persuade us to think as the writer does, reveals not only how and what the writer thinks, but also what he or she values. As E. B. White has noted, "no writer long remains incognito."

When we write about things "out there," our writing always reveals the form and likeness of our minds, just as every work of art reveals the creator as well as the ostensible subject. A portrait painting, for example, is not only about the sitter, it is also about the artist's perceptions of the sitter; hence the saying that every portrait is a self-portrait. Even photographs are as much about the photographer as they are about the subject. Richard Avedon said of his portraits of famous people, "They are all pictures of me, of the way I feel about the people I photograph."

A student's essay similarly, if it is written truly, is not exclusively about "*La Causa* and the New Chicana"; it is also about the perceptions and responses of the writer to both racism and sexism.

Style and Tone

Suppose we take a page of handwriting, or even a signature. We need not believe that graphology is an exact science to believe that the shape of the ink-lines on paper (apart from the meaning of the words) often tells us something about the writer. We look at a large, ornate signature, and we sense that the writer is confident; we look at a tiny signature written with the finest of pens, and we wonder why anyone is so self-effacing.

More surely than handwriting, the writer's style reveals, among other things, an attitude toward the self, toward the reader, and toward the subject. The writer's attitudes are reflected in what is usually called *tone*. It is difficult to separate style from tone but we can try. Most discussions of style concentrate on what might be thought of as ornament: figurative language ("a sea of troubles"), inversion ("A leader he is not"), repetition and parallelism ("government of the people, by the people, for the people"), balance and antithesis ("It was the best of times, it was the worst of times"). Indeed, for centuries style has been called "the dress of thought," implying that the thought is something separate from the expression; the thought, in this view, is dressed up in stylistic devices. But in most of the writing that we read with interest and pleasure, the stylistic devices are not ornamental but integral. When we talk about wit, sincerity, tentativeness, self-assurance, aggressiveness, objectivity, and so forth—and certainly when we talk about clarity—we can say we are talking about style, but we should recognize that style now is not a matter of ornamental devices that dress up some idea, but part of the idea itself. And "the idea itself" includes the writer's unified yet appropriately varied tone of voice.

To take a brief example: The famous English translation of Caesar's report of a victory,

I came, I saw, I conquered,

might be paraphrased thus:

After getting to the scene of the battle, I studied the situation. Then I devised a strategy that won the battle.

But this paraphrase loses much of Caesar's message; the brevity and the parallelism of the famous version, as well as the alliteration (*came, conquered*), convey tight-lipped self-assurance—convey, that is, the tone that reveals Caesar to us. And this tone is a large part of Caesar's message. Caesar is really telling us not only about what he did, but also about what sort of person he is. He is perceptive, decisive, and effective. The three actions, Caesar in effect tells us, are (for a man like Caesar) one. (The Latin original is even more tight-lipped and more unified by alliteration: *veni, vidi, vici.*)

Let's look now at a longer example, the opening sentence of Lewis Thomas's essay "On Natural Death":

> There are so many new books about dying that there are now special shelves set aside for them in bookstores, along with the health, diet and home-repair paperbacks and the sex manuals.

This sentence could have ended where the comma is placed: The words after "bookstores" are, it might seem, not important. One can scarcely argue that by specifying some kinds of "special shelves" Thomas clarifies an otherwise difficult or obscure concept. What, then, do these additional words do? They tell us nothing about death and almost nothing about bookshops, but they tell us a great deal about Thomas's *attitude* toward the new books on death. He suggests that such books are faddish and perhaps (like "the sex manuals") vulgar. After all, if he had merely wanted to call up a fairly concrete image of a well-stocked bookstore, he could have said "along with books on politics and the environment," or some such thing. His next sentence runs:

> Some of them are so packed with detailed information and step-by-step instructions for performing the function you'd think this was a new sort of skill which all of us are now required to learn.

Why "you'd think" instead of, say, "one might believe"? Thomas uses a colloquial form, and a very simple verb, because he wants to convey to us his commonsense, homely, down-to-earth view that these books are a bit pretentious—a pretentiousness conveyed in his use of the words "performing the function," words that might come from the books themselves. In short, when we read Thomas's paragraph we are learning as much about Thomas as we are about books on dying. We are hearing a voice, perceiving an attitude, and we want to keep reading, not only

Alexander Gardner, *Home of a Rebel Sharpshooter, Gettysburg. July 1863.*
© Bettmann/Corbis.

because we are interested in death but also because Thomas has managed to make us interested in Thomas, a thoughtful but unpretentious fellow.

Now listen to a short paragraph from John Szarkowski's *Looking at Photographs.* Szarkowski is writing about one of Alexander Gardner's photographs of a dead Confederate sharpshooter.

> Among the pictures that Gardner made himself is the one reproduced here. Like many Civil War photographs, it showed that the dead of both sides looked very much the same. The pictures of earlier wars had not made this clear.

Try, in a word or two, to characterize the tone (the attitude, as we sense it in the inflection of the voice) of the first sentence. Next, the tone of the second, and then of the third. Suppose the second and third sentences had been written thus:

> It showed that the dead of both sides looked very much the same. This is made clear in Civil War photographs, but not in pictures of earlier wars.

How has the tone changed? What word can you find to characterize the tone of the whole, as Szarkowski wrote it?

Acquiring Style

In the preceding pages we said that your writing reveals not only where you stand (your thesis) and how you think (the structure of your argument), but also who you are and how you take yourself (your tone). To follow our argument to its limit, we might say that everything in this book—including rules on the comma (the place in a sentence where you breathe)—is about style. We do. What more is there to say?

Clarity and Texture

Let's look first at a distinction Aristotle makes between two parts of style: that which gives clarity and that which gives texture. Exact words, concrete illustrations of abstractions, conventional punctuation, and so forth—matters we treat in some detail in the chapters on revising and editing—make for clarity. On the whole, this part of style is inconspicuous when present; when absent, the effect ranges from mildly distracting to ruinous. Clarity is the foundation of style. It can be achieved by anyone willing to make the effort.

Among the things that give texture, or individuality, are effective repetition, variety in sentence structure, wordplay, and so forth. This second group of devices, on the whole more noticeable, makes the reader aware of the writer's particular voice. These devices can be learned too, but seldom by effort alone. In fact, playfulness helps here more than doggedness. Students who work at this part of style usually enjoy hanging around words. At the same time, they're likely to feel that when they put words on paper, even in a casual letter to a friend, they're putting themselves on the line. Serious, as most people are about games they really care about, but not solemn, they'll come to recognize the rules of play in John Holmes's advice to young poets: "You must believe that your feelings and your words for your feelings are important. . . . That they are unique is a fact; that you believe they are unique is necessary."

Originality and Imitation

We conclude with a paradox: One starts to acquire an individual style by studying and imitating the style of others. The paradox isn't limited to writing. Stylists in all fields begin as apprentices. The young ball player imitates the movements of David Ortiz; the chess player hangs around the park or club watching the old pros, then finds a book that probably recommends beginning with Ruy Lopez's opening. When Millet was young he copied works by Michelangelo; when Van Gogh was young he copied works by Millet. The would-be writer may be lucky enough to have a teacher, one he can imitate; more likely he will, in W. H. Auden's words, "serve his apprenticeship in the library."

PART TWO

COLLEGE
WRITING

CHAPTER SEVEN

ANALYZING TEXTS

Analyzing an Image

Look at the drawing below by Pieter Brueghel the Elder, titled *The Painter and the Connoisseur* (done about 1565), and then jot down your responses to the questions that follow.

Albertina, Wien.

1. One figure is given considerably more space than the other. What may be implied by this fact?
2. What is the painter doing (besides painting)?
3. What is the connoisseur doing?
4. What does the face of each figure tell you about each man's character? The figures are physically close; are they mentally close? How do you know?

Now consider a student's brief discussion of the drawing.

> The painter, standing in front of the connoisseur and given more than two-thirds of the space, dominates this picture. His hand holds the brush with which he creates, while the connoisseur's hand awkwardly fumbles for money in his purse. The connoisseur apparently is pleased with the picture he is looking at, for he is buying it, but his parted lips give him a stupid expression and his eyeglasses imply defective vision. In contrast, the painter looks away from the picture and fixes his eyes on the model (reality) or, more likely, on empty space, his determined expression suggesting that he possesses an imaginative vision beyond his painting and perhaps even beyond earthly reality.

The author of this paragraph uses *analysis* to interpret the drawing, to discover its meaning. The paragraph doesn't simply tell us that the picture shows two people close together—that would be a *description*, not an analysis. This analytic paragraph separates the parts of the picture, pointing out that the two figures form a contrast. The paragraph explains why one figure gets much more space than the other, and it explains what the contrasting gestures and facial expressions imply. The writer of the comment has "read" or interpreted the drawing by examining how the parts function—that is, how they relate to the whole.

Analyzing Advertisements (Visual Rhetoric)

Most print advertisements rely on pictures: A happy family stands by an automobile and a few lines of text tell us to buy the car; an image of a sexy body accompanies an invitation to buy a particular perfume or some exercise equipment; a photograph of a starving child seeks to persuade us to contribute to a charity.

Ads for charities aside, most ads are images not so much of the product—a car, a perfume—as they are images of a desirable condition, a state, for instance, of happiness or sexual attractiveness or health. The ads are first of all selling an idea, such as "You deserve to be happy" (or sexy, or healthy). Once the ad has conveyed this point, it then hooks the product to it: If you buy this particular car, you and your family will have fun; if you use this perfume, you will attract a sexual partner. Cleaning the stove too much of a chore? Use *X* oven cleaner. Are you worried that you won't have enough money for your child's college tuition? Just open a savings plan with Bank *Y*, and find peace of mind.

Sometimes, no clear relation exists between the picture in an advertisement and the product it promotes. This may seem odd, but it's not. Advertisers want you to remember their products. The picture has served its purpose if it catches your attention and leads you to see and remember the product's name. (You may recall the recent television advertisement for Hardee's hamburgers, which featured Paris Hilton, in a bathing suit, washing a car.) Some very successful advertisements don't even mention the product itself. There's just an image—unusual, violent, shocking, amusing, or sexually explicit. The image creates a buzz, and the controversy gets people talking. Who placed the image? Why? Haven't they gone too far? Generally, advertisers are pleased when such questions are debated because the product is being noticed.

Even ads that appeal to reason ("proven," "doctors recommend," "more economical") use pictures as the hook. A solemn doctor in a lab coat, say, promotes a new drug for cholesterol; the text explains how it works and offers up facts and figures to support the drug manufacturer's claims. And ads for charities, which primarily appeal to emotion, even more obviously rely on pictures, using vivid images of suffering to appeal to our sense of pity or fairness or outrage—and sometimes all three at once.

If your instructor asks you to write an analysis of an advertisement, keep in mind that you will need to describe it accurately enough to enable someone who hasn't seen it to envision it. For an example of description and analysis at work in an academic essay on advertisements, see Dolores Hayden's "Advertisements, Pornography, and Public Space" on pages 131–135. The following checklist may also help you develop ideas for your analysis.

CHECKLIST FOR ANALYZING ADVERTISEMENTS

☐ What is your first impression of the ad? Excitement, perhaps conveyed by a variety of colors and large type? Dignity, perhaps conveyed by grays, lots of empty space, and smaller type?

☐ Who is the audience for the ad? Affluent young women? College students? Retired persons?

☐ Does the image appeal to an emotion—to your sense of fairness, pity, patriotism, envy, fear?

☐ Is the image intentionally shocking?

☐ Does the text make a logical, rational appeal?

☐ What does the text do? Does it convey information? Entertain?

☐ What is the relation of the image to the text? Does the image do most of the work, or is its job mostly to get you to read the text?

☐ Does the ad strike you as deceptive? Does it seem honest?

☐ How effective is it? Would you buy the product it promotes?

Analyzing Texts

Much of academic reading and writing is analytical. You read of the causes of a revolution, of the effects of inflation, or of the relative importance of heredity and environment; you write about the meaning of a short story, the causes and effects of poverty, the strengths and weaknesses of some proposed legislative action. And much of this reading and writing is based on the analysis of *texts*. As we note in Chapter 1, the word "text" derives from the Latin for "woven" (as in textile), and it has come to refer not only to words stitched together into sentences (whether novels or letters or advertisements), but also to all kinds of objects of interpretation: films, paintings, music videos, even food on a plate.

For that reason, much of our discussion in this chapter focuses on textual analysis. Of course writing an analysis of a drawing differs from writing an analysis of a poem (or, for that matter, from an analysis of a legislative proposal or an argument about the causes of inflation). Nevertheless, we believe that there are important similarities between these processes. In all cases,

• the writer must summarize or describe the object under scrutiny precisely, so that the reader is able to envision it,

- the writer must pay close attention to the details, what they imply, and how they relate to each other and to the whole, and

- the writer must be able to explain what the text *means*.

Keep in mind, too, that when academic writers write analytically, their purpose is to persuade the reader to see things *their* way: to understand the poem the way they do; to reach their conclusion about the causes of poverty; to adopt their position on the proposed legislative action. The analysis helps the writer to make a larger point: It provides the evidence for the argument. In Chapter 8, "Persuading Readers," we discuss argument in more detail. But for now, we'll focus on analysis and how it differs from summary and paraphrase.

Analysis Versus Summary and Paraphrase

Before we talk more about analysis, we should see how it differs from summary and paraphrase. A **summary** is a brief version of what a text adds up to. A film reviewer may summarize the plot of a film in a sentence or two, and a book reviewer may in a short paragraph summarize the plot of a novel or the argument of a book advocating reform of our welfare system. Similarly, a student may find that it is useful to summarize a text that will be later analyzed in an essay.

The Gettysburg Address: Summary, Paraphrase, Analysis

Summarizing

For convenience, we will focus on a piece of writing that you are probably familiar with, Lincoln's Gettysburg Address. And let's assume that your first-year composition instructor has asked you to analyze this text. Your analytic essay will be devoted chiefly to showing *how* the writing works. (Analysis, you will recall, is essentially the examination of the relationships of parts, showing how they function.) In this instance, you will probably show

- how the speech is organized (you may find that the basic pattern is birth, death, rebirth),

- how certain words set forth profound reverberations, and

- how the metaphors are related.

We will look at such things in a moment. Here is Lincoln's text:

Abraham Lincoln

The Gettysburg Address

Four score and seven years ago our fathers brought forth on this continent a new nation, conceived in liberty and dedicated to the proposition that all men are created equal. Now we are engaged in a great civil war, testing whether that nation or any nation so conceived and so dedicated can long endure. We are met on a great battlefield of that war. We have come to dedicate a portion of that field as a final resting-place for those who here gave their lives that that nation might live. It is altogether fitting and proper that we should do this. But in a larger sense, we cannot dedicate, we cannot consecrate, we cannot hallow this ground. The brave men, living and dead who struggled here have consecrated it far above our poor power to add or detract. The world will little note nor long remember what we say here, but it can never forget what they did here. It is for us the living rather to be dedicated here to the unfinished work which they who fought here have thus far so nobly advanced. It is rather for us to be here dedicated to the great task remaining before us—that from these honored dead we take increased devotion to that cause for which they gave the last full measure of devotion—that we here highly resolve that these dead shall not have died in vain, that this nation under God shall have a new birth of freedom, and that government of the people, by the people, for the people shall not perish from the earth.

You may want to begin your analytic essay with a summary of the text. Here, as a sample, is a student's summary:

```
Although we have come to dedicate a portion of
the battlefield at Gettysburg to the memory of
those who died here, our real task is to dedicate
ourselves to the preservation of the nation for
which they died--a nation in which the people govern
themselves.
```

In writing an essay, you might therefore as a lead-in to your analysis say (as the student did) something like this:

> In 1863 Lincoln was invited to speak briefly at the dedication of a cemetery at Gettysburg, Pennsylvania. His essential point is that although we have come to dedicate a portion of the battlefield at Gettysburg to the memory of those who died, our real task is to dedicate ourselves to the preservation of the nation for which they died--a nation in which the people govern themselves.

Or, you might choose to announce a bit more obviously that you are offering a summary, along these lines:

> Before we look at the ways in which Lincoln uses metaphor in the Gettysburg Address, a brief summary may be useful: Lincoln's essential point is that although we have come to dedicate a portion of the battlefield at Gettysburg to the memory of those who died in an effort to preserve the Union, our real task is to dedicate ourselves to the preservation of the nation for which they died--a nation in which the people govern themselves.

Paraphrasing

A **paraphrase** is something entirely different. Whereas a summary is much briefer than the original, a paraphrase is usually as long or longer because it is a restatement, a sort of translation into the same language. Thus, in the first sentence of the Gettysburg Address, Lincoln's "four-score and seven years ago" would be paraphrased as "eighty-seven years ago." (It happens that in this case the paraphrase—three words—is actually shorter than the original—five words—but usually a paraphrase is at least as long as the original.) Let's look again at the first sentence of the Gettysburg Address:

> Four score and seven years ago our fathers brought forth on this continent a new nation, conceived in Liberty and dedicated to the proposition that all men are created equal.

Here is a student's paraphrase:

```
Eighty-seven years ago (i.e., in 1776, the year of
the American Revolution) our ancestors introduced to
North America a new country; this country was brought
into existence ("conceived") by the male framers of
the Constitution who saw Liberty as the mother of the
new nation, and it was set apart or specially marked
("dedicated") as a nation in which all human beings
are regarded as equal.
```

Briefly, a paraphrase has two key features:

- It is as long as the original, and usually longer.
- It is usually designed to help a reader—or writer—understand a dense text.

Why paraphrase? First, a paraphrase can help clarify a difficult or obscure passage for your reader. Second, the act of paraphrasing can help you as the writer, by forcing you to slow down your reading and making you think carefully about each word. Careful reading is the first step in analytic thinking.

A RULE FOR WRITERS

In your own essays, do not paraphrase a source simply in order to avoid summarizing it or to avoid quoting it directly. If you merely restate a lucid source, changing words but in essence proceeding phrase by phrase, offering synonyms, you are **plagiarizing**, even if you begin saying something like "Jiménez has pointed out that. . . ." Why is such material plagiarism? Because all of the ideas and all of the structure of the thought, as well as some of the words, are someone else's. True, by acknowledging Jiménez ("Jiménez has pointed out") you are informing the reader that the ideas are not yours, but this acknowledgment does not tell the reader that you are using Jiménez's sentences, substituting some words. For additional information on plagiarism, see "Acknowledging Sources" (pp. 191–198).

In an analytic essay you should include a paraphrase only rarely, only when you think your readers may need some help in grasping the meaning of the text. If you simply want to remind your readers of the gist of a text you are responding to, it is better to summarize it rather than to paraphrase it. If you want them to see the text that you are analyzing, to experience it directly, quote the passage word for word, in quotation marks if it is short or set off and indented in block-quotation format if it is long.

Analyzing

An **analysis** of the Gettysburg Address—an attempt to show how it works, how it achieves its special effects—will not simply paraphrase the text but will make such points as these:

- "Four score and seven years" evokes the Bible, which in Psalm 90 speaks of human life as "three score years and ten"; Lincoln thus begins the speech by solemnly introducing a holy context.

- "Four score and seven" is not the only evocation of the Bible; Lincoln also uses "dedicate" (in the Bible the word commonly means "set aside for a divine purpose"), "consecrate," "hallow" (to make holy), "devotion" (this word contains the word "vow"), "under God"—words appropriate to the creation of a cemetery, and words suggesting that the dead soldiers were sacrifices to a divine purpose.

- The address moves from the past (the first sentence refers to the Revolution in 1776) to the present (for instance "now we are met," "we are engaged," "we cannot") and then to the future ("shall have a new birth," "shall not perish").

- A metaphor of birth begins the speech ("conceived" in the first sentence), and another ends the speech ("new birth" in the last sentence); somewhat fainter images of birth are also present in "brought forth" and "create."

- Alliteration (the repetition of initial sounds) helps to bind words together (*"f*our score . . . *f*athers . . . *f*orth; *n*ew *n*ation"), and moves the language from ordinary prose toward the more highly textured language of poetry.

- Triads also elevate the language beyond ordinary prose ("we cannot dedicate, we cannot consecrate, we cannot hallow," "of the people, by the people, for the people").

Observations such as these give a reader a sense not merely of the ideas of the address—that would be a paraphrase—but a sense of *how* the elements in the address work to create effects and meanings.

Paraphrasing and Summarizing Literary Texts

Paraphrase is especially useful in essays analyzing literature, where the meanings of words are often multiple. Let's look at a short work of literature, Shakespeare's Sonnet 116:

Let me not to the marriage of true minds
Admit impediments. Love is not love
Which alters when it alteration finds,
Or bends with the remover to remove.   4
O no, it is an ever-fixéd mark
That looks on tempests and is never shaken.
It is the star to every wandering bark
Whose worth's unknown, although his height be taken.   8
Love's not time's fool, though rosy lips and cheeks
Within his bending sickle's compass come;
Love alters not with his brief hours and weeks,
But bears it out even to the edge of doom.   12
If this be error and upon me proved,
I never writ, nor no man ever loved.

Shakespeare wrote this sonnet four hundred years ago, so it is not surprising that some of his words and phrases are not immediately clear. A student offered this paraphrase of the first six lines:

May I never concede ("admit") that obstacles can
alter the spiritual union of faithful ("true") minds.
Love cannot be considered true love if it changes
when it encounters change (for instance, when it sees
the beloved's loss of physical beauty, or when it
sees the beloved's economic circumstances change), or
if it withdraws or deviates or turns away when the
other party withdraws ("remove[s]") love. Love is a
permanent-standing thing ("ever-fixed mark"), like a
landmark or beacon, that observes disturbances but is
itself undisturbed ("never shaken").

Try paraphrasing the rest of the sonnet. (In line 7 "bark" means "ship"; in line 8 "height" means "altitude"; in line 9 "time's fool" is "plaything [i.e., victim] of time"; in line 10 "his" is "time's"; and in line 12 "edge of doom" is the "brink of Doomsday (Judgment Day)."

A summary of the first six lines would be notably different in content and length from a paraphrase. A student might write something like this:

```
I will never grant that true love changes when it
sees some sort of change in the beloved.
```

A RULE FOR WRITERS

Remember that a **summary** is often useful in an analytical or argumentative essay that responds to another argument because the summary reminds readers of the main points of a text. A **paraphrase** is useful if the original is particularly dense, either because it is highly metaphoric or because it is written in highly technical or obsolete language. An **analysis** is an examination of how the parts relate to the whole—for example, how certain words suggest an objective speaker, and how lengthy sentences suggest a highly educated speaker—or conversely, how lengthy sentences consisting of simple clauses linked by "and . . . and . . . and" may suggest a simple speaker.

Classifying and Thinking

Analysis (literally a separating into parts) is not only the source of much writing that seeks to explain but also a way of thinking, a way of arriving at conclusions (generalizations), a way of discovering meaning. Much of what we normally mean by analysis requires classifying ideas or things into categories and thinking about how the categories relate to each other.

When you think about choosing courses, for example, you classify the courses by subject matter, or by degree of difficulty ("Since I'm taking two hard courses, I ought to look for an easy one"), or by the hour at which they are offered, or by the degree to which they interest you, or by their merit as determined through the grapevine. In this case, you establish categories by breaking down the curriculum into parts, and by then putting into each category courses that significantly resemble each other but that are not identical. We need categories: We simply cannot get through life treating every object as unique.

Examples of Classifying

Suppose you were asked to write an essay putting forth your ideas about punishment for killers. You would need to distinguish between those killers whose actions are premeditated and those killers whose actions are not. And in the first category you might make further distinctions:

1. Professional killers who carefully contrive a death
2. Killers who are irrational except in their ability to contrive a death
3. Robbers who contrive a property crime and who kill only when they believe that killing is necessary in order to commit that crime

You can hardly talk usefully about capital punishment or imprisonment without making some such analysis of killers. You have, then, taken killers and *classified* them, for the sake of educating yourself and those persons with whom you discuss the topic. You have engaged in critical thinking. Unless you agree with the "Off with their heads" attitude of the mad Queen of Hearts, you will be satisfied with your conclusion only after you have tested it by dividing your topic into parts, each clearly distinguished from the others, and then showed how they are related.

Often the keenest analytical thinking considers not only what parts are in the whole, but also what is *not* there—what is missing in relation to a larger context that we can imagine. For example, if we analyze the female characters in the best-known fairy tales, we will find that most are either sleeping beauties or wicked stepmothers. These categories are general: "Sleeping beauties" includes all passive women valued only for their appearance, and "wicked stepmothers" includes Cinderella's cruel older sisters. (Fairy godmothers form another category, because they are not human beings.) Analysis helps us to discover the almost total absence of resourceful, productive women in the typical fairy tale. You might begin a thoughtful essay with a general statement to this effect and then support the statement—your thesis—with an analysis of "Cinderella," "Little Red Riding Hood," and "Snow White."

Cause and Effect

Analytical reasoning moving from cause to effect is also often expected in academic discussions, which are given to questions such as the following:

What part, if any, did oil play in our invasion of Iraq in 2003?

How does the death penalty affect jury verdicts?

Why do people enjoy horror movies?

What are the effects of billboard advertising?

Let's look at the first eight paragraphs of an essay, by the architect and scholar Dolores Hayden, that addresses the last question on the list, arguing from cause to effect.

Dolores Hayden
Advertisements, Pornography, and Public Space

1   Americans need to look more consciously at the ways in which the public domain is misused for spatial displays of gender stereotypes: These appear in outdoor advertising, and to a lesser extent in commercial displays, architectural decoration, and public sculpture. While the commercial tone and violence of the American city is often criticized, there is little analysis of the routine way that crude stereotypes appear in public, urban spaces as the staple themes of commercial art. Most Americans are accustomed to seeing giant females in various states of undress smiling and caressing products such as whiskey, food, and records. Male models also sell goods, but they are usually active and clothed—recent ad campaigns aimed at gay men seem to be the first major exception. Several geographers have established that men are most often shown doing active things, posed in the great outdoors; women are shown in reflective postures responding to male demands in interior spaces. As the nineteenth-century sexual double standard is preserved by the urban advertising, many twentieth-century urban men behave as if good women are at home while bad ones adorn the billboards and travel on their own in urban space; at the same time, many urban women are encouraged to think of emotionlessness, war-mongering, and sexual inexhaustibility as natural to the Marlboro cowboy, war heroes' statues, and every other male adult.

2   This double standard is the result of advertising practices, graphic design, and urban design. Sanctioned by the zoning laws, billboards are approved by the same urban planning boards who will not permit child care centers or mother-in-law apartments in many residential districts. But the problem with billboards is not only

aesthetic degradation. By presenting gender stereotypes in the form of nonverbal body language, fifty feet long and thirty feet high, billboards turn the public space of the city into a stage set for a drama starring enticing women and stern men.

3   Let us observe outdoor advertising and other urban design phenomena with similar effects, as they are experienced by two women on an urban commuting trip along the Sunset Strip in Los Angeles in June 1981. Standing on a street corner, the two women are waiting for a bus to go to work. The bus arrives, bearing a placard on the side advertising a local nightclub. It shows strippers doing their act, their headless bodies naked from neck to crotch except for a few blue sequins. The two women get on the bus and find seats for the ride along Sunset Boulevard. They look out the windows. As the bus pulls away, their heads appear incongruously above the voluptuous cardboard female bodies displayed on the side. They ride through a district of record company headquarters and film offices, one of the most prosperous in L.A.

4   Their first views reveal rows of billboards. Silent Marlboro man rides the range; husky, khaki-clad Camel man stares at green hills; gigantic, uniformed professional athletes catch passes and hit home runs on behalf of booze. These are the male images. Then, on a billboard for whiskey, a horizontal blonde in a backless black velvet dress, slit to the thigh, invites men to "Try on a little Black Velvet." Next, a billboard shows a well-known actress, reclining with legs spread, who notes that avocados are only sixteen calories a slice. "Would this body lie to you?" she asks coyly, emphasizing that the body language which communicates blatant sexual availability is only meant to bring attention to her thin figure. Bo Derek offers a pastoral contrast garbed in nothing but a few bits of fur and leather, as she swings on a vine of green leaves, promoting *Tarzan, the Ape Man.*

5   Next the bus riders pass a club called the Body Shop that advertises "live, nude girls." Two reclining, realistic nudes, one in blue tones in front of a moonlight cityscape, one in orange sunshine tones, stretch their thirty-foot bodies along the sidewalk. This is the same neighborhood where a billboard advertising a Rolling Stones' record album called "Black and Blue" made news ten years ago. A manacled, spread-legged woman with torn clothes proclaimed "I'm Black and Blue from the Rolling Stones—and I love it!" Members of a group called Women Against Violence Against Women (WAVAW) arrived with cans of spray paint and climbed the scaffolding to make

small, uneven letters of protest: "This is a crime against women." Demonstrations and boycotts eventually succeeded in achieving the removal of that image, but not in eliminating the graphic design problem. "Black and Blue" has been replaced by James Bond in a tuxedo, pistol in hand, viewed through the spread legs and buttocks of a giant woman in a bathing suit and improbably high heels, captioned "For Your Eyes Only."

6   When the two women get off the bus in Hollywood, they experience more gender stereotypes as pedestrians. First, they walk past a department store. In the windows mannequins suggest the prevailing ideals of sartorial elegance. The male torsos lean forward, as if they are about to clinch a deal. The female torsos, pin-headed, tip backward and sideways, at odd angles, as if they are about to be pushed over onto a bed. The themes of gender advertisements are trumpeted here in the mannequins' body language as well as on billboards. Next, the women pass an apartment building. Two neoclassical caryatids support the entablature over the front door. Their breasts are bared, their heads carry the load. They recall the architecture of the Erechtheum on the Acropolis in Athens, dating from the 5th century B.C., where the sculptured stone forms of female slaves were used as support for a porch in place of traditional columns and capitals. This is an ancient image of servitude.

7   After the neo-classical apartment house, the commuters approach a construction site. Here they are subject to an activity traditionally called "running the gauntlet," but referred to as "girl watching" by urban sociologist William H. Whyte. Twelve workers stop whatever they are doing, whistle, and yell: "Hey, baby!" The women put their heads down, and walk faster, tense with anger. The construction workers take delight in causing exactly this response: "You're cute when you're mad!" Whyte regards this type of behavior as charming, pedestrian fun in "Street Life," where he even takes pleasure in tracing its historic antecedents, but he has never been whistled at, hooted at, and had the dimensions of his body parts analyzed out loud on a public street.[1]

8   Finally, these women get to the office building where they work. It has two statues out front of women. Their bronze breasts culminate in erect nipples. After they pass this last erotic public display of

---

[1]William H. Whyte, "Street Life," *Urban Open Spaces* (Summer 1980); for a more detailed critique of hassling: Lindsy Van Gelder, "The International Language of Street Hassling," *Ms.* 9 (May 1981), 15–20, and letters about this article, *Ms.* (September 1981); and Cheryl Benard and Edith Schlaffer, "The Man in the Street: Why He Harasses," *Ms.* 9 (May 1981), 18–19.

women's flesh, sanctioned as fine art, they walk in the door to begin the day's work. Their journey has taken them through an urban landscape filled with images of men as sexual aggressors and women as submissive sexual objects.

Now let's analyze these paragraphs. In the first paragraph Hayden introduces the question her essay will address: "How do billboards and other outdoor representations of male and female bodies perpetuate gender stereotypes?" (our paraphrase). She points out that there has been "little analysis" of this problem, thus suggesting that it is worth investigating. In the last sentence of the second paragraph, she states an argument: "billboards turn the public space of the city into a stage set for a drama starring enticing women and stern men." Paragraphs 4 through 8 discuss the "causes." We note Hayden classifies these images fairly methodically: paragraphs 4 and 5 focus on billboards representing women as "available"; paragraph 6 focuses first on mannequins that represent women as vulnerable, and then on architectural elements that represent women as subservient; paragraph 8 focuses on bronze statues of female torsos.

In the next (and last) three paragraphs of the essay, Hayden discusses the effects of these representations: "women guard themselves," "men assume that ogling is part of normal public life," and the "sexual double standard" is maintained "in a brutal and vulgar way."

9   The transient quality of male and female interaction in public streets makes the behavior provoked by billboards and their public design images particularly difficult to attack. Psychologist Erving Goffman has analyzed both print ads and billboards as *Gender Advertisements* because art directors use exaggerated body language to suggest that consumers buy not products but images of masculinity or femininity. [2] If passers-by are driving at fifty miles per hour, these gender cues cannot be subtle. In *Ways of Seeing*, art historian John Berger describes the cumulative problem that gender stereotypes in advertising create for woman as "split consciousness." [3] While many women guard themselves, some men assume that ogling is part of normal public life. Women are always wary, watching men watch them, and wondering if and when something is going to happen to them.

[2]Erving Goffman, *Gender Advertisements* (New York: Harper Colphon, 1976), pp. 24–27; Nancy Henley, *Body Politics: Power, Sex, and Nonverbal Communication* (Englewood Cliffs, NJ: Prentice-Hall, 1977), p. 30; Marianne Wex, *Let's Take Back Our Space* (Berlin: Movimento Druck, 1979).
[3]John Berger et al., *Ways of Seeing* (Harmondsworth, England: BBC and Penguin, 1972), pp. 45–64.

10   Urban residents also encounter even more explicit sexual images in urban space. Tawdry strip clubs, X-rated films, "adult" bookstores and sex shops are not uncommon sights. Pornographic video arcades are the next wave to come. Pornography is a bigger, more profitable industry in the United States than all legitimate film and record business combined. [4] It spills over into soft-porn, quasi-porn, and tasteless public imagery everywhere. In the midst of this sex-exploitation, if one sees a real prostitute, there is mild surprise. Yet soliciting is still a crime. Of course, the male customer of an adult prostitute is almost never arrested, but the graphic designer, the urban designer, and the urban planner never come under suspicion for their contributions to a commercial public landscape that preserves the sexual double standard in a brutal and vulgar way.

11   Feminist Laura Shapiro calls our society a "rape culture." [5] Adrienne Rich has written of "a world masculinity made unfit for women or men." [6] But surely most Americans do not consciously, deliberately accept public space given over to commercial exploitation, violence and harassment of women. Indeed, the success of the "Moral Majority" displays how a few activists were able to tap public concern effectively about commercialized sexuality, albeit in a narrow, antihumanist way. In contrast, the example of the Women's Christian Temperance Union under Frances Willard's leadership, and the parks movement under Olmsted's,[7] show religious idealism, love of nature, and concern for female safety can be activated into dynamic urban reform movements that enlarge domestic values into urban values, instead of diminishing them into domestic pieties.

Analysis and Description

Analysis differs from description, as we note on page 120, but passages of description are commonly used in essays to support analysis of visual texts. In the essay "Advertisements, Pornography, and Public Space," for example, Dolores Hayden asks and answers the question "What are the

---

[4]Tom Hayden, *The American Future: New Visions Beyond Old Frontiers* (Boston: South End Press, 1980), p. 15.
[5]Laura Shapiro, "Violence: The Most Obscene Fantasy," in Jo Freeman, ed., *Women: A Feminist Perspective*, 2nd ed. (Palo Alto, CA: Mayfield, 1979), pp. 469–73.
[6]Ibid., p. 469.
[7]Frederick Law Olmsted (1822–1903) was an American landscape architect. Among his notable works are Central Park in Manhattan and Prospect Park in Brooklyn.

effects of representations of women in public space?"; as she answers this question, she presents us with brief but vivid descriptions of billboards, mannequins, and architectural elements. Although Hayden's essay includes some description, it is nevertheless primarily analytical. Reading it, we share the writer's thoughts, but these thoughts are not the random and fleeting notions of reverie. The thoughts have been organized for us; the effects of billboards and other images on both women and men have been classified and presented to us in an orderly and coherent account made vivid by passages of description. Even if we have never seen the advertisement for the James Bond film or the Rolling Stones album, we can visualize these images because Hayden has made them present to us. Through these passages, we share at least imaginatively in the experiences that gave rise to her thinking. And through description, if the communication between writer and reader has been successful, we are persuaded to share the writer's opinions.

Description at Work in the Analytic Essay

Hayden uses description in her essay to support her analysis of the effects of certain kinds of representations of women—the kind of analysis that might be written for a course in sociology or popular culture.

But because description is not analysis, if you are asked to analyze a painting for your art history class or an advertisement for your media studies class, it won't be enough simply to describe the thing in detail. It may be useful, then, to make some distinctions between the two processes, *description* and *analysis*. Hayden *describes* a billboard when she says, "a horizontal blonde in a backless black velvet dress, slit to the thigh, invites men to 'Try on a little Black Velvet'"; she *describes* mannequins in a department store window: "The female torsos, pin-headed, tip backward and sideways, at odd angles." She reports what any viewer might see if he or she looked closely enough. These statements don't offer evaluations, although Hayden's diction and tone—the words "slit" and "pin-headed," for example—do begin to shape our responses to these images. But when Hayden goes on to say that those mannequins look "as if they are about to be pushed over onto a bed" she is making an *inference*, she's telling her readers what the image *implies* or *suggests*; she is thinking critically about the image, *analyzing* it. Likewise, she *describes* the caryatids (columns in the shape of females) on the front door of an apartment building when she says,

Their breasts are bared, their heads carry the load.

But she's *analyzing* when she says,

> They recall the architecture of the Erechtheum on the Acropolis in Athens, dating from the 5th century B.C., where the sculptured stone forms of female slaves were used as support for a porch in place of traditional columns and capitals. This is an ancient image of servitude.

She's comparing (a common analytic procedure) the modern caryatids to those on the Acropolis, and she's offering an evaluation, a judgment: The caryatids at the entrance of the modern building present an "image of servitude." In another sense, she's explaining how the caryatids function. She not only answers the question "what do these images mean?" she explains *how* they mean.

Comparing

> If you want to really see something, look at something else.
>
> —*Howard Nemerov*

We began this chapter with a brief analysis of a Brueghel drawing. We *compared* Brueghel's handling of the two figures: the amount of space each figure occupied, their activities, their facial expressions, the directions of their gaze; we thereby arrived at an interpretation of the *meaning* of Brueghel's drawing. We might say that the drawing invites the comparison, and in so doing communicates Brueghel's understanding of the artist's vision, or of the value of art.

Writers, too, often use comparisons to explain a concept or idea or to arrive at a judgment or conclusion. As in drawing or painting, the point of a comparison in writing is not simply to list similarities or differences, but to explain something, to illuminate what the similarities and differences add up to. What the comparison—or analysis—adds up to is sometimes referred to as a *synthesis*—literally, a combining of separate elements to form a coherent whole.

Notice George Orwell's technique in the following paragraph, from an essay titled "England, Your England," written during World War II. Orwell clarifies our understanding of one kind of military march, the Nazi goose-step, by calling attention to how it differs from the march used by English soldiers. Notice, too, the point of his comparison, which he makes clear in his second sentence, and which resonates throughout the comparison.

One rapid but fairly sure guide to the social atmosphere of a country is the parade-step of its army. A military parade is really a kind of ritual dance, something like a ballet, expressing a certain philosophy of life. The goose-step, for instance, is one of the most horrible sights in the world, far more terrifying than a dive-bomber. It is simply an affirmation of naked power; contained in it, quite consciously and intentionally, is the vision of a boot crashing down on a face. Its ugliness is part of its essence, for what it is saying is "Yes, I *am* ugly, and you daren't laugh at me," like the bully who makes faces at his victim. Why is the goose-step not used in England? There are, heaven knows, plenty of army officers who would be only too glad to introduce some such thing. It is not used because the people in the street would laugh. Beyond a certain point, military display is only possible in countries where the common people dare not laugh at the army. The Italians adopted the goose-step at about the time when Italy passed definitely under German control, and, as one would expect, they do it less well than the Germans. The Vichy government, if it survives, is bound to introduce a stiffer parade-ground discipline into what is left of the French army. In the British army the drill is rigid and complicated, full of memories of the eighteenth century, but without definite swagger; the march is merely a formalised walk. It belongs to a society which is ruled by the sword, no doubt, but a sword which must never be taken out of the scabbard.

—George Orwell

Organizing Short Comparisons

An essay may be devoted entirely to a comparison, say of two kinds of tribal organization. But such essays are relatively rare. More often, an essay includes only a paragraph or two of comparison—for example, explaining something unfamiliar by comparing it to something familiar. Let's spend a moment discussing how to organize a paragraph that makes a comparison—though the same principles can be applied to entire essays.

The first part may announce the topic, the next part may discuss one of the two items being compared, and the last part may discuss the other. We can call this method *lumping*, because it presents one item in a lump, and then the other in another lump. Thus Orwell says all that he wishes to say about the goose-step in one lump, and then says what he wishes to say about the British parade-step in another lump. But in making a comparison a writer may use a different method, which we'll call *splitting*. The discussion of the two items may run throughout the paragraph, the writer perhaps devoting alternate sentences to each.

Because almost all writing is designed to help the reader see what the writer has in mind, it may be especially useful here to illustrate these two structures, lumping and splitting, with two paragraphs that compare two sculptures. The first comparison of a Japanese statue of a Buddha with a Chinese statue of a bodhisattva (a slightly lower spiritual being, dedicated to saving humankind) treats the Buddha first, and then the bodhisattva. As you will see, it is an example of lumping.

> The Buddha, recognizable by a cranial bump that indicates a sort of supermind, sits erect and austere in the lotus position (legs crossed, each foot with the sole upward on the opposing thigh), in full control of his body. The carved folds of his garments, in keeping with the erect posture, are severe, forming a highly disciplined pattern that is an outward expression of his remote, constrained, austere inner nature. The bodhisattva, on the other hand, sits in a languid, sensuous posture known as "royal ease," the head pensively tilted downward, one knee elevated, one leg hanging down. He is accessible, relaxed, and compassionate.

The structure is, simply this:

> The Buddha (posture, folds of garments, inner nature)
> The bodhisattva (posture, folds of garments, inner nature)

If, however, the writer had wished to split rather than to lump, she would have compared an aspect of the Buddha with an aspect of the bodhisattva, then another aspect of the Buddha with another aspect of the bodhisattva, and so on, perhaps ending with a synthesis to clarify the point of the comparison. The paragraph might have read like this:

> The Buddha, recognizable by a cranial bump that indicates a sort of supermind, sits erect and austere, in the lotus position (legs crossed, each foot with the sole upward on the opposing thigh), in full control of his body. In contrast, the bodhisattva sits in a languid, sensuous posture known as "royal ease," the head pensively tilted downward, one knee elevated, one leg hanging down. The carved folds of the Buddha's garments, in keeping with his erect posture, are severe, forming a highly disciplined pattern, whereas the bodhisattva's garments hang naturalistically. Both figures are spiritual but the Buddha is remote, constrained, and austere; the bodhisattva is accessible, relaxed, and compassionate.

Shaka, the Historical Buddha, Japan, Heian period, late 10th–early 11th century; cherry with polychrome and gold; single woodblock construction; 83 cm (height of figure); 72.5 cm (height of hairline).

Guanyin, China, Jin Dynasty, 12th century; wood with traces of polychrome and gold, 141 × 88 × 88 cm.

In effect the structure is this:

> The Buddha (posture)
>
> The bodhisattva (posture)
>
> The Buddha (garments)
>
> The bodhisattva (garments)
>
> The Buddha and the bodhisattva (synthesis)

Whether in any given piece of writing you should compare by lumping or by splitting will depend largely on your purpose and on the complexity of the material. We can't even offer the rule that splitting is good for brief, relatively obvious comparisons, lumping for longer, more complex ones, though such a rule usually works. We can, however, give some advice:

1. If you split, reread your draft with two points in mind:
   - *Imagine your reader*, and ask yourself if it is likely that this reader can keep up with the back-and-forth movement. Make sure (perhaps by a summary sentence at the end) that the larger picture is not obscured by the zigzagging.
   - *Don't leave any loose ends.* Make sure that if you call attention to points 1, 2, and 3 in *X*, you mention all of them (not just 1 and 2) in *Y*.
2. If you lump, do not simply comment first on *X* and then on *Y*.
   - *Let your reader know where you are going*, probably by means of an introductory sentence.
   - *Don't be afraid in the second half to remind your reader of the first half.* It is legitimate, and even desirable, to relate the second half of the comparison to the first half. A comparison organized by lumping will not break into two separate halves if the second half develops by reminding the reader how it differs from the first half.

Longer Comparisons

Now let's think about a comparison that extends through two or three paragraphs. If you are comparing the indoor play (for instance, board games or play with toys) and the sports of girls with those of boys, you can, for example, devote one paragraph to the indoor play of girls, a second paragraph to the sports of girls, a third to the indoor play of boys, and a fourth to the sports of boys. If you are thinking in terms of comparing girls and boys, such an organization uses lumps, girls first and then boys (with a transition such as "Boys on the other hand . . ."). But you might split, writing four paragraphs along these lines:

Indoor play of girls

Indoor play of boys

Sports of girls

Sports of boys

Or you might organize the material into two paragraphs:

Play and sports of girls

Play and sports of boys

There is no rule, except that the organization and the point of the comparison be clear.

Consider these paragraphs from an essay by Sheila Tobias on the fear of mathematics. The writer's thesis in the essay is that although this fear is more commonly found in females than in males, biology seems not to be the cause. After discussing some findings (for example, that girls compute better than boys in elementary school, and that many girls tend to lose interest in mathematics in junior high school), the writer turns her attention away from the schoolhouse. Notice that whether a paragraph is chiefly about boys or chiefly about girls, the writer keeps us in mind of the overall point: reasons why more females than males fear math.

1   Not all the skills that are necessary for learning mathematics are learned in school. Measuring, computing, and manipulating objects that have dimensions and dynamic properties of their own are part of the everyday life of children. Children who miss out on these experiences may not be well primed for math in school.

2   Feminists have complained for a long time that playing with dolls is one way of convincing impressionable little girls that they may only be mothers or housewives—or, as in the case of the Barbie doll, "pinup girls"—when they grow up. But doll-playing may have even more serious consequences for little girls than that. Do girls find out about gravity and distance and shapes and sizes playing with dolls? Probably not.

3   A curious boy, if his parents are tolerant, will have taken apart a number of household and play objects by the time he is ten, and, if his parents are lucky, he may even have put them back together again. In all of this he is learning things that will be useful in physics and math. Taking parts out that have to go back in requires some examination of form. Building something that stays up or at least stays put for some time involves working with structure.

4   Sports is another source of math-related concepts for children which tends to favor boys. Getting to first base on a not very well hit grounder is a lesson in time, speed, and distance. Intercepting a football thrown through the air requires some rapid intuitive eye calculations based on the ball's direction, speed, and trajectory. Since physics is partly concerned with velocities, trajectories, and collisions of objects, much of the math taught to prepare a student for physics deals with relationships and formulas that can be used to express motion and acceleration.

A few points about the organization of these paragraphs:

- Paragraph 1 offers a generalization about "children"—that is, about boys and girls.
- Paragraph 2 discusses the play of girls with dolls in the context of its relevance—irrelevance, really—to mathematics.
- Paragraph 3 discusses the household play of boys, again in the context of mathematics.
- Paragraph 4 discusses the outdoor sports of boys, but notice that girls are not forgotten, for its first sentence is "Sports is another source of math-related concepts for children which tends to favor boys."

In short, even when there is a sort of seesaw structure, boys on one end and girls on the other, we never lose sight of the thesis that comprises both halves of the comparison.

Ways of Organizing an Essay Devoted to a Comparison

What happens if you want to organize a comparison or contrast that runs through an entire essay, say a comparison between two political campaigns, or between the characters in two novels. Remember that you are writing a comparison not merely as an exercise but in order to make a significant point—let's say, to demonstrate the superiority of X to Y.

Probably your first thought, after making some jottings in which you perhaps draw up two lists, will be to lump rather than to split—that is, to discuss one half of the comparison and then to go on to the second half. We'll discuss this useful method of organization in a moment, but here we want to point out that many instructors and textbooks disapprove of such an organization, arguing that the essay too often breaks into two parts and that the second part involves a good deal of repetition of categories set up in the first part. They prefer splitting. Let's say you are comparing the narrator of *Huckleberry Finn* with the narrator of *The Catcher in the Rye*, in order to show that despite superficial similarities, they are very different, and that the difference is partly the difference between the nineteenth century and the twentieth. An organization often recommended is something like this:

1. First similarity (the narrator and his quest)

    a. Huck

    b. Holden

2. Second similarity (the corrupt world surrounding the narrator)

   a. Society in *Huckleberry Finn*

   b. Society in *The Catcher in the Rye*

3. First difference (degree to which the narrator fulfills his quest and escapes from society)

   a. Huck's plan to "light out" to the frontier

   b. Holden's breakdown

And so on, for as many additional differences as seem relevant. Here is another way of splitting and organizing a comparison:

1. First point: the narrator and his quest

   a. Similarities between Huck and Holden

   b. Differences between Huck and Holden

2. Second point: the corrupt world

   a. Similarities between the worlds in *Huck* and *The Catcher*

   b. Differences between the worlds in *Huck* and *The Catcher*

3. Third point: degree of success

   a. Similarities between Huck and Holden

   b. Differences between Huck and Holden

But a comparison need not employ either of these methods of splitting. There is even the danger that an essay employing either of them may not come into focus until the essayist stands back from the seven-layer cake and announces, in the concluding paragraph, that the odd layers taste better. In your preparatory thinking you may want to make comparisons in pairs, but you must come to some conclusions about what these add up to before writing the final version. The final version should not duplicate the thought processes; rather, it should be organized so as to make the point clearly and effectively.

A RULE FOR WRITERS

The point of a comparison is not to list pairs of similarities or differences, but to illuminate a topic.

Although in a long essay you cannot postpone until page 30 a discussion of the second half of the comparison, in an essay of, say, fewer than ten pages, nothing is wrong with setting forth half of the comparison and then, in the light of what you've already said, discussing the second half. True, an essay that uses lumping will break into two unrelated parts if the second half makes no use of the first or fails to modify it; but the essay will hang together if the second half looks back to the first half and calls attention to differences that the new material reveals.

The danger of organizing the essay into two unrelated lumps can be avoided if in formulating your thesis you remember that your aim is to call attention to the unique features of something by holding it up against something similar but significantly different. If the differences are great and apparent, a comparison is a waste of effort. ("Blueberries are different from elephants. Blueberries do not have trunks. And elephants do not grow on bushes.") Indeed, a comparison between essentially and evidently unlike things can only obscure, for by making the comparison the writer implies there are significant similarities, and readers can only wonder why they do not see them. The essays that do break into two halves are essays that make *un*instructive comparisons: The first half tells the reader five things about baseball, the second half tells the reader five unrelated things about football.

CHECKLIST FOR REVISING COMPARISONS

☐ Is the point of the comparison—your reason for making it—clear? (See p. 137.)

☐ Do you cover all significant similarities and differences? (See p. 141.)

☐ Is the comparison readable—that is, is it clear and yet not tediously mechanical? (See p. 141.)

☐ Is lumping or splitting the best way to make this comparison? (See pp. 143–145.)

☐ If you are offering a value judgment, is it fair? Have you overlooked weaknesses in your preferred subject, and strengths in your less preferred subject?

Process Analysis

Popular writing offers many examples of the form of writing known as **process analysis**. Newspaper articles explain how to acquire a home aquarium or how to "detail" your car to improve its resale value; magazine articles explain how to begin a program of weight training or how to make a safe exit in an airplane emergency. The requirements a writer must follow when preparing such an article, sometimes called a **directive process analysis**, can be simply stated:

- Know the material thoroughly.
- Keep your audience in mind.
- Set forth the steps clearly, usually in chronological order.
- Define unfamiliar terms.

Explaining a process is common in academic writing too, though usually the explanation is of how something happens or has happened, and it is thus sometimes called an **informative process analysis**. The writer's purpose is for the reader to understand the process, not to perform it. You may find yourself reading or writing about a successful election strategy or a botched military campaign. In an exam you may be explaining your plan to solve a mathematical problem, or you may be explaining how the imagery works in a Shakespearean sonnet. You might write an essay on the camera techniques Hitchcock used in a sequence, or a term paper based on your research in marine biology. Once again, you will need to keep your reader in mind, to organize your explanation clearly and logically, and, of course, to write with expert knowledge of your subject.

The essay below reports on a lecture that was, from the evidence, an entertaining example of an *informative process analysis*.

Anne Hebald Mandelbaum

It's the Portly Penguin That Gets the Girl, French Biologist Claims

1   The penguin is a feathered and flippered bird who looks as if he's on his way to a formal banquet. With his stiff, kneeless strut and natural dinner jacket, he moves like Charlie Chaplin in his heyday dressed like Cary Grant in his.

2   But beneath the surface of his tuxedo is a gallant bird indeed. Not only does he fast for 65 days at a time, sleep standing up, and forsake all others in a lifetime of monogamy, but the male penguin also guards, watches over, and even hatches the egg.

3   We owe much of our current knowledge of the life and loves of the king and emperor penguins to—*bien sûr*—a Frenchman. Twenty-eight-year-old Yvon Le Maho is a biophysiologist from Lyons who visited the University last week to discuss his discoveries and to praise the penguin. He had just returned from 14 months in Antarctica, where he went to measure, to photograph, to weigh, to take blood and urine samples of, to perform autopsies on—in short, to study the penguin.

4   Although his original intent had been to investigate the penguin's long fasts, Monsieur Le Maho was soon fascinated by the amatory aspect of the penguin. Copulating in April, the female produces the egg in May and then heads out to sea, leaving her mate behind to incubate the egg. The males huddle together, standing upright and protecting the 500-gram (or 1.1-pound) egg with their feet for 65 days. During this time, they neither eat nor stray: each steadfastly stands guard over his egg, protecting it from the temperatures which dip as low as −40 degrees and from the winds which whip the Antarctic wilds with gusts of 200 miles an hour.

5   For 65 days and 65 nights, the males patiently huddle over the eggs, never lying down, never letting up. Then, every year on July 14th—Bastille Day, the national holiday of France—the eggs hatch and thousands of penguin chicks are born, M. Le Maho told his amused and enthusiastic audience at the Biological Laboratories.

6   The very day the chicks are born—or, at the latest, the following day—the female penguins return to land from their two-and-a-half month fishing expedition. They clamber out of the water and toboggan along the snow-covered beaches toward the rookery and their mates. At this moment, the males begin to emit the penguin equivalent of wild, welcoming cheers—*"comme le cri de trompette,"* M. Le Maho later told the *Gazette* in an interview—"like the clarion call of the trumpet."

7   And, amid the clamorous thundering of 12,000 penguins, the female recognizes the individual cry of her mate. When she does, she begins to cry to him. The male then recognizes *her* song, lifts the newborn chick into his feathered arms, and makes a beeline for the female. Each singing, each crying, the males and females rush

toward each other, slipping and sliding on the ice as they go, guided all the while by the single voice each instinctively knows.

8   The excitement soon wears thin for the male, however, who hasn't had a bite to eat in more than two months. He has done his duty and done it unflaggingly, but even penguins cannot live by duty alone. He must have food, and quickly.

9   Having presented his mate with their newborn, the male abruptly departs, heading out to sea in search of fish. The female, who has just returned from her sea-going sabbatical, has swallowed vast quantities of fish for herself and her chick. Much of what she has eaten she has not digested. Instead, this undigested food becomes penguin baby food. She regurgitates it, all soft and paplike, from her storage throat right into her chick's mouth. The chicks feed in this manner until December, when they first learn to find food on their own.

10   The penguins' reproductive life begins at age five, and the birds live about 25 years. Their fasting interests M. Le Maho because of its close similarities with fasting in human beings. And although many migratory birds also fast, their small size and indeed their flight make it almost impossible to study them closely. With the less-mobile and non-flying penguin, however, the scientist has a relatively accessible population to study. With no damage to the health of the penguin, M. Le Maho told the *Gazette*, a physiobiologist can extract blood from the flipper and sample the urine.

11   "All fasting problems are the same between man and the penguin," M. Le Maho said. "The penguin uses glucose in the brain, experiences ketosis as does man, and accomplishes gluconeogenesis, too." Ketosis is the build-up of partially burned fatty acids in the blood, usually as a result of starvation; gluconeogenesis is the making of sugar from non-sugar chemicals, such as amino acids. "The penguin can tell us a great deal about how our own bodies react to fasting conditions," M. Le Maho said.

12   He will return to Antarctica, M. Le Maho said, with the French government-sponsored *Expéditions Polaires Françaises* next December. There he will study the growth of the penguin chick, both inside the egg and after birth; will continue to study their mating, and to examine the penguin's blood sugar during fasting.

13   During the question-and-answer period following his talk, M. Le Maho was asked what the female penguin looks for in a mate. Responding, M. Le Maho drew himself up to his full five-foot-nine and said, *"La grandeur."*

Explaining an Analysis

As we have suggested, the writer of an analytical essay arrives at a thesis by asking questions and answering them, by separating the topic into parts and by seeing—often through the use of lists and scratch outlines— how those parts relate. Or, we might say, analytic writing presupposes detective work: The writer looks over the evidence, finds some clues, pursues the trail from one place to the next, and makes the arrest. Elementary? Perhaps.

You may recall that Sherlock Holmes customarily searches for evidence, finds it, and then—and this is important—explains it to his listener, usually Dr. Watson. When you write an analytic essay, you are Holmes, and your reader is Watson. Even when as a writer, after preliminary thinking you have solved a problem—that is, focused on a topic and formulated a thesis—you are, as we have said before, not yet done. It is, alas, not enough simply to present the results of your analytical thinking to a reader who, like Dr. Watson, will surely want to know "How in the world did you deduce that?" And like Holmes, writers are often impatient; we long to say with him "I have no time for trifles." But the real reason for our impatience is, as Holmes is quick to acknowledge, that "It was easier to know it than to explain why I know it." But explaining to readers why or how, presenting both the reasoning that led to a thesis and the evidence that supports the reasoning, is the writer's job.

In your preliminary detective work (that is, in reading, taking notes, musing, jotting down some thoughts, and writing rough drafts) some insights (perhaps including your thesis) may come swiftly, apparently spontaneously, and in random order. You may be unaware that you have been thinking analytically at all. In preparing your essay for your reader, however, you become aware, in part because *you must become aware*. To replace your reader's natural suspicion with respect for your analysis, you must explain your reasoning in an orderly and interesting fashion, and you must present your evidence.

CHAPTER EIGHT

PERSUADING READERS

To persuade readers is to convince them of the merit of your point of view, whether you're arguing against censorship, or for state-sponsored lotteries, or in favor of a particular interpretation of a short story. To be persuasive, you must present *reasonable arguments*, supported with *evidence*. In academic essays, the distinction between argument and analysis is often blurry. In the preceding chapter, for example, Dolores Hayden's analytic essay ("Advertisements, Pornography, and Public Space") does more than assert that certain kinds of images appear in certain places. It sets forth an **argument:** We ought not to allow public space to be given over to the harassment of women. The writer supports that argument with **evidence,** a report of images that she has observed, images that she subjects to careful **analysis.** In Chapter 10, "Writing the Research Essay," we'll examine an essay in which the writer uses **analysis** and **argument** in roughly equal proportion. In this chapter, after a brief comment on persuasion by emotional appeal, we'll focus on the elements of argument: on the distinction between claims and evidence, on the importance of defining terms and of avoiding fallacies, and on the use of wit in persuasive writing.

Emotional Appeals

It is often said that good argumentative writing appeals only to reason and logic (Greek: *logos*), never to emotion (*pathos*), and that any sort of emotional appeal is illegitimate, irrelevant, fallacious. Logic textbooks may even stigmatize with Latin labels the various sorts of emotional appeal—for instance, *argumentum ad populam* (appeal to the prejudices

of the mob, as in "Come on, we all know that schools don't teach anything anymore") and *argumentum ad misericoridam* (appeal to pity, as
in "No one can blame this poor kid for stabbing a classmate because his
mother was often institutionalized and his father beat him").

True, appeals to emotion may get in the way of the facts of the case;
they may blind the audience by stimulating tears. When an emotional
argument confuses the issue or shifts attention away from the facts of the
issue, we can reasonably speak of the fallacy of emotional appeal. But no
fallacy is involved when an emotional appeal heightens the facts, bringing
them home to the audience rather than masking them. If we are talking
about legislation that would govern police actions, it is legitimate to show
a photograph of the battered, bloodied face of a victim of alleged police
brutality. Of course such a photograph cannot tell if the subject threatened
the officer with a gun or repeatedly resisted an order to surrender. But it
can tell us that the victim was severely beaten and (like a comparable
description in words) evoke in us emotions that may properly enter into
our decision about what sorts of limitations on police actions are appropriate. Similarly, an animal rights activist who is arguing that calves are cru-
elly confined might reasonably tell us the size of the pen in which the
beast—unable to turn around or even to lie down—is kept. Others may
argue that calves don't much care about turning around or have no right
to turn around, but the verbal description, which unquestionably makes
an emotional appeal, can hardly be called fallacious or irrelevant.

In appealing to emotions, then:

• Do not falsify (especially by oversimplifying) the issue.
• Do not distract attention from the facts of the case.

For the most part, you should focus on the facts and concentrate on
offering reasons (essentially, statements linked with "because"), but
you may also legitimately bring the facts home to your readers by seeking to induce in them the appropriate emotions. Your words will be fallacious only if you stimulate emotions that are not rightly connected
with the facts of the case.

Making Reasonable Arguments

Persuasive writing that offers evidence and relies chiefly on reasoning
rather than on appeals to the emotions is usually called *argument*. What
distinguishes argument from exposition is this: Whereas both consist of

statements, in argument some statements are offered as *reasons* for other statements. Another way of characterizing argument is that argument assumes there is or may be substantial disagreement between informed readers. To overcome this disagreement, the writer of an argument offers reasons that seek to convince by their validity. Here, for example, is C. S. Lewis arguing against vivisection, the experimentation on live animals for scientific research:

> A rational discussion of this subject begins by inquiring whether pain is, or is not, an evil. If it is not, then the case against vivisection falls. But then so does the case for vivisection. If it is not defended on the ground that it reduces human suffering, on what ground can it be defended? And if pain is not an evil, why should human suffering be reduced? We must therefore assume as a basis for the whole discussion that pain is an evil, otherwise there is nothing to be discussed.
>
> Now if pain is an evil then the infliction of pain, considered in itself, must clearly be an evil act. But there are such things as necessary evils. Some acts which would be bad, simply in themselves, may be excusable and even laudable when they are necessary means to a greater good. In saying that the infliction of pain, simply in itself, is bad, we are not saying that pain ought never to be inflicted. Most of us think that it can rightly be inflicted for a good purpose—as in dentistry or just and reformatory punishment. The point is that it always requires justification. On the man whom we find inflicting pain rests the burden of showing why an act which in itself would be simply bad is, in those particular circumstances, good. If we find a man giving pleasure it is for us to prove (if we criticize him) that his action is wrong. But if we find a man inflicting pain it is for him to prove that his action is right. If he cannot, he is a wicked man.

And here is Supreme Court Justice Louis Brandeis, concluding his justly famous argument that government may not use evidence illegally obtained by wiretapping:

> Decency, security and liberty alike demand that government officials shall be subjected to the same rules of conduct that are commands to the citizen. In a government of laws, existence of the government will be imperiled if it fails to observe the law scrupulously. Our Government is the potent, the omnipresent teacher. For good or for ill, it teaches the whole people by its example. Crime is contagious. If the Government becomes a lawbreaker, it breeds contempt for law; it invites every man to become a law unto himself; it invites anarchy. To declare that in the

administration of the criminal law the end justifies the means—to declare that the Government may commit crimes in order to secure the conviction of a private criminal—would bring terrible retribution. Against that pernicious doctrine this Court should resolutely set its face.

Notice here that Brandeis's reasoning is highlighted by his forceful style. Note the resonant use of parallel constructions ("Decency, security and liberty," "For good or for ill," "it breeds . . . it invites," "To declare . . . to declare") and the variation between long and short sentences. Note too the wit in his comparisons: Government is a teacher, crime is like a disease.

Claims and Evidence

Evidence is what a writer offers in support of a **claim**—an assertion, usually that something is true, or right, or good. Evidence usually comes in the form of examples, testimony, and statistics.

Three Kinds of Claims: Claims of Fact, Value, and Policy

We can usually distinguish between two kinds of claims, claims of fact and claims of value, and we can sometimes distinguish these from a third kind of claim, claims of policy.

Claims of Fact

Claims of fact assert that something is or was or will be. They include, for instance, arguments about cause and effect, correlation, probability, and states of affairs. The following examples can be considered claims of fact:

Vanilla is the most popular flavor of ice cream in the United States.

Pornography stimulates violence against women.

Pornography has the potential of leading to violence.

Pornography serves a useful social purpose because it offers a harmless release of impulses that might otherwise be released in such activities as molestation or rape.

Capital punishment reduces crime.

Capital punishment does not reduce crime.

To support a claim of this sort, you must provide evidence. Such evidence might, for instance, be testimony (for instance, your own experience, or statements by men who have said that pornography stimulated them to violence), or it might be statistics (gathered from a report in a scholarly journal). Even if the claim has to do with the future—let's say the claim that gun control will not reduce crime—you try to offer evidence. For example, you might gather information about the experiences of other countries, or even of certain states, that have adopted strict regulations concerning the sale of guns. The implication is that if a policy had a particular effect in one place, it will have the same effect in another. Opponents may point out that results in, say, Miami, are no guarantee of the same results in, say, Chicago, but our point is that even claims for future facts must offer evidence.

Claims of Value

Claims of value concern what is right or wrong, good or bad, better or worse than something else:

> Country music deserves to be taken seriously.
>
> Capital punishment is barbaric.
>
> Euthanasia is immoral.

Some claims of value may be mere expressions of taste: "Vanilla is better than chocolate." It is hard to imagine how one could go about supporting such a claim—or refuting it. One probably can do no better than reply with the Latin proverb, "*De gustibus non est disputandum.*" (There is no disputing about tastes.) Notice, however, that the claim that vanilla is better than chocolate is quite different from the claim that most Americans prefer vanilla to chocolate. The last statement is a claim of fact, not of value, and it can be proved or disproved with evidence—for example, with information provided by the makers of ice cream.

Claims of value that go beyond the mere expression of taste—for instance, claims of morality or claims of artistic value—are usually supported by appeals to standards. ("The Patriot Act is bad *because* governments should not restrict the rights of individuals," or "Hip-hop music is good *because* it is complex."). In supporting claims of value, writers usually appeal to standards that they believe are acceptable to their readers. Here are some examples:

Sex-education programs in schools are inappropriate *because* aspects of moral education should properly be given only by parents.

Sex-education programs in schools are appropriate *because* society has a duty to provide what most parents obviously are reluctant to provide.

Doctors should be permitted to end a patient's life if the patient makes such a request, *because* each of us should be free to make the decisions that most concern us.

Euthanasia is unacceptable *because* only God can give or take life.

In arguing a claim of value, be sure you have clearly in your mind the standards that you believe support the claim. You may find it appropriate to explain *why* you hold these standards, and *how* adherence to these standards will be of benefit.

Claims of Policy

Claims of policy assert that a policy, law, or custom should be initiated or altered or dropped. Such claims usually are characterized by words like "should," "must," and "ought."

Children should be allowed to vote, if they wish to.

A course in minority cultures ought to be required.

The federal tax on gasoline must be raised.

In defending an unfamiliar claim of policy, you may want to begin by pointing out that there is a problem that is usually overlooked. For instance, if you urgently believe that children should have the right to vote—a view almost never expressed—you'll probably first have to convince your audience that there really is an arguable issue here, an issue concerning children's rights, an issue that deserves serious thought.

In defending a claim of policy you will probably find yourself providing information, just as you would do in support of a claim of fact. For instance, if your topic is children and the vote, you might point out that until 1920 women could not vote in the United States, the usual arguments being that they were mentally unfit and that they would vote the way their men told them to vote. Experience has proved that these low estimates of the capabilities of the disenfranchised were absurd.

But in defending a claim of policy you will probably have to consider values as well as facts. Thus, in arguing for an increase in the gasoline tax, you might want not only to provide factual information about how much money a five-cents-per-gallon tax would raise, but also to argue that such an increase is *fairer* than an alternative such as reducing Social Security benefits.

Three Kinds of Evidence: Examples, Testimony, Statistics

Writers of arguments seek to persuade by offering evidence. There are three chief forms of evidence used in argument:

- Examples
- Testimony, the citation of authorities
- Statistics

We'll briefly consider each of these.

Examples

The word *example* is from the Latin *exemplum*, which means "something taken out." An example is the sort of thing, taken from among many similar things, that one selects and holds up for view, perhaps after saying "For example," or "For instance."

Three categories of examples are especially common in written arguments:

- Real examples
- Invented instances
- Analogies

Real examples are actual instances that have occurred. If, say, we are arguing that gun control won't work, we point to those states that have adopted gun control laws and that nevertheless have had no reduction in crimes using guns. Or, if we want to support the assertion that a woman can be a capable head of state, we may find ourselves pointing to women who actually served as heads of state, such as Golda Meir and Indira Ghandi (prime ministers of Israel and India) and to Margaret Thatcher (prime minister of England).

The advantage of using real examples is, clearly, that they are real. Of course, an opponent might stubbornly respond that Golda Meir, Indira Gandhi, and Margaret Thatcher for some reason or other could not function as the head of state in *our* country. Someone might argue, for instance, that the case of Golda Meir proves nothing, since the role of women in Israeli society is different from the role of women in the United States (a country in which a majority of the citizens are Christians). And another person might argue that much of Mrs. Gandhi's power came from the fact that she was the daughter of Nehru, an immensely popular Indian statesman. Even the most compelling real example inevitably will in some ways be special or particular, and in the eyes of some readers may not seem to be a fair example.

Consider, for instance, a student who is arguing that peer review should be part of a writing course. The student points out that he or she found it of great help in high school. An opponent argues that things in college are different—college students should be able to help themselves, even highly gifted college students are not competent to offer college-level instruction, and so on. Still, as the feebleness of these objections (and the objections against Meir and Gandhi) indicates, real examples can be very compelling.

Invented instances are exempt from the charge that, because of some detail or other, they are not relevant as evidence. Suppose, for example, you are arguing against capital punishment, on the grounds that if an innocent person is executed, there is no way of even attempting to rectify the injustice. If you point to the real case of *X*, you may be met with the reply that *X* was not in fact innocent. Rather than get tangled up in the guilt or innocence of a particular person, it may be better to argue that we can suppose—we can imagine—an innocent person convicted and executed, and we can imagine that evidence later proves the person's innocence.

Invented instances have the advantage of presenting an issue clearly, free from all of the distracting particularities and irrelevancies that are bound up with any real instance. But invented instances have the disadvantage of being invented, and they may seem remote from the real issues being argued.

Analogies are comparisons pointing out several resemblances between two rather different things. For instance, one might assert that a government is like a ship, and in times of stress—if the ship is to weather the storm—the authority of the captain must not be questioned.

But don't confuse an analogy with proof. An analogy is an extended comparison between two things; it can be useful in exposition, for it explains the unfamiliar by means of the familiar: "A government is like a ship, and just as a ship has a captain and a crew, so a government has . . ."; "Writing an essay is like building a house; just as an architect must begin with a plan, so the writer must. . . ." Such comparisons can be useful, helping to clarify what otherwise might be obscure, but their usefulness goes only so far. Everything is what it is, and not another thing. A government is not a ship, and what is true of a captain's power need not be true of a president's power; and a writer is not an architect. Some of what is true about ships may be roughly true of governments, and some of what is true about architects may be true of writers, but there are differences too. Consider the following analogy between a lighthouse and the death penalty:

> The death penalty is a warning, just like a lighthouse throwing its beams out to sea. We hear about shipwrecks, but we do not hear about the ships the lighthouse guides safely on their way. We do not have proof of the number of ships it saves, but we do not tear the lighthouse down.

> —*J. Edgar Hoover*

How convincing is Hoover's analogy as an argument—that is, as a reason for retaining the death penalty?

Testimony

Testimony, or the citation of authorities, is rooted in our awareness that some people are recognized as experts. In our daily lives we constantly turn to experts for guidance: We look up the spelling of a word in the dictionary, we watch weather forecasts on television, we take an ailing cat to the vet for a checkup. Similarly, when we wish to become informed about controversial matters, we often turn to experts, first to help educate ourselves, and then to help convince others.

Don't forget that *you* are an authority on many things. For example, today's newspaper includes an article about the cutback in funding for the teaching of the arts in elementary and secondary schools. Art educators are responding that the arts are not a frill, and that in fact the arts provide the analytical thinking, teamwork, motivation, and self-discipline that most people agree are needed to reinvigorate American schools. If you have been involved in the arts in school—for instance, if you studied painting or learned to play a musical instrument—you are in a position to evaluate these claims. Similarly, if you have studied in a bilingual educational program, your own testimony will be invaluable in any discussion of the merits of bilingual programs.

There are at least two reasons for offering testimony in an argument. The obvious one is that expert opinion carries some weight with any audience; the less obvious one is that a change of voice (if the testimony is not your own) in an essay may afford the reader a bit of pleasure. No matter how engaging your own voice may be, a fresh voice—whether that of Thomas Jefferson, Ruth Bader Ginsburg, or Alice Walker—may provide a refreshing change of tone.

But, of course, there are dangers:

- The words of authorities may be taken out of context or otherwise distorted.
- The authorities may not be authorities on the present topic.

Quite rightly we are concerned with what Jefferson said, but it is not clear that his words can be fairly applied, on one side or the other, to such an issue as abortion or drilling for oil in Alaska. Quite rightly we are concerned with what Einstein said, but it is not clear that his eminence as a physicist constitutes him an authority on, say, world peace.

Statistics

Statistics, another important form of evidence, are especially useful in arguments concerning social issues. For example, if we want to argue for raising the driving age, we will probably do some research and will offer statistics about the number of accidents caused by people in certain age groups.

But a word of caution: The significance of statistics may be difficult to assess. For instance, opponents of gun control legislation have pointed out, in support of the argument that such laws are ineffectual, that homicides in Florida *increased* after Florida adopted gun control laws. Supporters of gun control laws cried "Foul," arguing that in the years after adopting these laws Miami became (for reasons having nothing to do with the laws) the cocaine capital of the United States, and the rise in homicide was chiefly a reflection of murders involved in the drug trade. That is, a significant change in the population has made a comparison of the figures meaningless. This objection seems plausible, and probably the statistics therefore should carry little weight.

A Note on Definition in the Persuasive Essay

To argue a point or to explain an idea, writers frequently need to provide definitions. Defining the terms of an argument is one of the persuasive writer's most useful strategies: A writer making an argument for or against abortion would be likely at some point in the essay to define the term "life."

The words may be *specialized* or unfamiliar to the writer's intended audience—for example, the words "venture capitalist" or "enterprise zones." Or, a writer might define a word that the audience may think it knows but that (in the writer's opinion) the audience may misunderstand. For instance, you might argue that the words "insurgent" and "terrorist" are not synonyms, and then go on to define each word, showing the differences between them.

In addition to defining a word because it is specialized ("venture capitalist"), or because we want to distinguish it from another word ("insurgent" and "terrorist"), we may define a word because the word has many meanings, and we want to make sure that readers take the word in a particular way. A word like "ability," for example, may require defining in a discussion of the Scholastic Aptitude Test. To argue that the SAT does or does not measure "academic ability," the writer and reader need, in a sense, to agree on a specific meaning for "ability." This kind of definition, where the writer specifies or stipulates a meaning ("By *ability* I mean . . ."), is called a **stipulative definition.**

The word *stipulate*, by the way, comes from a Latin word meaning "to bargain." Explaining a word's *etymology*, its history or its origin, as we have just done, is often an aid in definition.

In short, when defining a word or term, writers have many options, and they need to take into account both their own purposes in writing and their readers' needs.

Definition at Work

In the following brief essay student Lena Flora defines the term *political correctness*.

The Plight of the Politically Correct

Political correctness is a style of language, an attitude, and a standard of ethics that people have now been struggling with for years. Part of the reason for this struggle lies in the fact that no one is exactly sure what is and what is not politically correct. The phrase political correctness might be defined as "conformity to a body of liberal or radical opinion, especially on social matters." Political correctness also involves the avoidance of anything, even established vocabulary, that might be construed as discriminatory or pejorative. In effect, political correctness seems to mean taking every word in the English language, scrutinizing it for any way that it could possibly offend any one person, and using this criterion to ban its use in day-to-day speech. For example, I can no longer grow up and be a fireman, a policeman, a mailman, or a woman. I may not even be allowed to call myself female. Does this mean that I am fated to call myself testosteronally-challenged, or maybe x-chromosomally gifted? Am I a chauvinist pig if I like to be known as a woman, or if I refer to my daughter as my little girl? By some strict politically correct standards, yes. Also, political correctness forces me to refrain from using many adjectives I might use to describe myself. I am not Oriental, short, or near-sighted. Instead, I am an Asian-American, vertically-challenged, and distant-visually-challenged person of feminine gender. I certainly don't feel challenged in any of these areas, only in the area of speaking with political correctness.

How Much Evidence Is Enough?

If you allow yourself ample time to write your essay, you probably will turn up plenty of evidence to illustrate your arguments, such as examples drawn from your own experience and imagination, from your reading, and from your talks with others. Evidence will not only help to clarify and to support your assertions, but it will also provide a concreteness that will be welcome in a paper that might be on the whole fairly abstract. Your sense of your audience will have to guide you as you select your evidence. Generally speaking, a single example may not fully illuminate a difficult point, and so a second example, a clincher, may be desirable. If you offer a third or fourth example you probably are succumbing to a temptation to include something that tickles your fancy. If it is as good as you think it is, the reader probably will accept the unnecessary example and may even be grateful. But before you heap up examples, try to imagine yourself in your reader's place, and ask if the example is needed. If it is not needed, ask yourself if the reader will be glad to receive the overload.

One other point: On most questions, say on the value of bilingual education or on the need for rehabilitation programs in prisons, it's not possible to make a strictly logical case, in the sense of an absolutely air-tight proof. Don't assume that it is your job to make an absolute proof. What you are expected to do is to offer a reasonable argument.

Two Kinds of Reasoning: Induction and Deduction

We have just said that you are expected to offer a reasonable argument, which means that your essay will probably demonstrate two kinds of thinking, inductive and deductive. **Induction** is the process of reasoning from particular to general, or drawing a conclusion about all members of a class from a study of some members of the class. Every elephant I have seen is grayish, so by induction (from Latin for "lead into," "lead up to") I conclude that all elephants are grayish. And here we get to what is called *logos*, reasoning, as opposed to *pathos*, emotion.

Here's another example: I have met ten graduates of Vassar College and all are females, so I conclude that all Vassar graduates are females. This conclusion, however, happens to be incorrect; Vassar originally admitted only women, but it now admits men. Induction is valid only if the sample is representative.

Because we can rarely be certain that a sample is representative, induced conclusions are usually open to doubt. Still, we live our lives largely by induction; we have dinner with a friend, we walk the dog, we write home for money—all because these actions have produced certain results in the past and we assume that actions of the same sort will produce results consistent with our earlier experience. Nelson Algren's excellent advice must have been arrived at inductively: "Never eat at a place called Mom's, and never play cards with a man called Doc." In developing our argument, we draw on experience—"Policy X has been successful in all ten instances where it was tried, so we can assume it will probably succeed here too"—but we must understand that we are not dealing with certainties.

Deduction (from Latin for "lead down from") is the process of reasoning from premises to a logical conclusion. Here is the classic example:

"All men are mortal" (the major premise);

"Socrates is a man" (the minor premise);

"Therefore Socrates is mortal" (the conclusion).

Such an argument, which takes two truths and joins them to produce a third truth, is called a *syllogism* (from Greek for "a reckoning together"). Deduction moves from a general statement to a specific application; it is, therefore, the opposite of induction, which moves from specific instances to a general conclusion.

Notice that if a premise of a syllogism is not true, one can reason logically and still come to false conclusion. Example: All teachers are members of a union; Jones is a teacher; Therefore Jones is a member of a union. Although the formal process of reasoning is correct here, the major premise is false—not all teachers are members of a union—and so the conclusion is worthless. (Jones may or may not be a member of a union.) In other words, "Garbage in, garbage out."

Avoiding Fallacies

Let's further examine writing reasonable arguments by considering some obvious errors in reasoning. In logic these errors are called **fallacies** (from a Latin verb meaning "to deceive"). As Tweedledee says in *Through the Looking-Glass*, "If it were so, it would be; but as it isn't, it ain't. That's logic."

To persuade readers to accept your opinions you must persuade them that you are reliable; if your argument includes fallacies, thoughtful readers will not take you seriously. More important, if your argument includes fallacies, you are misleading yourself. When you search your draft for fallacies, you are reading it critically, searching for ways to improve the quality of your thinking. Here are nine fallacies to avoid.

1. False authority. Don't try to borrow the prestige of authorities who are not authorities on the topic in question—for example, a heart surgeon speaking on politics. Similarly, some former authorities are no longer authorities, because the problems have changed or because later knowledge has superseded their views. Adam Smith, Jefferson and Eleanor Roosevelt, remain persons of genius, but an attempt to use their opinions when you are examining modern issues—even in their fields— may be questioned. Remember the last words of John B. Sedgwick, a Union Army general at the Battle of Spotsylvania in 1864: "They couldn't hit an elephant at this dist—." In short, before you rely on an authority, ask yourself if the person in question *is* an authority on the topic. And don't let stereotypes influence your idea of who is an authority. Remember the Yiddish proverb: "A goat has a beard, but that doesn't make him a rabbi."

2. False quotation. If you do quote from an authority, don't misquote. For example, you may find someone who grants that "there are strong arguments in favor of abolishing the death penalty"; but if she goes on to argue that, on balance, the arguments in favor of retaining it seem stronger to her, it is dishonest to quote her words so as to imply that she favors abolishing it.

3. Suppression of evidence. Don't neglect evidence that is contrary to your own argument. You owe it to yourself and your reader to present all the relevant evidence. Be especially careful not to assume that every question is simply a matter of *either/or*. There may be some truth on both sides. Take the following thesis: "Grades encourage unwholesome competition, and should therefore be abolished." Even if the statement about the evil effect of grading is true, it may not be the whole truth, and therefore it may not follow that grades should be abolished. One might point out that grades do other things too: They may stimulate learning, and they may assist students by telling them how far they have progressed. One might nevertheless conclude, on balance, that the fault outweighs the benefits. But the argument will be more persuasive now that the benefits of grades have been considered.

Concede to the opposition what is due it, and then outscore the opposition. If you don't discuss the opposing evidence, your readers will keep wondering why you do not consider this point or that, and may consequently dismiss your argument. Confronting the opposition will almost surely strengthen your own argument. As Edmund Burke said 200 years ago, "He that wrestles with us strengthens our nerves, and sharpens our skill. Our antagonist is our helper."

4. Generalization from insufficient evidence. In rereading a draft of an argument that you have written, try to spot your own generalizations. Ask yourself if a reasonable reader is likely to agree that the generalization is based on an adequate sample.

A visitor to a college may sit in on three classes, each taught by a different instructor, and may find all three stimulating. That's a good sign, but can we generalize and say that the teaching at this college is excellent? Are three classes a sufficient sample? If all three are offered by the Biology Department, and if the Biology Department includes only five instructors, perhaps we can tentatively say that the teaching of biology at this institution is good. If the Biology Department contains twenty instructors, perhaps we can still say, though more tentatively, that this sample indicates that the teaching of biology is good. But what does the sample say about the teaching of other subjects at the college?

It probably does say something—the institution may be much concerned with teaching across the board—but then again it may not say a great deal, since the Biology Department may be exceptionally concerned with good teaching.

5. The genetic fallacy. Don't assume that something can necessarily be explained in terms of its birth or origin, its genesis. "He wrote the novel to make money, so it can't be any good" is not a valid inference. The value of a novel does not depend on the author's motivations in writing it. Indeed, the value or worth of a novel needs to be established by reference to other criteria. Neither the highest nor the lowest motivations guarantee the quality of the product. Another example: "Capital punishment arose in days when people sought revenge, so now it ought to be abolished." Again an unconvincing argument: Capital punishment may have some current value; for example, it may serve as a deterrent to crime. But that's another argument, and it needs evidence if it is to be believed.

6. Begging the question and circular reasoning. Don't assume the truth of the point that you should prove. The term *begging the question* is a trifle odd. It means, in effect, "You, like a beggar, are asking me to grant you something at the outset."

Consider two examples: "The barbaric death penalty should be abolished"; "This senseless language requirement should be dropped." Both statements assume what they should prove—that the death penalty is barbaric and that the language requirement is senseless. You can of course make assertions such as these, but you must go on to prove them.

Circular reasoning is usually an extended form of begging the question. What ought to be proved is covertly assumed: "*X* is the best-qualified candidate for the office, because the most informed people say so." Who are the most informed people? Those who recognize *X*'s superiority. Circular reasoning, then, normally includes intermediate steps absent from begging the question, but the two fallacies are so closely related that they can be considered one. Here's another example: "I feel sympathy for her because I identify with her." Despite the "because," no reason is really offered. What follows "because" is merely a restatement, in slightly different words, of what precedes; the shift of words, from "feel sympathy" to "identify with," has misled the writer into thinking she is giving a reason.

7. *Post hoc ergo propter hoc* (Latin for "after this, therefore because of this"). Don't assume that because *X* precedes *Y*, *X* must cause *Y*. For exam-

"Look, maybe you're right, but for the sake of argument let's assume you're wrong and drop it."

ple: "He went to college and came back a boozer; college corrupted him." He might have taken up liquor even if he had not gone to college. Another example: "When a fifty-five-mile-per-hour limit was imposed in 1974, after the Arab embargo on oil, the number of auto fatalities decreased sharply, from 55,000 deaths in 1973 to 46,000 in 1974, so it is evident that a fifty-five-mile-per-hour limit—still adhered to in some states— saves lives." Not quite. Because gasoline was expensive after the embargo, the number of miles traveled decreased. The number of fatalities *per mile* remained constant. The price of gas, not the speed limit, seems responsible for the decreased number of fatalities. Moreover, the national death rate has continued to fall. Why? Several factors are at work: seat-belt and child-restraint laws, campaigns against drunk driving, improved auto design, and improved roads. Medicine, too, may have improved so that today doctors can save accident victims who in 1974 would have died. In short, it probably is impossible to isolate the correlation between speed and safety.

8. *Argumentum ad hominem* (Latin for "argument toward the man"). Here the argument is directed toward the person rather than toward the issue. Don't shift from your topic to your opponent. A

speaker argues in favor of legalizing abortions and her opponent, instead of facing the merits of the argument, attacks the character or the associations of the opponent: "When you were married, you had an extra-marital affair and became pregnant, didn't you?"

9. False assumption. Consider the Scot who argued that Shakespeare must have been a Scot. Asked for his evidence, he replied, "The ability of the man warrants the assumption." Or take a statement such as "She goes to Yale, so she must be rich." Possibly the statement is based on faulty induction (the writer knows four Yale students, and all four are rich) but more likely he is just passing on a cliché. The Yale student in question may be on a scholarship, may be struggling to earn the money, or may be backed by parents of modest means who for eighteen years have saved money for her college education.

The errors we have discussed are common. In revising, try to spot them and eliminate or correct them. You have a point to make, and you should make it fairly. If it can be made only unfairly, you do an injustice not only to your reader but also to yourself; you should try to change your view of the topic. You don't want to be like the politician whose speech had a marginal note: "Argument weak; shout here."

Wit

In addition to using sound argument and other evidence, writers often use wit, especially irony, to persuade. In irony, the words convey a meaning somewhat different from what they explicitly say. Wry understatement is typical. Here, for instance, is Thoreau explaining why in *Walden*, his book about his two years in relative isolation at Walden Pond, he will talk chiefly about himself:

> In most books, the *I*, or first person, is omitted; in this it will be retained; that, in respect to egotism, is the main difference. We commonly do not remember that it is, after all, always the first person that is speaking. I should not talk so much about myself if there were anybody else whom I knew as well. Unfortunately, I am confined to this theme by the narrowness of my experience.

Notice the wry apology in Thoreau's justification for talking about himself: He does not know anyone else as well as he knows himself. Similarly, in "unfortunately" ("Unfortunately, I am confined to this theme by the narrowness of my experience") we again hear a wry voice. After all, Thoreau knows, as we know, that *no one* has experience so deep or broad that he or she knows others better than himself or herself. Thoreau's presentation of himself as someone who happens not to have had the luck of knowing others better than himself is engagingly clever.

Avoiding Sarcasm

Because writers must, among other things, persuade readers that they are humane, sarcasm has little place in persuasive writing. Although desk dictionaries usually define sarcasm as "bitter, caustic irony" or "a kind of satiric wit," if you think of a sarcastic comment that you have heard you will probably agree that "a crude, sneering remark" is a better definition. Lacking the wit of good satire and the carefully controlled mockery of irony, sarcasm usually relies on gross overstatement and intends simply to humiliate. *Sarcasm* is derived from a Greek word meaning "to tear flesh" or "to bite the lips in rage," altogether an unattractive business. Sarcasm is unfair, for it dismisses an opponent's arguments with ridicule rather than with reason; it is also unwise, for it turns the reader against the speaker or writer. Readers hesitate to ally themselves with a writer who apparently enjoys humiliating the opposition. A sarcastic remark can turn the hearers against the speaker and arouse sympathy for the victim. In short, sarcasm usually doesn't work.

Tone and Ethical Appeal

Although this chapter is chiefly about persuasion in the sense of rational discourse—the presentation of reasons in support of a thesis or conclusion—there are other forms of persuasion. We've already mentioned one of them: the *appeal to emotion*. The *appeal to force* is another: As Al Capone put it, "You can get a lot more done with a kind word and a gun, than with a kind word alone." But, in a sense, kind words themselves can do quite a lot. The writer's **tone,** or voice, matters. A moment ago we cautioned against the use of sarcasm, on the grounds that the satirist is perceived as an unattractive character, and this caution can now be put into a larger context, something that Aristotle called the **ethical appeal,** from *ethos*, the Greek work for "character." The ethical appeal is based on the idea that effective speakers and writers convey by their tone the suggestion that they are good people, specifically that they are

- informed,
- intelligent,

- benevolent, and
- honest.

Because they are perceived as trustworthy, their words inspire confidence in their listeners and their readers. When we read an argument, we hear or sense a *voice* or *persona* behind the words, and our assent to the argument depends partly on the extent to which we trust this speaker, this voice, this character.

How can you inspire this trust? To begin with, you should indeed be informed, intelligent, benevolent, and honest. Still, possession of these qualities does not guarantee that you will convey them in your writing. You will have to revise your drafts so that these qualities become apparent to your audience—so that nothing in your essay causes your reader to doubt your knowledge, intelligence, good intentions, and integrity. A blunder in logic, a misleading quotation, a sarcastic remark—all such slips can cause readers to withdraw their trust from the writer.

It's generally not persuasive to present as villains or fools all persons who hold views different from your own, especially if some of them are your readers. Recognize opposing views, assume they are held in good faith, state them fairly, and be temperate in arguing your own position: "If I understand their view correctly . . ."; "It seems reasonable to conclude that . . ."; "Perhaps, then, we can agree that. . . ."

A RULE FOR WRITERS:

When you argue, be courteous and be respectful of your topic, of your audience, and of the people who hold views you are arguing against.

A Note on Critical Thinking

To think critically is to adopt a skeptical or questioning view, especially about our own opinions. It is easy to be skeptical when we hear the opinions of others—"What is your evidence for that?" "Says who?" "Why should I grant your assumptions, even for the sake of argument?"—but it is difficult for us to question our own assumptions because they seem so obviously true. For example, it once seemed obvious to many people that lawmakers should not get paid, or paid well. The idea was that a man (it was obvious that women should not be making laws) should seek public office not to make money but rather to serve the community. The idea is high-minded, but the consequence

"Please forgive Edgar. He has no verbal skills."

was that only the rich could afford to run for, and to hold, office. Experience proved that many officeholders, however high-minded, had chiefly their own interests at heart. They may indeed have thought that their actions were always for the good of the nation, but inevitably they tended to see things from a particular point of view, the point of view of the rich, in America more specifically the point of view of rich, white Protestant males.

Thinking critically, then, involves questioning even your own cherished assumptions, things that seem "self-evident," "obvious," "clearly true." It involves imagining yourself as someone who does not share these assumptions and then questioning the arguments you have presented. For example, are the statistics you offer current? Even if they are, can they be interpreted differently? To ask such questions of others may open you to the charge of negativeness, but the charge is unfair if you adopt the same questioning manner when you consider your own arguments, especially your assumptions and your evidence. In short, to think critically is to be skeptical not only of the assumptions, arguments, and conclusions of others but also of your own—thus to remain open to assuming a modified or new position.

Organizing an Argument

As we have said earlier, writers find out what they think partly by means of the act of putting words on paper. But in presenting arguments for their readers, writers rarely duplicate their own acts of discovery. To put it another way, the process of setting forth ideas, and supporting them, does not follow the productive but untidy, repetitive, often haphazard process of preliminary thinking. For instance, a point that did not strike us until the middle of the third draft may, in the final version, appear in the opening paragraph. Or an example that seemed useful early in our thinking may, in the process of revision, be omitted in favor of a stronger example. Through a series of revisions, large and small, we try to work out the best strategy for persuading our readers to accept our reasoning as sound, our conclusion as valid. Unfortunately, we find, an argument cannot be presented either as it occurs to us or all at once.

No simple formula governs the organization of all effective argumentative essays. An essay may begin by announcing its thesis and then set forth the supporting reasons. Or it may begin more casually, calling attention to specific cases, and then generalize from these cases. Probably it will then go on to reveal an underlying unity that brings the thesis into view, and from here it will offer detailed reasoning that supports the thesis.

As the writer of a persuasive essay, you almost always have to handle, in some sequence or other, the following matters:

- The context of the argument (for instance, an explanation of why the issue should be considered, or reconsidered)
- The thesis
- The evidence that supports the thesis
- The counterevidence
- The response to counterclaims and counterevidence (either a refutation or a concession that there *is* merit to the counterclaims but not as much as to the writer's thesis)
- Some sort of reaffirmation, perhaps that the topic needs attention or that the thesis advanced is the most plausible or the most workable or the most moral, or that the ball is now in the reader's court

Three methods of organizing arguments are fairly common, and one or another may suit an essay you're working on.

1. Begin with the context of the argument, then set forth the thesis statement and work from the simplest argument up to the most complex, taking account of opposing arguments as you set forth your own arguments. Such an arrangement will keep your reader with you, step by step.

2. After setting forth the context and your thesis, arrange the arguments in order of increasing strength. The danger in following this plan is that you may lose the reader from the start, because you begin with a weak argument. Avoid this problem by telling your reader that indeed the first argument is relatively weak (if it is terribly weak, it isn't an argument at all, so scrap it), but that you offer it for the sake of completeness or because it is often given, and that you will soon give the reader far stronger arguments. Face the opposition to this initial argument, grant that opposition as much as it deserves, and salvage what is left of the argument. Then proceed to the increasingly strong arguments, devoting at least one paragraph to each. Introduce each argument with an appropriate transition ("another reason," "even more important," "most convincing of all"). State it briefly, summarize the opposing view, and then demolish this opposition. With this organization, your discussion of each of your own arguments ends affirmatively.

3. After sketching the background and stating your thesis in an introductory paragraph, mass all of the opposing arguments, and then respond to them one by one.

CHECKLIST FOR REVISING DRAFTS
OF PERSUASIVE ESSAYS

☐ Are the terms clearly defined? (See pp. 159–160.)

☐ Is the thesis stated promptly and clearly? (See pp. 171–172.)

☐ Are the assumptions likely to be shared by your readers? If not, are they reasonably argued rather than merely stated? (See pp. 165–167.)

☐ Are the facts verifiable? Is the evidence reliable? (No out-of-date statistics, no generalizations from insufficient evidence?) (See pp. 156–159.)

☐ Is the reasoning sound? (See pp. 163–167.)

☐ Are the authorities really authorities on this matter?
(See p. 163.)

☐ Are all of the substantial counterarguments recognized and
effectively responded to? (See p. 164.)

☐ Does the essay make use, where appropriate, of concrete examples?
(See pp. 156–157.)

☐ Is the organization effective? Does the essay begin in a compelling
way, keep the thesis in view, and end interestingly? (See pp.
171–172.)

☐ Is the tone appropriate? (Avoid sarcasm. Present yourself as
fair-minded, and assume that those who hold a view opposed to
yours are also fair-minded.) (See pp. 167–169.)

Persuasion at Work: Two Writers Consider Torture

We present below two essays, the first arguing that torture should not be
authorized under any circumstances, even in the case of a "ticking
bomb," and the second arguing that because torture is inevitable and
necessary, it should be legalized so that it can be regulated. Following
each essay, we offer a brief analysis of the writer's persuasive devices
and strategies.

Philip B. Heymann
Torture Should Not Be Authorized

*Philip B. Heymann, a former U.S. deputy attorney general in the
Clinton administration, is a professor at Harvard Law School. His most recent
publications include* Preserving Liberty in an Age of Terror *(with Juliette
Kayyem, 2005), and* Terrorism, Freedom, and Security *(2003). The
following essay was published in the* Boston Globe *in 2002 and represents
Heymann's position in his ongoing debate with Alan Dershowitz about the
authorization of torture. Dershowitz's response appears on pages 176–178.*

1   Authorizing torture is a bad and dangerous idea that can easily be made to sound plausible. There is a subtle fallacy embedded in the traditional "ticking bomb" argument for torture to save lives.

2   That argument goes like this. First, I can imagine dangers so dire that I might torture or kill guilty or innocent persons if I was quite sure that was necessary and sufficient to prevent those dangers. Second, very many feel this way, although differing in the circumstances and the certainty level they would want. Therefore, the "ticking bomb" argument concludes, everyone wants a system for authorizing torture or murder; we need only debate the circumstances and the level of certainty.

3   This conclusion, leading to abandonment of one of the few worldwide legal prohibitions, leaves out the fact that I do not have faith in the authorizing system for finding the required circumstances with any certainty because the costs of errors are born by the suspect tortured, not by those who decide to torture him. The conclusion also ignores the high probability that the practice of torture will spread unwisely if acceptance of torture with the approval of judges is substituted for a flat, worldwide prohibition.

4   The use of torture would increase sharply if there were "torture warrants." Any law enforcement or intelligence official who tortures a prisoner in the United States now is very likely to be prosecuted and imprisoned.

5   Punches may be thrown, but anything we think of as "torture" is considered an inexcusable practice. That revulsion will disappear if we make torture acceptable and legal whenever a judge accepts the judgment of intelligence officials that: (1) there is a bomb; (2) the suspect knows where it is; (3) torture will get the truth, not a false story, out of him before the bomb explodes; (4) the bomb won't be moved in the meantime. Every individual who believes in his heart, however recklessly, that those conditions (or others he thinks are just as compelling) are met will think there is nothing seriously wrong with torture.

6   Professor Alan Dershowitz wants to bet that judges will say "no" in a high enough percentage of cases of "ticking bombs" that whatever moral force their refusal has will offset the legitimating and demoralizing effects of authorizing occasional torture. It's a bad bet.

7   Judges have deferred to the last several thousand requests for national security wiretaps and they would defer here. The basis of their decisions, information revealing secret "sources and methods" of intelligence gathering, would not be public. And if the judge

refused, overrode the judgment of agents who thought lives would be lost without torture, and denied a warrant, why would that decision be more likely to be accepted and followed by agents desperate to save lives than the flat ban on torture we now have?

8   How many false positives do you want to accept? You would get six false positives out of ten occasions of torture even in the extraordinarily unlikely event that the intelligence officers convince the judge that they were really 80 percent sure of each of the above four predictions.

9   And even if you would tolerate this number of false positives if torture were in fact the only way to get the needed information to defuse the bomb, there are frequently other promising ways (such as emergency searches or stimulating conversations over tapped phones) that will be abandoned or discounted if torture is available.

10   Finally, if we approve torture in one set of circumstances, isn't every country then free to define its own exceptions, applicable to Americans as well as its own citizens? Fear of that led us to accept the Geneva Convention prohibiting torture of a prisoner of war, although obtaining his information might save dozens of American lives.

11   As to preventing terrorism, torture is an equally bad idea. Torture is a prescription for losing a war for support of our beliefs in the hope of reducing the casualties from relatively small battles.

12   Dershowitz misunderstands my argument. I do not accept torture either "off the books" with a wink at the secret discretion of the torturers or on the open authority of the judges from whom they might seek authorization. I predict so many types of harms to so many people and to the nation from any system that authorizes torture, either secretly or openly, that I would prohibit it.

13   The overall, longer-term cost of any system authorizing torture, openly or tacitly, would far outweigh its occasional, short-term benefits.

An Analysis of Heymann's Argument

In his essay, Philip Heymann argues against the position that torture is acceptable if the circumstances are extreme—if, say, a suspect seems to have information about a "ticking bomb" that might be obtained if he or she were tortured—and if the torture has been approved by judges. Heymann makes his **thesis** clear in the first line of his essay, with a **claim of value:** "Authorizing torture is a bad and dangerous idea." He introduces the **counterargument** in paragraph 1: The "ticking bomb" argument "can easily be made to sound plausible," he says, but it contains a **"fallacy."** He presents the counterargument itself in paragraph 2. In paragraph 3, he present his **reasons** for thinking his opponent's position to be flawed: (1) authorities are more likely to make mistakes when deciding if a suspect is to be tortured, because the suspect, not the authority, will bear the burden of a mistake; and (2) "torture warrants" will lead to the erosion of our sense that torture is unacceptable and cause the spread of a practice that now is universally condemned. He develops this point with more reasons in paragraphs 4 and 5. In paragraph 6, he contests Alan Dershowitz's implied **claim of fact,** that judges would authorize torture infrequently. Heymann counters this claim by presenting **evidence,** a **claim** about the future based on **facts** already evident: Judges frequently authorize requests for otherwise illegal wiretaps when national security is thought to be in jeopardy. In paragraphs 8 and 9, he raises the issue of "false positives" (and we note that he does not tell us the source of his **statistics** here). In succeeding paragraphs, he presents more **reasons** in support of his central claim: authorizing torture in the United States will lead to the spread of torture in other countries (paragraph 10), and it will generate more bad will toward us (paragraph 11). He concludes with perhaps his strongest point, **a claim of fact,** that the costs of authorizing torture will far outweigh the benefits.

Alan M. Dershowitz
Yes, It Should Be "On the Books"

Alan Dershowitz is Professor of Law at Harvard University, where he has taught since 1964. His most recent publications include Preemption: A Knife that Cuts Both Ways *(2006),* The Case for Peace *(2005), and* America on Trial: Inside the Legal Battles that Transformed Our Nation— From the Salem Witches to the Guantanamo Detainees *(2004).*

1   Professor Philip Heymann and I share a common goal: to eliminate torture from the world, or at the very least to reduce it to an absolute minimum. The real disagreement between us seems to be

over whether the use of torture, under these extreme circumstances, would be worse if done in secret without being incorporated into our legal system—or worse if it required a torture warrant to be issued by a judge. This is truly a choice of evils, with no perfect resolution. However, I insist that any extraordinary steps contemplated by a democracy must be done "on the books." Of course there is the risk of false positives and ever expanding criteria. But these evils would exist whether torture was conducted off or on the books. A carefully designed judicial procedure is more likely to reduce the amount of torture actually conducted, by creating accountability and leaving a public record of every warrant sought and granted.

2   The legal historian John Langbein has shown that there was far more torture in Medieval France than England because in France the practice was left to the discretion of local officials, whereas in England it required an extraordinary warrant, which was rarely granted. Heymann suggests that "any law enforcement and intelligence official who tortures a prisoner in the United States now is very likely to be prosecuted and imprisoned." I believe that a police officer who tortured and successfully prevented a terrorist attack would not be prosecuted, and if he were, he would be acquitted.

3   Indeed, in a case decided in 1984, the Court of Appeals for the 11th circuit commended police officers who tortured a kidnapper into disclosing the location of his victim. Although there was no evidence that the victim's life was in imminent danger, the court described the offending police officers as "a group of concerned officers acting in a reasonable manner to obtain information in order to protect another individual from bodily harm or death." Elsewhere in the opinion, they described the "reasonable manner" as including "choking him until he revealed where [the victim] was being held." These police officers were not prosecuted. Under my proposal, no torture warrant could have been granted in such a case.

4   Our nation has had extensive experience with "off the book" actions. President Nixon authorized an off the book "plumbers" operation to break into homes and offices. President Reagan authorized an off the book foreign policy that culminated in the Iran-Contra debacle. President[s] Eisenhower and Kennedy apparently authorized off the book attempts to assassinate Fidel Castro. The road to tyranny is paved by executive officials authorizing actions which they deem necessary to national security,

without subjecting these actions to the check and balance of legislative approval, judicial imprimatur, and public accountability. We are a nation of laws, and if the rule of law means anything, it means that no action regardless of how unpalatable, must ever be taken outside of the rule of law. If the action is to be taken, it must be deemed lawful. If it cannot be deemed lawful it should not be taken.

5   Unless we are prepared to authorize the issuance of a torture warrant in the case of the ticking bomb, we should not torture, even if that means that innocent people may die. If we want to prevent the death of hundreds of innocent people by subjecting one guilty person to nonlethal pain, then we must find a way to justify this exception to the otherwise blanket prohibition against torture. All the evils of torture would be multiplied if we were to accept the way of the hypocrite, by proclaiming loudly that we are against it but subtly winking an eye of approval when it is done.

6   Hypocrisy, too, is contagious. Several years ago, an Israeli prime minister reprimanded security officials for bringing him "unwanted information of misdeeds by Shin Bet" (the Israeli FBI). A wise professor commented on this action in the following words: "That strategy is extremely dangerous to democratic values, because it is designed to prevent oversight and to deny accountability to the public."

7   That wise professor was Philip Heymann.

An Analysis of Dershowitz's Argument

Unlike Heymann's direct, even confrontational opening ("Authorizing torture is a bad and dangerous idea"), the **tone** of Dershowitz's opening is almost conciliatory. He presents himself as a trustworthy speaker who wants something good and reasonable and who acknowledges that there is no easy solution, "no perfect resolution." He says that he essentially agrees with his opponent. He and Heymann both think that torture is bad; they simply disagree on whether torture with warrants is worse than torture conducted illegally, in secret. Dershowitz implies that Heymann supports the latter: This seems to us to **falsify** Heymann's position. Heymann clearly asserts that he is against torture.

Dershowitz's **thesis** appears in the last sentence of his opening paragraph. He supports his thesis with **evidence** in paragraphs 2 and 3. In these paragraphs, he uses legal historians and recent case records to support his **claim** that authorizing torture actually reduces it and to contest Heymann's claim that, under the current laws, authorities who torture suspects are punished. In paragraph 4, he makes an **analogy** between "off the books" torture to other "off the books" activities (Watergate, Iran-Contra, plots to murder Fidel Castro). Here he suggests that requiring warrants for torture will prevent "tyranny" by enabling legislative checks and balances to operate. The analogy seems powerful—but is it relevant? We don't think so. The activities he lists were and are illegal. They never would or could have been legally authorized. Torture is now against the law. Dershowitz proposes rewriting the law to make warranted torture legal.

He concludes by suggesting that those who don't support his position are hypocrites because they are willing to protest torture while also "subtly winking an eye of approval when it is done." He doesn't call Heymann himself a hypocrite (reasonable speakers don't call people names). But he comes close to doing so in his conclusion, when he quotes Heymann's comments, in another context, in favor of accountability. If Heymann is in favor of accountability when it comes to the Israeli secret police, Dershowitz suggests, he should be in favor of the accountability that Dershowitz claims would result from requiring warrants for torture.

As we have seen in the two preceding essays, offering airtight proof on a controversial matter may be an impossible proposition. Virginia Woolf put it this way: "When a subject is highly controversial . . . one cannot hope to tell the truth. One can only show how one came to hold whatever opinion one does hold."

CHAPTER NINE

USING SOURCES

> Research is formalized curiosity. It is
> poking and prying with a purpose.
> —*Zora Neale Hurston*

Why Use Sources?

In preparing to write, academic writers use sources to enlarge and refine their ideas. These sources can include facts, opinions, and the ideas of others, recorded in print or in bytes, and in the form of books, articles, lectures, reports, reviews, and interviews. Research essays—which are also sometimes called "researched essays" or "documented essays"—are based in part on such sources, and you'll write them in many of your college courses.

Even an essay that is primarily persuasive or analytical may be in part based on research. For example, if you have been asked to write an essay in which you state your position on legalizing gambling or on the use of torture in times of threats to national security, you will probably need to take into consideration the arguments of others who have written on the topic. If you've been asked to analyze a novel by Kate Chopin, it may be useful to read what current literary critics have said about it. If you don't consider any source, you risk taking a very uninformed position. Considering what others have said and developing your own position in relation to their ideas is central to academic writing.

Not everyone likes research, of course. There are hours spent reading books and articles that prove to be contradictory or irrelevant. When the project is large, you may feel that there isn't enough time to read all the material that's available—or even to get your hands on it. Regardless of the scope of the project, some of the books may be dull. The poet William Butler Yeats, though an indefatigable worker on projects that interested him, engagingly expressed an indifference to the obligation that confronts every researcher: to look carefully at all the relevant evidence. Running over the possible reasons why Jonathan Swift did not marry (that he had syphilis, for instance, or that he feared he would transmit a hereditary madness), Yeats says: "Mr. Shane Leslie thinks that Swift's relation to Vanessa was not platonic, and that whenever his letters speak of a cup of coffee they mean the sexual act; whether the letters seem to bear him out I do not know, for those letters bore me."

Though research sometimes requires one to read boring things, those who engage in it feel, at other times, an exhilaration, a sense of triumph at becoming expert on something. When you know what others have said about your topic, you are in a position to say: "Here is how other people have thought about this question; their ideas are all very interesting, but I see the matter differently. Let me tell you what *I* think."

In the example below, the second paragraph of a research essay we reprint in full in the next chapter, a student does just that. In the essay, Beatrice Cody argues against interpretations of Chopin's novel *The Awakening* as a feminist political statement—the prevailing view. Instead, she contends that the suicide of Chopin's protagonist, Edna Pontellier, "resulted from the torments of her individual psyche, her inability to cope with the patriarchal expectations, which most women in fact were able to tolerate."

> It is difficult to say how Chopin wished The
> Awakening to be interpreted. Heroines who explore
> their own individuality (with varying degrees of suc-
> cess and failure) abound in her work (Shinn 358);
> Chopin herself, though married, was a rather nontra-
> ditional wife who smoked cigarettes, and, like Edna
> Pontellier, took walks by herself (Nissenbaum
> 333-34). One might think therefore that Chopin was
> making a political statement in The Awakening about
> the position of women in society based on her own
> rejection of that position. But aside from slim bio-
> graphical evidence and the assertions of some critics
> such as Larzer Ziff and Daniel S. Rankin that Chopin
> sympathized with Edna, we have no way of knowing
> whether she regarded this protagonist as a victim of
> sexist oppression or simply, to quote her family

doctor in the novel itself, as "a sensitive and
highly organized woman [... who] is especially peculiar" (66). It is therefore necessary to explore the
two possibilities, using evidence from the novel to
determine whether Edna Pontellier's awakening is
political or peculiarly personal in nature.

Note the authority with which the student writes as she (respectfully)
calls into question the conclusions of others who have written about the
novel she's studied and researched. She has read enough to know that
the biographical evidence supporting a feminist reading of *The
Awakening* is "slim"; she has found enough evidence to say (persuasively, we think) that "It is . . . necessary to explore" the matter further.
She knows a lot about her topic. She has become, over the course of several weeks, a kind of expert on it.

There can be great satisfaction in knowing enough about a topic to
contribute to the store of knowledge and ideas about it. There can also
be great satisfaction in simply learning to use the seemingly infinite
resources now available to researchers—in print or electronic formats—
as well as in learning to document and to acknowledge your research
accurately and responsibly.

In this chapter we discuss

- how to find and evaluate sources, both print and electronic;
- how to take useful notes;
- how to use others' ideas to help you develop your own; and
- how to paraphrase, summarize, and quote the work of others, so that
  their words and ideas are distinct from yours.

What Is a Source?
Primary and Secondary Materials

Sources are usually divided into two categories, primary and secondary.
A **primary source** is the real subject of study; a **secondary source** is a
critical or historical account written about a primary source. For example, if you want to know whether Shakespeare's attitude toward Julius
Caesar was highly traditional or highly original, or a little of each, you
would read *Julius Caesar*, other Elizabethan writings about Caesar, and
translations of Latin writings known to the Elizabethans. These are primary sources. In addition to these, you would read secondary sources

such as modern books on Shakespeare and on Elizabethan attitudes toward Rome and toward monarchs.

Similarly, the primary material for an essay on Kate Chopin's novel *The Awakening* is of course the novel itself; the secondary material consists of such things as biographies of Chopin and critical essays on the novel. But the line between these two kinds of sources is not always sharp. For example, if you are concerned with the degree to which *The Awakening* is autobiographical, primary materials include not only the novel and also Chopin's comments on her writing but perhaps also the comments of people who knew her. Thus the essays—based on interviews with Chopin—that two of her friends published in newspapers probably can be regarded as primary material because they were contemporary with the novel and because they give direct access to Chopin's views, while the writings of later commentators constitute secondary material.

Developing a Research Topic

Your instructor may assign a topic, in which case, you'll be saved some work. (On the other hand, you may find yourself spending a lot of time with material you don't find exciting. On yet another hand, you may become interested in something you'd otherwise never have known about.) More likely, you'll need to develop your own topic, a topic related to the subject of the course for which the research essay has been assigned. Some possibilities:

- Perhaps you've read Maxine Hong Kingston's *The Woman Warrior* (1976) for a Women's Studies course, and you have become interested in Confucian or Buddhist ideas that inform the narrative.

- Perhaps your government course has touched on the internment of Japanese-Americans during World War II, and you'd like to know more about what happened.

- Perhaps you've read Chopin's *The Awakening* for a literature course, and you're wondering what readers thought about the novel when it was first published.

Any of these interests could well become a topic for a research essay. But how do you find the relevant material?

Finding Sources

We can't give you a roadmap or a recipe for finding the sources you need. The number of possible topics is infinite, as is the number of sources. Research approaches vary widely. And the Internet—the vast interconnection of computer networks that has made an extraordinary amount of information available to researchers and everyone else— complicates things further. By its very nature, the Internet is constantly changing; guides to research on the Internet are generally out of date even before they appear in print.

Nevertheless, we do have some general suggestions. One good rule of thumb is to begin with what you already know, with what you already have at hand. For instance, the textbook for your government course may cite official documents on the relocation and internment of Japanese-Americans. Or your edition of Chopin's *The Awakening* may contain an introduction that references some critical essays on the novel; it's also likely to contain a selected bibliography, a list of books and articles about Chopin and her work. If you have already identified a few titles, you can go directly to your library's online catalog and begin your search there. (We'll have a bit more to say about online searches in a moment.)

If, however, you know very little about the topic, and haven't yet identified any possible sources (let's say you know nothing or almost nothing about Confucianism, but Maxine Hong Kingston's *The Woman Warrior* has made you want to learn about it), it's not a bad idea to begin with an encyclopedia—the *Encyclopaedia Britannica*, perhaps—which you'll find online through your library's e-resources Web page, and in hardcopy form in the library's reference area. In addition to providing basic information about your topic, encyclopedia articles usually include cross-references to other articles within the encyclopedia, as well as suggestions for further reading. These suggestions can help you begin to compose a list of secondary sources for your essay. And of course you need not limit yourself to one encyclopedia. There are hundreds of invaluable specialized encyclopedias, such as *Encyclopedia of Anthropology*, *Encyclopedia of Crime and Justice*, *Encyclopedia of Psychology*, *Encyclopedia of Religion* (a good place to go for an introduction to Confucianism), and *Kodansha Encyclopedia of Japan*. Several of them are certain to be available in your library's reference area or through your library's central information system.

The Library's Central Information System

All libraries used to work in more or less the same way. Each one had a card catalog, a set of hundreds of little drawers containing thousands (even millions) of alphabetically arranged three-by-five cards. When you wanted a book, you went to the card catalog and looked it up by title, author, or subject. Because books would of course differ from library to library, the cards would also of course differ, but the system in every library was pretty much the same.

In recent years, online catalogs have replaced card catalogs in college, university, and public libraries. And the on-line catalog constitutes only a tiny fraction of the information available to you through your institution's library. With the help of enormous databases such as JSTOR, LexisNexis, and Project Muse, you can search thousands of academic journals, newspapers, and magazines. From a computer terminal in your library (or from home via an Internet connection), you can access bibliographies and indexes, full-text versions of encyclopedias, dictionaries, and academic journals, the catalogs of *other* libraries—and much more.

Unlike card catalogs, each library's central information system is a bit different. Resources differ from one library to the next. And like the Internet itself, your library's central information system is changing every day. For these reasons, perhaps the best advice we can give you about learning to find books and articles in your library is to go to your college or university's research librarian and ask for help.

Using the Internet

As we've noted, the Internet can be a tremendous resource for researchers. But because anyone, anywhere, can post pretty much anything, the information available on the Internet can be difficult to evaluate. When you're working with secondary sources that have been published in journals or in book form, for the most part you're working with material that experts in that field have judged to be worth reading. Before it's published, an article in a journal such as *Society* or *College English*, for example, will have been read by a number of reviewers (most or all of them college professors in the field), as well as by members of an advisory board and several editors. If *Society* or *College English* is in your institution's library—and we bet it is—it's there in part because librarians have decided it is worth including in the serials collection. An article in one of these journals may have weaknesses, but several experts have thought it was pretty good.

Much of the information available on the Internet has not been similarly vetted. Advertisements coexist with course syllabi. By entering the relevant keyword into a search engine such as Google or Yahoo! you could (if you wanted to) access a chat group on Heath Ledger as easily as you could find photographs of people's pets. Or an interview with Jamaica Kincaid. Or the full text of *Romeo and Juliet.* Or an essay on your research topic, written by your professor—or by the person who sits next to you in your biology class.

How do you judge what may be worth considering? In part by using the analytic skills we discuss elsewhere in this book. The following checklist will help you focus your analysis.

"On the Internet, nobody knows you're a dog."

CHECKLIST FOR EVALUATING WEB SITES

☐ Who produced the site (a teacher, a commercial entity, a student)?

☐ Who sponsored the site?

☐ For whom is the author writing? Who is the intended audience?

☐ Can you tell if the author of the document is an authority in the field? (Perhaps the document is linked to the author's home page.)

☐ Does he or she reference other critics or writers? Good ones?

☐ Is the text well written?

☐ Do arguments seem well supported, or is the document full of vague generalizations?

☐ When was the site created or last updated?

For more on this matter, we recommend (appropriately enough) that you consult documents available on the Web, such as "Evaluating Information Found on the Internet" (http://milton.mse.jhu.edu:8001/research/education/net.html). It *should* still be available—but that's the other problem with Internet sources: What's here today may be gone tomorrow.

Reading and Taking Notes on Secondary Sources

Almost all researchers—professionals as well as beginners—find that they end up with some notes that are irrelevant, and, on the other hand, find, when drafting the paper, that they vaguely remember certain material they now wish they had taken notes on. Especially in the early stages of a project, when the topic and thesis may still be relatively unfocused, it's hard to know what is noteworthy and what is not. You simply have to flounder a bit.

It may be helpful to skim an article or book all the way through the first time around without taking notes. By the time you reach the end, you may find it isn't noteworthy. Or you may find a useful summary near the end that will contain most of what you can get from the piece. Or you may find that, having a sense of the whole, you can now quickly reread the piece and take notes on the chief points that concern you.

Even if you follow this procedure, a certain amount of inefficiency is inevitable; therefore plenty of time should be allowed. And it's worth keeping in mind that different people really do work differently. We list here three strategies for taking notes; we suspect that, over time, you'll develop your own.

- Take notes using four-by-six-inch cards, writing on one side only, because material on the back of a card is usually neglected when you come to write the paper. (Taking notes by hand offers several advantages—not least of which is that you don't need access to a computer to do it.)

- Take notes on your computer, keeping a separate file for each book or article. Material can be easily moved from one file to another as the organization of the essay begins to take shape.

- Don't take notes—or take very few notes. Photocopy secondary material you think you might use, if it is brief, and underline and annotate that material as you read and think about it. Material from electronic sources can be downloaded and later printed out and annotated as well. In fact, it's advisable to download any information you access online. Online sources can disappear; but if you download or print the source, you'll be able to check it if necessary, and will be able to produce it if there are any questions about your use of it. The disadvantage here is obvious: This method uses a lot of paper. But there are two big advantages. Passages from the sources are transcribed (or, in the cases of downloaded material, moved) only once, into the draft itself, so there's less risk of mistakes and distortions. And the research—the collecting of information—can go very quickly.

A RULE FOR WRITERS

It's crucial that you think carefully about the material you're collecting and that you annotate it thoroughly. If you don't—that is, if you merely download and print—you'll find yourself with a pile of paper, and no idea of what to do with it.

A Guide to Note-Taking

1. Scan the work before you start taking notes. Before assiduously taking notes from the first paragraph onward, or highlighting long passages, try to get a sense of the author's thesis. You may find an early paragraph that states the thesis outright; you may also find a concluding paragraph that offers a summary of the evidence that supports the thesis. Having gained a general idea of the work, you can now take notes sparingly while you read the material carefully and critically.

Verrett, pp. 152-154 ✓   botulism argument
                                  search for substitute
p.152 Industry and gov't approved nitrite as color
fixer. Now shifting ground, saying it prevents
botulism. Verrett points out "legal snag." New
approval needed for new use.
(Thus public hearing and unwanted attention)

p.154 "... the industry--USDA-FDA coalition seems
firm in its position that there is no substitute for
nitrate, now or ever. Their posture is misdirected
at defending nitrites devising ways to keep it
in food rather than ways to get it out." ✓

              Verrett and Carper, _Eating May Be Hazardous_

2. Read critically. Read thoughtfully, continually asking yourself if the author supports assertions with adequate evidence. Be especially sure to ask what can be said *against* assertions that coincide with your own beliefs. The heart of critical thinking is a willingness to face objections to one's own beliefs.

3. Be sure to record the title and author of the source. If you're using notecards, specify the source in an abbreviated form in the upper-left corner. If you're taking notes on your computer, make a separate file for each book or article, and use the author's name and the first significant word of the title to identify the file. If you're using photocopies or downloaded material, make sure that you also photocopy the bibliographic information—which usually appears in full on the title page of a book and often (but not always) appears on the first page of a journal article. (And be sure to make a record of the full span of the article, not just the pages that you have copied.)

4. Write summaries, not paraphrases (that is, write abridgments rather than restatements, which in fact may be as long as or longer than the original). As we note in our chapter on analyzing texts, there is rarely any point to paraphrasing. Generally speaking, either quote exactly (and put the passage in quotation marks, with a notation of the source, including the page number or numbers) or summarize, reducing a page or even an entire article or chapter of a book to a few sentences that can be written on a notecard, typed into your computer, or squeezed into the margin of a photocopied page. Even when you summarize, record your source (including the page numbers), so that you can give appropriate credit in your essay.

5. Quote sparingly. Of course in your summary you will sometimes quote a phrase or a sentence—putting it in quotation marks—but quote sparingly. You are not simply transcribing what you read; rather you are assimilating knowledge and you are thinking, and so for the most part your source should be chewed and digested rather than swallowed whole. Thinking now, while taking notes, will also help you later to avoid plagiarism. If, on the other hand, when you take notes you simply copy material at length, later when you are writing the essay you may be tempted to copy it yet again, perhaps without giving credit. Likewise, if you simply photocopy pages from articles or books, or download material from the Internet, and then merely underline some passages without annotating your reading, you probably will not be thinking; you will just be underlining. But if you make a terse summary you will be forced to think and to find your own words for the idea.

6. Quote accurately. After copying a quotation, check your transcription against the original, and correct any misquotation. Verify the page number also. If a quotation runs from the bottom of, say, page 306 to the top of 307, make a distinguishing mark (for instance two backslashes after the last word of the first page), so that if you later use only part of the quotation, you will know the page on which it appeared.

7. Use ellipses to indicate the omission of any words within a sentence. If the omitted words are at the end of the quoted sentence, put a period immediately at the point where you end the sentence, and then add three spaced periods.

```
If the ... words are at the end of the quoted sen-
tence, put a period immediately at the point where
you end....
```

8. Use square brackets to indicate your additions to the quotations. Here is an example:

```
Here is an [uninteresting] example.
```

9. *Do not* change even an occasional word when copying a passage, even if you think you will be later putting it into your own words. Notes of this sort may find their way into your essay, your reader will sense a style other than your own, and suspicions (and perhaps even charges) of plagiarism will follow. (For a detailed discussion of plagiarism, see pp. 191–198).

10. Comment on your notes. Consider it your obligation to *think* about the material as you take notes, evaluating it and using it as a stimulus to further thought. For example, you may want to say "Tyler seems to be generalizing from insufficient evidence," or "Corsa made the same point five years earlier"; but make certain that later you will be able to distinguish between these comments and the notes summarizing or quoting your source. A suggestion: Surround all comments recording your responses with double parentheses, thus: ((Is there evidence for this assertion?)).

11. Write a keyword on each card or at the beginning of each section of notes in your computer file. A brief key—for example "effect on infants' blood"—can help you to tell at a glance what is on the card or in the file.

A RULE FOR WRITERS

Quote directly only those passages that are particularly effective, or crucial, or memorable. In your finished essay these quotations will provide authority and emphasis.

Acknowledging Sources

Using Sources Without Plagiarizing

Your purpose as an academic writer is to develop *your own ideas* about the topic you are writing about. Secondary sources will help you shape and develop your thoughts about your topic, but your purpose is to develop an argument and an analysis that is your own. It is crucial, then, to be clear about the distinction between your words and ideas and those of your sources. Not to do so is to risk charges of **plagiarism.** To plagiarize is to use someone else's words or ideas without attributing them to a source; it is to pass off someone else's work as your own. It is, in short, theft. The institutional consequences of plagiarism vary from school to school, and from case to case. In the university where one of us teaches, students who are found guilty of plagiarism are, among other things, banned from the campus for a year. At other schools, students can be expelled permanently; at still others, they simply receive a failing grade for the course and are put on academic probation.

A RULE FOR WRITERS

Respect for your readers and for your sources requires that you acknowledge your indebtedness for material when

- you quote directly from a work, or
- you paraphrase or summarize someone's words (the words of your paraphrase or summary are your own, but the ideas are not), or
- you use an idea that is not common knowledge.

Most commonly, the words, ideas, and information you'll cite in a research essay will come from printed and electronic sources. But you must also acknowledge the advice of peer editors and ideas that come from lectures and class discussions, unless your instructor tells you not to do so. (We explain how to format the citations for all these sources in Chapter 14.)

Let's suppose you are going to make use of William Bascom's comment on the earliest responses of Europeans to African art:

The first examples of African art to gain public attention were the bronzes and ivories which were brought back to Europe after the sack of Benin by a British military expedition in 1897. The superb technology of the Benin bronzes won the praise of experts like Felix von Luschan who wrote in 1899, "Cellini himself could not have made better casts, nor anyone else before or since to the present day." Moreover, their relatively realistic treatment of human features conformed to the prevailing European aesthetic standards. Because of their naturalism and technical excellence, it was at first maintained that they had been produced by Europeans—a view that was still current when the even more realistic bronze heads were discovered at Ife in 1912. The subsequent discovery of new evidence has caused the complete abandonment of this theory of European origins of the bronzes of Benin and Ife, both of which are cities in Nigeria.

—*William Bascom,* African Art in Cultural Perspective
(New York: Norton, 1973), p. 4

Acknowledging a Direct Quotation A student wanting to use some or all of Bascom's words might write something like this:

> According to William Bascom, when Europeans first encountered Benin and Ife works of art in the late nineteenth century, they thought that Europeans had produced them, but the discovery of new evidence "caused the complete abandonment of this theory of European origins of the bronzes of Benin and Ife, both of which are cities in Nigeria" (4).

In this example, the writer introduces Bascom with a signal phrase ("According to William Bascom"); then she summarizes several sentences from Bascom; then she uses quotation marks to indicate the passage that comes directly from Bascom's book. Note that the summary does *not* borrow Bascom's language and it does *not* borrow his sentence structure; the words and their arrangement are all the writer's own. Note also that what appears inside the quotation marks is an exact transcription of Bascom's words: Within the quotation marks the writer has not changed any word endings, or omitted any words, or inserted any punctuation of her own. (The "4" inside parentheses at the end of the passage is the page reference. Again, we explain how to use the MLA system of parenthetic citation in Chapter 14.)

Acknowledging a Paraphrase or Summary Summaries (abridgments) are usually superior to paraphrases (rewordings, of approximately the same length as the original) because summaries are briefer. As we explain in Chapter 7, "Analyzing Texts," when you are using secondary sources, you will for the most part be writing summaries, not paraphrases—unless the language of the source is especially complex. If Bascom's sentences had been obscure—for instance, if they used highly technical language—there would have been a reason to paraphrase them. In that case, the writer of the essay would explicitly have said she was paraphrasing Bascom, and she would have explained why.

Occasionally you may find that you cannot summarize a passage in your source and yet you don't want to quote it word for word—perhaps because it is too technical or because it is poorly written. In that case, you need to paraphrase the passage—that is, you need to put it into your own words. Even though you have put the idea into your own words, you must give credit to the source because the idea is not yours. *Both summaries and paraphrases must be acknowledged.* In both cases, the author must be identified by name, and the location of the source—a page reference if you are using a print source—must be given.

Here is an example of an **acceptable summary:**

> William Bascom, in <u>African Art</u>, points out that the
> first examples of African art brought to Europe--Benin
> bronzes and ivories--were thought by Europeans to be
> of European origin, because they were realistic and
> well made, but evidence was later discovered that
> caused this theory to be abandoned (4).

The summary is adequate, and the page reference indicates where the source is to be found. But if the writer had omitted the signal phrase "William Bascom, in *African Art*, points out that," the result would have been plagiarism. Not to give Bascom credit would be to plagiarize, even if the words are the writer's own. The offense is just as serious as not acknowledging a direct quotation.

The following paragraph is an example of an **unacceptable summary.** The writer uses too much of Bascom's language, and she follows his organization of the material: She has not turned the material into her own writing. And she gives Bascom no credit for his ideas.

> The earliest examples of African art to become widely
> known in Europe were bronzes and ivories that were
> brought to Europe in 1897. These works were thought
> to be of European origin, and one expert said that
> Cellini could not have done better work. Their tech-
> nical excellence, as well as their realism, fulfilled
> the European standards of the day. The later discov-
> ery of new evidence at Benin and Ife, both in
> Nigeria, refuted this belief.

Again, one problem here is that all the *ideas* are Bascom's—and his name appears neither in a signal phrase nor in a citation. Another problem is that the writer doesn't put the passage entirely into her own words. Rather, she simply substitutes one phrase for another, maintaining much of the structure and organization of Bascom's sentences. The writing is Bascom's, in a thin disguise. She substitutes

> "The earliest examples of African art"

for Bascom's

"The first examples of African art";

she substitutes

"to become widely known"

for

"to gain public attention";

she substitutes

"Their technical excellence, as well as their realism"

for

"their naturalism and technical excellence."

The writer here is plagiarizing—perhaps without even knowing it. This form of plagiarism, where a writer simply substitutes his or her own phrases here and there but retains the form and content of the original passage, is one of the most common forms of plagiarism that writing instructors see. Much of it occurs, we believe, because students don't know it's wrong—and because they don't see their job as developing their *own* ideas in relation to their sources.

As we have noted, it is unlikely that a writer would paraphrase a passage that is as straightforward and as free of technical language as Bascom's: the main reason for paraphrasing is to clarify a text that might be confusing to a reader—a literary text, for example, or a particularly complex or technical piece of writing. In the following example, a passage that contains an **acceptable paraphrase** of a sentence from Darwin's *Origin of Species*, the student clarifies a key point in Darwin's argument:

Before discussing the relationship between Darwin's
observations of animal life and his views of the nature
of human society, it may be helpful to clarify the
meaning of a key sentence in The Origin of Species.
Darwin says, in Chapter 3, I should premise that I use
the term Struggle for Existence in a large and
metaphorical sense, including dependence of one being

```
on another, and including (which is more important) not
only the life of the individual, but success in leaving
progeny.
In other words, Darwin notes that he wishes to say in
advance that his phrase "Struggle for Existence" is to
be understood in a figurative way to indicate not only
how the survival of a creature is dependent on other
creatures, but also to refer to the importance of pro-
ducing offspring.
```

The paraphrase clarifies the terms that might have been obscure in the original ("premise" means "say in advance"; "progeny" means "off-spring"), and it is entirely in the student's own language. If the student had borrowed any of Darwin's phrases or significant words, the paraphrase would have been inadequate. Here is an example of an **unacceptable paraphrase** of Darwin's sentence:

```
In other words, Darwin says that he wants to posit
that he will use the term Struggle for Existence in a
grand and poetical way, to mean dependence of one
being on another, as well as--more significantly--its
success in leaving offspring.
```

Note that several phrases are lifted directly from the source (for example, "use the term Struggle for Existence" and "dependence of one being on another"); note also the cheesy substitution of "posit" for "premise" and "grand and poetical" for "large and metaphorical." The source (Darwin) is identified, and in a way, the problems *seem* minor: It's just a sentence, after all. But if there were a pattern of such problems in a student essay, if there were several such sentences, the student would be open to charges of plagiarism.

Acknowledging an Idea   Let's say you have read an essay in which Irving Kristol argues that journalists who pride themselves on being tireless critics of national policy are in fact irresponsible critics because they have no policy they prefer. If this strikes you as a new idea and you adopt it in an essay—even though you set it forth entirely in your own words and with examples not offered by Kristol—you must acknowledge your debt to Kristol. *Not to acknowledge such borrowing is plagiarism.* Your readers will not think the less of you for naming your source; rather, they will be grateful to you for telling them about an interesting writer.

Fair Use of Common Knowledge

If in doubt as to whether or not to give credit (either with formal documentation or merely in a phrase such as "Carol Gilligan says . . . "), give credit. But as you begin to read widely in your field or subject, you will develop a sense of what is considered common knowledge.

Unsurprising definitions in a dictionary can be considered common knowledge, and so there is no need to say "According to Webster, a novel is a long narrative in prose." (That's weak in three ways: It's unnecessary, it's uninteresting, and it's inexact since "Webster" appears in the titles of several dictionaries, some good and some bad.)

Similarly, the date of Freud's death can be considered common knowledge. Few can give it when asked, but it can be found out from innumerable sources, and no one need get the credit for providing you with the date. Again, if you simply *know*, from your reading of Freud, that Freud was interested in literature, you need not cite a specific source for an assertion to that effect, but if you know only because some commentator on Freud said so, and you have no idea whether the fact is well known or not, you should give credit to the source that gave you the information. Not to give credit—for ideas as well as for quoted words—is to plagiarize.

A RULE FOR WRITERS

Material that is regarded as common knowledge, such as the date of Freud's death, is not cited because all sources can be expected to give the same information—*but if you are in doubt about whether something is or is not common knowledge, cite your source.*

"But How Else Can I Put It?"

If you have just learned—say from an encyclopedia—something that you sense is common knowledge, you may wonder how to change into your own words the simple, clear words that this source uses in setting forth this simple fact. For example, if before writing an analysis of a photograph of Buffalo Bill and Sitting Bull, you look up these names in the *Encyclopaedia Britannica*, you will find this statement about Buffalo Bill (William F. Cody): "In 1883 Cody organized his first Wild West exhibition." You could not use this statement as your own, word for word, without feeling uneasy. But to put in quotation marks such a routine statement of what can be considered common knowledge, and to cite a source for it, seems pretentious. After all, the *Encyclopedia Americana* says much the same thing in the same routine way: "In 1883 . . . Cody organized Buffalo Bill's Wild West." It may be that the word "organized" is simply the most obvious and the best word, and perhaps you will end up using it. Certainly, to change "Cody organized" into "Cody presided over the organization of" or "Cody assembled" or some such thing in an effort to avoid plagiarizing would be to make a change for the worse and still to be guilty of plagiarism. What, then, can you do? You won't get yourself into this mess of wondering whether to change clear, simple wording into awkward wording if in the first place, when you take notes, you *summarize* your sources, thus: "1883: organized Wild West," or "first Wild West: 1883." Later (even if only thirty minutes later), when drafting your paper, if you turn this nugget—probably combined with others—into the best sentence you can, you will not be in danger of - plagiarizing, even if the word "organized" turns up in your sentence.

Of course, even when dealing with material that can be considered common knowledge—and even when you have put it into your own words—you probably *will* cite your source if you are drawing more than just an occasional fact from a source. For instance, if your paragraph on Buffalo Bill uses half a dozen facts from a source, cite the source. You do this both to avoid charges of plagiarism and to protect yourself in case your source contains errors of fact.

CHECKLIST FOR AVOIDING PLAGIARISM

☐ In taking notes, did you indicate clearly when you were quoting directly, when you were paraphrasing, and when you were summarizing? Did you record the sources of all online material that you cut and pasted into your notes? (See pp. 187–191.)

☐ Are all quotations enclosed within quotation marks and acknowledged? (See p. 193.)

☐ Are all changes within quotations indicated by square brackets for additional words or punctuation and ellipses (. . .) for omissions? Are quotations otherwise exact? Have you transcribed quoted passages *precisely* as they appear in the source? (See p. 190)

☐ Are the sources for all ideas that are not your own acknowledged, and are these ideas set forth in your own words and with your own sentence structure? (See p. 191.)

☐ Does the list of sources include all the sources (online as well as print) that you have used?

CHAPTER TEN

WRITING THE
RESEARCH ESSAY

> For every event, there is a cause and effect.
> For every crime, a motive. And for every
> motive, a passion. The art of research is the
> ability to look at the details, and see the
> passion.
>
> —*Bill Pullman as Daryl Zero,*
> *in* The Zero Effect

When you use sources, you are not simply emptying on the table the contents of a shopping cart filled at the scholar's supermarket, the library. You are cooking a meal. You must have a point, an opinion, a thesis. A thesis, as we described it in Chapter 1, is an idea about which intelligent readers might *disagree*. When you use sources in a research essay, you are working to establish and develop such an idea in the context of what others have thought about your topic. Your readers should feel they are moving toward the thesis with you, rather than reading a report, an anthology of commentary on a topic. Writers of reports—the kind of paper many of us wrote in high school—tend to use sources in one way: to *support* their main point. (And often, the main point turns out to have been made in one or more of the sources.) When you write a research essay, on the other hand, you use sources in a range of ways, among them:

- To establish the context of an argument, the position *against* which you'll be arguing.
- To provide the history of a problem or idea or event, or helpful background information—on an author's life, for example.

- To provide evidence to support a claim you're making.
- To provide evidence to support—or to dispute—a claim made by another critic or scholar or researcher.

Research makes you an expert on your topic; you now know what others have to say about it. But as you have thought about what the secondary sources have said about your primary material, it's likely that you've noticed contradictions and gaps, that you agree with some opinions and arguments and disagree with others, that you've begun to develop your own ideas about your topic.

Writing the Essay

Beyond referring you to the rest of this book, we can offer only seven pieces of advice:

1. **With a tentative thesis in mind, begin by rereading your notes and sorting them by topic.** Put together what belongs together. Don't hesitate to reject interesting material that now seems irrelevant or redundant. After sorting, re-sorting, and rejecting, you will have a kind of first draft without writing a draft.

2. **From your notes, make a first outline.** Although you can't yet make a paragraph outline, you may find it useful to make a fairly full outline, indicating not only the sequence of points but also the quotations that you will use. In sketching the outline, of course you will be guided by your *thesis*. As you worked, you probably modified your tentative ideas in the light of what your further research produced, but by now you ought to have a relatively firm idea of what you want to say. Without a thesis you will have only the basis for a *report*, not a potential essay.

3. **Transcribe or download quotations, even in the first draft, exactly as you want them to appear in the final version.** Of course this takes some time, and the time will be wasted if, as may well turn out, you later see that the quotation is not really useful. (On the other hand, the time has not really been wasted, since it helped you ultimately to delete the unnecessary material.)

If at this early stage you just write a note reminding yourself to include the quotation—something like "here quote Jackson on undecided voters"—when you reread the draft you won't really know how the page sounds. You won't, for instance, know how much help your reader needs by way of a lead-in to the quotation, or how much discussion should follow. Only if you actually see the quotation are you in the position of your audience, and it's a good idea to try to imagine your audience, even at this early stage.

4. Include, right in the body of the draft, all of the relevant citations. This way, when you come to revise, you don't have to start hunting through your notes to find who said what, and where. You can, for the moment, enclose these citations within diagonal lines, or within double parentheses—anything to remind you that they will be your documentation.

5. Resist the urge to include every note in your essay. As we suggest in Chapter 1, writing is a way of discovering ideas. Consequently, as you write your first draft, your thesis will inevitably shift, and notes that initially seemed important will now seem irrelevant. Don't stuff them into the draft, even if you're concerned about meeting a page requirement: Readers know padding when they see it.

6. Resist the urge to do more research. As you draft, you may also see places where another piece of evidence, another reference to a source, or another example would be useful. And you may feel compelled to head back to the library. We think that for now you should resist that urge too: It may simply be procrastination in disguise. Continue writing this first draft if possible, and plan to incorporate new material in a later draft.

7. As you revise your draft, make sure that you do not merely tell the reader "A says ... B says ... C says ...." Rather, by using a lead-in or signal phrase such as "A claims," "B provides evidence that," "according to C," "D concedes that," you help the reader to see the role of the quotation in your paper. Further, after quoting or summarizing a source, you should normally comment on it, thereby making clear the relation between your own ideas and those of the source.

CHECKLIST FOR REVISING DRAFTS OF RESEARCH ESSAYS

- [ ] Is the tentative title informative and focused?
- [ ] Does the paper make a point, or does it just accumulate other people's ideas? (See pp. 199–200.)
- [ ] Does it reveal the thesis early? (See pp. 10–11; 171–172.)
- [ ] Are claims supported by evidence? (See pp. 156–159.)
- [ ] Are all the *words* and *ideas* of the sources accurately attributed? (See pp. 191–198.)

☐ Are quotations introduced adequately with signal phrases (such as "according to Ziff," or "Smith contends," or "Johnson points out") to indicate who is speaking? (See p. 201.)

☐ Are all of the long quotations necessary, or can some of them be effectively summarized? (See p. 194.)

☐ Are quotations discussed adequately? (See p. 201; see also Chapter 7, "Analyzing Texts.")

☐ Does the paper advance in orderly stages? Can your imagined reader easily follow your thinking? (See Chapter 2, "Drafting and Revising.")

☐ Is the documentation in the correct form? (See Chapter 14, "Documenting Sources.")

A Sample Research Essay (MLA Format)

We began Chapter 10 with a paragraph from the following research essay, "Politics and Psychology in *The Awakening*." We noted that Beatrice Cody used her research to help her develop her *own* position on the novel. As you read her essay, be alert to the range of sources Cody has chosen, and to the range of ways in which she uses them: to establish the critical position she'll be arguing against, to give helpful background on Chopin's life, to provide information on the responses of Chopin's contemporaries to the novel, and so on.

Note: Cody uses the Modern Language Association (MLA) form of in-text citations, which are clarified by a list headed "Works Cited." We explain the MLA system in detail in Chapter 14, "Documenting Sources." In that chapter we also explain and illustrate the American Psychological Association (APA) form of in-text citations, and we offer information on several other systems of documentation.

Beatrice Cody
Ms. Bellanca
Writing 125
12 April 2006

Politics and Psychology in
The Awakening

Title announces focus and scope of essay.

1   At first glance, Kate Chopin's novel The Awakening (1899) poses no problem to the feminist reader. It is the story of Edna Pontellier, a woman living at the turn of the century who, partly through a half-realized summer romance, discovers that sensual love, art, and individuality mean more to her than marriage or motherhood. When she concludes that there can be no compromise between her awakened inner self and the stifling shell of her outer life as a wife and mother, she drowns herself. In such a summary, Edna appears to be yet another victim of the "Feminine Mystique" described by Betty Friedan in the 1950's, a mind-numbing malaise afflicting the typical American housewife whose husband and society expected her to care for family at the expense of personal freedom and fulfillment. However, it is possible that the events leading to Edna's tragic death were not caused solely by the expectations of a sexist society pre-dating Friedan's model, in which a wife was not only dutiful to but also the "property" of her husband (Culley 119),

Plot summary helps orient readers unfamiliar with novel.

204 • *Part Two: College Writing*

Cody 2

Citation includes title because there are two works by Chopin on Works Cited list.

and a mother not only stayed home but also sacrificed even the "essential" for her children (Chopin Awakening 48). Perhaps Edna's suicide resulted from the torments of her individual psyche, her inability to cope with the patriarchal expectations, which most women in fact were able to tolerate.

Clear statement of thesis.

Citation 2 includes name because author isn't cited in the sentence itself.

It is difficult to say how Chopin wished The Awakening to be interpreted. Heroines who explore their own individuality (with varying degrees of success and failure) abound in her work (Shinn 358); Chopin herself, though married, was a rather nontraditional wife who smoked cigarettes, and, like Edna Pontellier, took walks by herself (Nissenbaum 333-34). One might think therefore that Chopin was making a political statement in The Awakening about the position of women in society based on her own rejection of that position. But aside from slim biographical evidence and the assertions of some critics such as Larzer Ziff and Daniel S. Rankin that Chopin sympathized with Edna, we have no way of knowing whether she regarded this protagonist as a victim of sexist oppression or simply, to quote her family doctor in the novel itself, as "a sensitive and highly organized woman... [who] is especially peculiar" (66). It is therefore necessary to explore the two possibilities, using

Sources are paraphrased here. Although the words of the sources aren't used, ideas must be acknowledged.

Brackets around "who" indicate that word has been added.

Citation includes page number because title and author are clear from context.

Cody 3

evidence from the novel to determine
whether Edna Pontellier's awakening is
political or peculiarly personal in
nature.

3   It does not take a deeply feminist
awareness to detect the dominant,
controlling stance Edna's husband,
Leonce, assumes in their marriage.
Throughout the novel Chopin documents
the resulting injustices, both great and
small, which Edna endures. In one
instance Leonce comes home late at night
after Edna has fallen asleep, and, upon
visiting their sleeping children,
concludes that both of them are
feverish. He wakes Edna so that she may
check on them, despite her assertion
that the children are perfectly well.
He chides her for her "inattention" and
"habitual neglect of the children"
(7)--rather than respecting her ability
as their mother to judge the state of
their health or attending to them
himself--and reduces her to tears. She
defers to his judgment, looking at the
boys as he had asked, and, finding them
entirely healthy, goes out to the porch
where "an indescribable oppression
... filled her whole being with a
vague anguish" (8). Though in some ways
inconsequential, actions such as these
epitomize Leonce Pontellier's attitude
toward women and particularly toward
his wife. It is his belief that she has
a certain role and specific duties

... (three spaced periods) indicate that words have been omitted from sentence.

Cody 4

(those of a woman) which must be done well--according to his (a man's) standards. Although he would probably claim to love Edna, he does not seem to regard her as an autonomous individual; she is the mother of his children, the hostess of such "callers" as he deems appropriate (i.e., the ones who will bring him influence and esteem) (51) and essentially another decoration in his impeccably furnished house (50). When Edna's awakening leads her to abandon household chores in favor of painting, Chopin exposes Leonce's sexism:

Prose quotations longer than four typed lines are indented one inch from the left margin and double-spaced.

> Mr. Pontellier had been a rather courteous husband so long as he met a certain tacit submissiveness in his wife. But her new and unexpected line of conduct completely bewildered him ... her absolute disregard for her duties as a wife angered him. (57)

Block quotations are not enclosed within quotation marks. Note that the period precedes the parenthetic citation in a block quotation.

4   It would seem from such evidence that Chopin intended The Awakening to depict the wrongs that women suffered at the hands of men in her society. Taking this cue from Chopin, many twentieth-century critics choose to view it in a political light. Larzer Ziff, for example, claims that the novel "rejected the family as the automatic equivalent of feminine self

Cody 5

Cody quotes opposing views. Note smooth integration of quoted passages. The verbs "claims," "noting," and "states" clearly signal quotations.

fulfillment, and on the very eve of the twentieth century it raised the question of what woman was to do with the freedom she struggled toward" (175). Winfried Fluck, noting Edna's "preference for semi-conscious states of being ... sleeping, dreaming, dozing, or the moment of awakening" (435), argues that she is enacting "a radical retreat from the imprisonment of all social roles" (435). Marie Fletcher states that "[Edna's] suicide is the last in a series of rebellions which structure her life, give it pathos, and make of the novel...an interpretation of the 'new woman'" (172)--"the emerging suffragist/woman professional of the late nineteenth century" (Culley 118). Even in 1899 an anonymous reviewer in the New Orleans Times-Democrat noticed the political implications of the novel, declaring in his own conservative way that

> a woman of twenty-eight, a wife and twice a mother who is pondering upon her relations to the world about her, fails to perceive that the relation of a mother to her children is far more important than the gratification of a passion which experience has taught her is ... evanescent, can hardly be said to be fully awake. (150)

Cody 6

5   These critics lead us to focus on the socio-political implications of the novel, and on the questions it raises about a woman's role and responsibility: when if ever does a woman's personal life become more important than her children? or, how does Edna embody the emancipated woman? But I believe that more than just the social pressure and politics of the late nineteenth century were acting on Edna. It was the inherent instability of her own psyche, exacerbated by the oppression she suffered as a woman, that drove her to swim out to her death at the end of The Awakening.

Clear transition ("despite").

6   Despite the feminist undertones discernible in Chopin's work, a strong sense prevails that Edna's tragedy is unique, a result of her own psychology, not only of societal oppression. Throughout the novel Chopin describes Edna's agitated state of mind and drops hints about her upbringing and family life before marriage. Upon piecing all the clues to her personality together one gets a troubling, stereotypical picture. Edna's widowed father is a stern colonel from Kentucky who "was perhaps unaware that he had coerced his own wife into her grave" (71). From the scenes in which he appears one deduces that he is harsh and authoritative with his family; the narrator's comment about his wife implies that perhaps

In this paragraph and the next, Cody develops her argument by analyzing the text of the novel.

Cody 7

he was abusive (no doubt
psychologically, possibly physically)
as well. He gambles compulsively on
horseracing (69), which denotes an
addictive personality. He also
makes his own very strong cocktails--
"toddies"--which he drinks almost
all day long (71). He retains the
appearance of sobriety, however,
which indicates a high tolerance built
up over much time. From this evidence
one may assume that he suffers
from alcoholism.

7   The rest of Edna's family--two
sisters--fit the mold of the
dysfunctional family that a violent,
alcoholic parent tends to create. Her
oldest sister seems to be the hyper-
responsible, over-functioning
"perfect" daughter. She served as a
surrogate mother to Edna and her
younger sister, and is described by
Edna's husband as the only daughter
who "has all the Presbyterianism
undiluted" (66). Edna's younger sister
is, predictably, exactly the opposite:
Leonce Pontellier describes her as a
"vixen" (66). She has rebelled against
all of the rules and expectations that
the eldest daughter obeys and
fulfills. Edna, the middle child, is
hence a curious case. Chopin tells us
that "even as a child she had lived
her own small life all within herself"
(15). In such family situations the

middle child is usually rather
introverted. Where the two other
siblings strive compulsively either to
correct or create problems, the sibling
in the middle passively escapes from
her painful family situation by
withdrawing into herself (Seixas and
Youcha 48-49).

Evidence from experts offered in support of thesis.

8   So far this simplistic but
relatively reliable delineation of
personalities works for Edna's
character. Later in life she perpetuates
the patterns of her dysfunctional family
by marrying a man who almost mirrors her
father in personality; he is simply a
workaholic rather than an alcoholic.
Edna gives birth to two children, "a
responsibility which she had blindly
assumed" (20) in her typically passive
way. The first time she truly examines
her role in this marriage and indeed in
the world at large occurs on Grand Isle,
a resort island where she and her family
are vacationing for the summer. There
she begins to spend a great deal of time
with a young man named Robert Lebrun,
and a mutual desire gradually arises
between them. This desire, and the
general sensuality and openness of the
Creole community to which she is
exposed, bring about Edna's sexual,
artistic, and individual awakening.
Although the reader is excited and
inspired by this awakening in Edna--a
woman learning to shed the fetters

of both her oppressive marriage and society in general--the way it takes control of her life is disturbingly reminiscent of mental illness. She becomes infatuated with Robert, devotes an inordinate amount of time to painting, and seeks out classical music, which wracks her soul in a torturous ecstasy.

9   Throughout her awakening, she experiences myriad moods and feelings that she had never felt before in her docile, passive state. Many of these moods manifest themselves in the form of mysterious, troubling voices: "the voices were not soothing that came to her from the darkness and the sky above and the stars" (53); "she felt like one who has entered and lingered within the portals of some forbidden temple in which a thousand muffled voices bade her begone" (84). Behind the veil of metaphor here one can detect hints of an almost schizoid character. Chopin even describes Edna as two selves, which naturally befits a woman undergoing an emotional transformation, but which also denotes a distinctly schizophrenic state of mind: "she was becoming herself and daily casting aside that fictitious self which we assume like a garment with which to appear before the world" (57); "she could only realize that she herself--her present

self--was in some way different from
the other self" (41). Chopin phrases
her descriptions of Edna in such a
way that they could in fact describe
either a woman gaining her emotional
autonomy or a woman losing her mind.

10   As compelling as I find the
suggestion of Edna's insanity, I must
admit that her struggle between self-
hood and motherhood is one too common
to all women to be passed off as the
ravings of a madwoman. As to which
interpretation she preferred, Chopin
offered few clues. For example, in
February 1898 Chopin responded to a
question, posed by the society page of
the St. Louis Post-Dispatch, about the
possible motives for a recent rash of
suicides among young high-society
women. Rather than the pressure of
society as a likely motive, she
suggests a "highly nervous" disposition
(qtd. in Toth 120). Indeed, she asserts
that "leadership in society is a
business ... there is nothing about it that
I can see that would tend to produce an
unhealthy condition of mind. On the
contrary, it prevents women from
becoming morbid, as they might, had
they nothing to occupy their attention
when at leisure" (qtd. in Toth 120).
Perhaps, then, we are to suppose that a
combination of psychic instability and
extensive leisure, rather than the
oppression of her society, caused Edna

Parenthetic reference to an indirect source. (The quotation from Chopin appears on page 120 of Toth's book.)

Cody 11

to take her own life. And yet this
same response in the Post-Dispatch
includes a counter-question to the
editor: "Business men commit suicide
every day, yet we do not say that
suicide is epidemic in the business
world. Why should we say the feeling
is rife among society women, because
half a dozen unfortunates, widely
separated, take their own lives?"
(qtd. in Toth 120). Her implicit
criticism of the double standard
suggests that Chopin was aware of the
politics of gender relations in her
own society in addition to the
existence of an "hysterical tendency"
in some women (qtd. in Toth 120). One
cannot therefore discount the
possibility that Chopin meant Edna's
suicide to be in part a reaction to
her society's rigid and limiting
expectations of women.

11   Chopin received such harsh
criticism of Edna Pontellier's sexual
freedom and attitude toward family
that, when The Awakening was published,
if not before, she must have had some
idea of how controversial the issue of
her protagonist's personal freedom
really was: her hometown library banned
the book, and Chopin herself was banned
from a St. Louis arts club (Reuben).
Her critics tend to believe that she
sympathized unreservedly with her
headstrong heroine; but even the

*Citation of
online
source.
(Source is
unpagi-
nated, so
citation gives
only the
author's
name.)*

Cody 12

retraction she published soon after her
novel does not reveal whether she
viewed Edna as oppressed or mentally
ill. Apparently written for the benefit
of her scandalized reviewers, the
retraction ironically relieves Chopin
of all responsibility for Edna's
"making such a mess of things and
working out her own damnation" (159).
Again, as in her ambiguous response to
the Post-Dispatch, Chopin leaves
curious readers unsatisfied, and the
motive of Edna's suicide unclear.

12   It is left to the reader therefore
to decide whether Edna is a martyr to a
feminist cause--the liberation of the
American housewife--or the victim of a
psychological disturbance that drives
her to suicide. I believe that it is
best not to dismiss either possibility.
To begin with, one cannot deny that in
the nineteenth century few options other
than marriage and child-rearing were
open to women. These narrow options were
the result of a societal structure in
which men socially, economically, and
sexually dominated women. In the twenty-
first century we can look back at
Chopin's time and feel confident in
condemning this state of affairs, but
from contemporary criticism of The
Awakening alone, it is clear that this
political view was not so widely
accepted at the turn of the century.
Perhaps Chopin had an unusually clear

and untimely insight into what we now
consider the sexism of her society,
but she chose to condemn it only
implicitly by portraying it as a fact
of life against which her unbalanced
heroine must struggle and perish. As
Larzer Ziff puts it, "Edna Pontellier
is trapped between her illusions and
the condition which society
arbitrarily establishes to maintain
itself, and she is made to pay" (175).
Chopin fused the political and the
personal in Edna Pontellier, who, like
most women in the world, suffers not
only from the pressures of a society
run by and for men, but also from her
own individual afflictions.

Sources are listed in alphabetical order by author.

"Works Cited" is centered.

Begin Works Cited list on new page. Continue pagination.

Works Cited

Three hyphens indicate another work by the author named immediately above.

Chopin, Kate. <u>The Awakening</u>. 1899. Ed. Margaret Culley. New York: Norton, 1976.

---."Retraction." 1899. Rpt. in <u>The Awakening</u>. By Kate Chopin. 159.

Short form of citation. Articles by Culley and Fletcher are reprinted in the Norton edition of The Awakening. *The full citation for the volume appears under* Chopin.

Culley, Margaret. "The Context of <u>The Awakening</u>." In <u>The Awakening</u>. By Kate Chopin. 119-22.

Second and subsequent lines of entry are indented 5 spaces.

Fletcher, Marie. "The Southern Woman in the Fiction of Kate Chopin." Rpt. in <u>The Awakening</u>. By Kate Chopin. 170-73.

Fluck, Winfried. "'The American Romance' and the Changing Functions of the Imaginary." <u>New Literary History</u> 27.3 (1996): 415-57. <u>Project Muse</u>. JHU. 1 Apr. 2006. http://muse:jhu.edu:80/journals/ new literary history /v27/ 27.3fluck.html.

Online source (paginated).

"New Publications." <u>New Orleans Times-Democrat</u>. Rpt. in <u>The Awakening</u>. By Kate Chopin. 150.

Signed entry in a reference work with alphabetically arranged entries.

Nissenbaum, Stephen. "Chopin, Kate O'Flaherty." <u>Notable American Women, 1607-1950: A Biographical Dictionary</u>. Cambridge, MA: Harvard University Press, 1971.

Online source (unpaginated).

Rankin, Daniel S. "Influences Upon the Novel." Rpt. in <u>The Awakening</u>. By Kate Chopin. 163-65.

Cody 15

Reuben, Paul P. "Chapter 6: 1890-1910:
Kate Chopin (1851-1904)." PAL:
Perspectives in American
Literature--A Research and
Reference Guide. 2 Apr. 2006.
http://www.csustan.edu/english/
reuben/pal/chap6/chopin.html.

Seixas, Judith S., and Geraldine
Youcha. Children of Alcoholism: A
Survivor's Manual. New York:
Harper, 1985.

Shinn, Thelma J. "Kate O'Flaherty
Chopin." American Women Writers:
A Critical Reference Guide from
Colonial Times to the Present. New
York: Unger, 1979 ed.

Journal article.
Toth, Emily. "Kate Chopin on Divine
Love and Suicide: Two Rediscovered
Articles." American Literature 63
(1991): 115-21.

Ziff, Larzer. Excerpt from The American
1890s: Life and Times of a Lost
Generation, 279-305. Rpt. in The
Awakening. By Kate Chopin. 173-75.

A Brief Analysis of Cody's Use of Sources

In our introductory comments, we noted that Cody uses sources in a range of ways in this essay. Here, we will point to some of the specific ways in which she uses the ideas of others to develop her argument about the novel and to enrich her analysis of it:

- In paragraph 1, Cody alludes to Betty Friedan's concept of the "feminine mystique" to help explain the prevailing interpretation of the novel. Note that the reference to Freidan is general; the idea of the "feminine mystique" is treated as **common knowledge.**

- In paragraph 2, Cody draws on Chopin's biography to help develop the interpretation she'll be arguing against. She's **granting the**

opposition what's due to it; she's establishing the merit of the point of view against which she's arguing. (One wouldn't, after all, want to waste time arguing against a foolish position.) She also **quotes the authorities,** the critics Ziff and Rankin, she'll go on to dispute.

- At the end of paragraph 2, Cody **quotes a passage from the novel, evidence** that helps **support** her thesis (stated at the end of paragraph 1) that Edna's suicide in part "resulted from the torments of her individual psyche."

- In paragraphs 3 and 4, Cody **analyzes evidence** from the novel, from contemporary reviews, and from current criticism, that **does not support** her argument, but rather supports the "socio-political" interpretation of *The Awakening.* (Again, she's establishing the merit of the **counterargument.**)

- In paragraph 6, Cody **analyzes** the text of the novel, focusing now on **evidence** that **supports** her position—for example, Chopin's representation of Edna's family members.

- In paragraph 7, Cody refers to what might be called **expert testimony:** a discussion in a psychology textbook that supports her interpretation of Edna's dysfunctional family as a cause of Edna's own disturbed psyche.

- In paragraph 10, Cody quotes from Chopin herself to give a somewhat different perspective on Edna's character; she thereby enriches her analysis of Chopin's protagonist.

- In paragraph 12, Cody uses a quotation from Larzer Ziff, a critic she's been disagreeing with until now, in part to support her larger point. We note that at the end of the essay, she develops a position that strikes a balance between the argument she's been putting forth, and the prevailing view of the novel. Our last impression of Cody, therefore, is that she is a thoughtful and reasonable critic.

A Sample Research Essay (APA Format)

In the following research essay, student Jacob Alexander uses the APA form of in-text citations, which are clarified by a list headed "References." Our annotations in the margins of the essay point to noteworthy features of Alexander's use of sources and of the system of citation; a brief analysis of the essay follows it. For instructions on using the APA citation format, see Chapter 14, "Documenting Sources," pages 323–331.

1/2"

Nitrite   1

Quadruple space   5 spaces

Nitrite: Preservative or Carcinogen?

Jacob Alexander

Writing 1B: Environmental Issues

Professor Louis

May 2, 2006

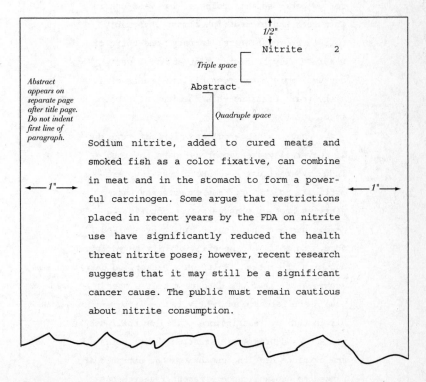

1/2"

Nitrite   2

Triple space

Abstract

Quadruple space

Abstract appears on separate page after title page. Do not indent first line of paragraph.

← 1" →   ← 1" →

Sodium nitrite, added to cured meats and smoked fish as a color fixative, can combine in meat and in the stomach to form a powerful carcinogen. Some argue that restrictions placed in recent years by the FDA on nitrite use have significantly reduced the health threat nitrite poses; however, recent research suggests that it may still be a significant cancer cause. The public must remain cautious about nitrite consumption.

Nitrite: Preservative or Carcinogen?

1   According to Julie Miller Jones, a professor of food and nutrition and the author of Food Safety, "average Americans eat their weight in food additives every year" (cited in Murphy, 1996, p. 140). There are approximately fifteen thousand additives currently in use (National Cancer Institute Fact Sheet [NCI], 1996); many of them are known to be dangerous. Of these, nitrites may be among the most hazardous of all. In this country, ham, bacon, corned beef, salami, bologna, lox, and other cold cuts and smoked fish almost invariably contain sodium nitrite. In fact, one-third of the federally inspected meat and fish we consume--more than seven billion pounds of it every year--contains this chemical (Jacobson, 1987, p. 169).

2   Just how dangerous are nitrites, and why-- if they really are dangerous--does the food industry still use them? Both questions are difficult to answer. Some experts say that nitrites protect consumers from botulism, a deadly disease that can be caused by spoiled food, and that "the benefits of nitrite additives outweigh the risks" (Edlefsen & Brewer, no date). Others argue that the dangers nitrites once posed have been significantly reduced--even eliminated--by restrictions placed on their use by the Food and Drug Administration. Nevertheless, the evidence has long suggested that nitrites are linked to stomach cancer; recent research has

Page number and short form of title appear on every page

An indirect reference. Alexander consulted Murphy, who quotes Jones.

Citation gives author because Jacobson is not named in the text. Note format: author, date of publication, and page number preceded by a "p."

This online source did not provide a date of publication.

Nitrite   4

A reference to two sources. The writer is summarizing whole works, so no page numbers are given.

linked nitrites to leukemia and brain tumors as well (Warrick, 1994; Legator & Daniel, 1995). Perhaps the only certain conclusions one can reach are that the effects of nitrite on the human body are still to some degree uncertain-- and that to protect themselves, consumers must be cautious and informed.

Clear statement of thesis.

3   That nitrite is a poison has been clear for almost three decades. In 1974, Jacqueline Verrett, who worked for the FDA for fifteen years, and Jean Carper reported on several instances of people poisoned by accidental overdoses of nitrites in cured meats:

Quotations of more than forty words must be indented one inch from the left margin. Block quotations do not require quotation marks at beginning and end.

> In Buffalo, New York, six persons were hospitalized with "cardiovascular collapse" after they ate blood sausage which contained excessive amounts of nitrites.... In New Jersey, two persons died and many others were critically poisoned after eating fish illegally loaded with nitrites. In New Orleans, ten youngsters between the ages of one and a half and five became seriously ill . . . after eating wieners or bologna overnitrited by a local meat-processing firm; one wiener that was obtained later from the plant was found to contain a whopping 6,570 parts per million. In Florida, a three-year-old boy died after eating hot dogs with three times greater nitrite concentration than the government allows. (pp. 138-39)

Note that a period precedes the parenthetical citation in a block quote.

Nitrite   5

4   The chemical has the unusual and
difficult-to-replace quality of keeping meat a
fresh-looking pink throughout the cooking,
curing, and storage process (Assembly of Life
Science, 1982, p. 3). The nitrous acid from the
nitrite combines with the hemoglobin in the
blood of the meat, fixing its red color so that
the meat does not turn the tired brown or gray
natural to cured meats.

5   Unfortunately, it does much the same thing
in humans. Although most of the nitrite passes
through the body unchanged, a small amount is
released into the bloodstream. This combines
with the hemoglobin in the blood to form a
pigment called methemoglobin, which cannot carry
oxygen. If enough oxygen is incapacitated, a
person dies. The allowable amount of nitrite in
a quarter pound of meat has the potential to
incapacitate between 1.4 and 5.7 percent of the
hemoglobin in an average-sized adult (Verrett &
Carper, 1974, pp. 138-39). One of the problems
with nitrite poisoning is that infants under a
year, because of the quantity and makeup of
their blood, are especially susceptible to it.

6   If the consumer of nitrite isn't acutely
poisoned (and granted, such poisonings are
rare), his or her blood soon returns to normal
and this particular danger passes: the chemical,
however, has long-term effects, as research
conducted in the 1970's clearly established.
Nitrite can cause headaches in people who are
especially sensitive to it, an upsetting symptom

considering that in rats who ate it regularly
for a period of time it has produced lasting
"epileptic like" changes in the brain--
abnormalities which showed up when the rats
were fed only a little more than an American
fond of cured meats might eat (Wellford, 1973,
p. 173). Experiments with chickens, cattle,
sheep, and rats have shown that nitrite, when
administered for several days, inhibits the
ability of the liver to store vitamin A and
carotene (Hunter, 1972, p. 90). And finally,
Nobel laureate Joshua Lederberg points out that,
in microorganisms, nitrite enters the DNA.
"If it does the same thing in humans," he says,
"it will cause mutant genes." Geneticist Bruce
Ames adds, "If out of one million people, one
person's genes are mutant, that's a serious
problem.... If we're filling ourselves now with
mutant genes, they're going to be around for
generations" (cited in Zwerdling, 1971,
pp. 34-35).

7   By far the most alarming characteristic of
nitrite, however, is that in test tubes, in
meats themselves, in animal stomachs, and in
human stomachs--wherever a mildly acidic
solution is present--it can combine with amines
to form nitrosamines. And nitrosamines are
carcinogens. Even the food industry and the
agencies responsible for allowing the use of
nitrite in foods admit that nitrosamines cause
cancer. Edlefsen and Brewer, writing recently
for the National Food Safety Database, note that

Nitrite   7

*An online
source. (The
authors and
title are
named in
the sentence;
the source
has no date
or page
numbers.)*

"over 90 percent of the more than 300 known
nitrosamines in foods have been shown to cause
cancer in laboratory animals." They continue:
"No case of human cancer has been shown to
result from exposure to nitrosamines," but they
acknowledge that "indirect evidence indicates
that humans would be susceptible" (no date).

8   It is important to note that nitrite
alone, when fed to rats on an otherwise
controlled diet, does not induce cancer. It must
first combine with amines to form nitrosamines.
Considering, however, that the human stomach has
the kind of acidic solution in which amines and
nitrites readily combine, and considering as
well that amines are present in beer, wine,
cereals, tea, fish, cigarette smoke, and a long
list of drugs including antihistamines,
tranquilizers, and even oral contraceptives, it
is hardly surprising to find that nitrosamaines
have been found in human stomachs.

9   When animals are fed amines in combination
with nitrite, they developed cancer with a
statistical consistency that is frightening,
even to scientists. Verrett and Carper report
that after feeding animals 250 parts per million
(ppm) of nitrites and amines, William Lijinsky,
a scientist at Oak Ridge National Laboratory,

> found malignant tumors in 100 percent of
> the test animals within six months....
> "Unheard of," he says.... "You'd usually
> expect to find 50 percent at the most.
> And the cancers are all over

Nitrite   8

the place--in the brain, lung, pancreas,
stomach liver, adrenals, intestines. We
open up the animals and they are a
bloody mess." [He] believes that
nitrosamines, because of their incredible
versatility in inciting cancer, may be
the key to an explanation for the mass
production of cancer in seemingly dissimilar populations. In other words,
nitrosamines may be a common factor in
cancer that has been haunting us all
these years. (1974, p. 136)

    Verrett and Carper (1974, pp. 43-46) list
still more damning evidence. Nitrosamines have
caused cancer in rats, hamsters, mice, guinea
pigs, dogs, and monkeys. It has been proven
that nitrosamines of over a hundred kinds cause
cancer. Nitrosamines have been shown to pass
through the placenta from the mother to cause
cancer in the offspring. Even the lowest levels
of nitrosamines ever tested have produced cancer in animals. When animals are fed nitrite
and amines separately over a period of time,
they develop cancers of the same kind and at
the same frequency as animals fed the corre-
sponding nitrosamines already formed.

10   To address these problems (and in response
to intense public concern), in 1978, the FDA
ruled that a reducing agent, such as ascorbic

*This online
source did
not provide a
date of
publication.*
acid, must be added to products containing
nitrite; the reducing agent inhibits the formation of nitrosamines (Edlefsen & Brewer, no

date). And in the last two decades, at least,
the furor over nitrite seems as a consequence
to have abated. In fact, a 1997 article published by the International Food Information
Council Foundation (a group primarily sponsored
by the food industry, according to information
provided by its Website), celebrates nitrite as
a "naturally-derived" substance that, according
to the American Academy of Science, has never
been found to cause cancer. On the contrary,
the anonymous author states, nitrite does many
good things for consumers; it may even help to
fight cancer: "it safeguards cured meats against
the most deadly foodborne bacterium known to
man" and helps with "promoting blood clotting,
healing wounds and burns and boosting immune
function to kill tumor cells."

11   Other experts are less certain that reducing agents have entirely solved the nitrosamine
problem. The Consumer's Dictionary of Food
Additives notes that one common agent, sodium
ascorbate, which is added to the brine in which
bacon is cured, "offers only a partial barrier
because ascorbate is soluble in fatty tissues"
(Winter, 1994, p. 282). But in the wake of several studies it is unclear that "inhibiting"
the formation of nitrosamines actually makes
nitrites safe to consume.

No citation is given here because all information is included in the sentence itself.

12   The Los Angeles Times reports that one of
these studies, conducted by John Peters, an
epidemiologist at USC, found that "children who
eat more than 12 hot dogs per month have nine

Nitrite   10

times the normal risk of developing childhood
leukemia" (Warrick, 1994). Interestingly, the
study was focused not on nitrites, but rather on
electromagnetic fields. "Dietary exposure to
processed or cured meats was part of a little
side questionnaire to our study on electro
magnetic fields," Peters said. "We were as
surprised as anyone by the hot dogs findings.

An indirect reference. The writer quotes Warrick quoting Peters.

. . . It was the biggest risk for anything we saw
in the study--about four times the risk for
EMF's" (cited in Warrick, 1994).

13   In another of these recent studies, hot
dogs were linked to brain tumors: researchers
found that "children born to mothers who ate at
least one hot dog per week while pregnant have
twice the risk of developing brain tumors, as do
children whose fathers ate too many hot dogs

Authors are named in the sentence and the online source isn't paginated. Only publication date is cited.

before conception" (Warrick, 1994).
Dr.M.Legator and Amanda Daniel comment that
"these studies confirm thirty years worth
of scientific research on the cancer causing
properties of preserved meats and fish" (1995).

14   The question, then, is why nitrite
continues to be used in so much of the meat
Americans consume. Although nitrite adds a small
amount to flavor, it is used primarily for
cosmetic purposes. Food producers are of course
also quick to point out that nitrite keeps
people safe from botulinum in cured meats, an
argument to which the public may be particularly
susceptible because of a number of recent and
serious food scares. Nevertheless, some evidence

Nitrite   11

suggests that the protection nitrite offers is
both unnecessary and ineffective.

15   Michael Jacobson explains the preservative
action of nitrite:

> Nitrite makes botulinum spores sensitive
> to heat. When foods are treated with
> nitrite and then heated, any botulinum
> spores that may be present are killed. In
> the absence of nitrite, spores can be
> inactivated only at temperatures that ruin
> the meat products. . . . Nitrite's
> preservative action is particularly
> important in foods that are not cooked
> after they leave the factory, such as ham,
> because these offer an oxygen-free
> environment, the kind in which botulinum
> can grow. The toxin does not pose a danger
> in foods that are always well cooked, such
> as bacon, because the toxin would be
> destroyed in cooking.
>
> Laboratory studies demonstrate
> clearly that nitrite can kill botulinum,
> but whether it actually does in
> commercially processed meat has been
> called into question. Frequently, the
> levels used may be too low to do
> anything but contribute to the color.
> (1987, p. 165)

Bratwurst and breakfast sausage are manufac-
tured now without nitrite because they don't
need to be colored pink; bacon is always cooked
thoroughly enough to kill off any botulinum

Nitrite   12

spores present. Certainly there are other ways
of dealing with botulism. High or low temperature prevents botulism. What nitrite undoubt-
edly does lower, however, is the level of care
and sanitation necessary in handling meat.

16   Clearly, the use of nitrite adds immeasur-
ably to the profit-making potential of the meat
industry, but why does the federal government
allow this health hazard in our food? In the
first place, nitrite and nitrate have been used
for so long that it is hard for lawmakers to get
past their instinctive reaction, "But that's the
way we've always done it." Indeed, the Romans
used saltpeter, a nitrate, to keep meat and, as
early as 1899, scientists discovered that the
nitrate breaks down into nitrite and that it is
the nitrite which actually preserves the red

Note that a
reference to a
single page is   color in meats (Jacobson, 1987, pp. 164-65).
preceded by
"p." and that   Thus, by the time the U.S. Department of Agri-
a reference to
two or more   culture and the Food and Drug Administration got
pages is
preceded by   into the business of regulating food, they
"pp."
tended to accept nitrite and nitrate as givens.

A second reason for the inadequacy of
regulation is that government mechanisms for
protecting the consumer are full of curious
loopholes. In 1958 Congress passed the Food
Additive Amendment, including the Delaney
Clause, which clearly states that additives
should be banned if they induce cancer in laboratory animals. Unfortunately, however, the
amendment does not apply to additives that were
in use before it was passed, so, since nitrite

Nitrite   13

and nitrate had already been in use for a long time, they were automatically included on the list of chemicals "Generally Recognized as Safe." To complicate matters further, nitrite in meat is regulated by the USDA, while nitrite in fish is under the jurisdiction of the FDA. And these agencies generally leave it to industry--the profit-maker--to establish whether or not an additive is safe. The final irony in this list of governmental errors is that the FDA depends heavily, for "independent" research and advice, on the food committees of the National Academy of Sciences, which Daniel Zwerdling claims are "like a Who's Who of the food and chemical industry" (1971, p. 34). (This, of course, is the organization cited in the anonymous web posting quoted above, the organization that holds that "nitrite levels in cured meat have not been linked to the development of human cancers.")

Because the author is named in the sentence, the citation gives only the date and page number.

17   Clearly, consumers need to be informed; clearly, it is unwise to count on government agencies for protection against the dangers food additives may pose. Some experts continue to argue that nitrite is safe enough; Edelfson and Brewer, for example, cite a 1992 study by J. M. Jones that suggests that drinking beer exposes a consumer to more nitrite than does eating bacon--and that new car interiors are a significant source of nitrite as well.[1] Others recom-

An explanatory footnote.

[1]Presumably the exposure here results from contact, not ingestion.

Nitrite   14

mend caution. One expert advises: "If you must eat nitrite-laced meats, include a food or drink high in vitamin C at the same time--for example, orange juice, grapefruit juice, cranberry juice, or lettuce" (Winter, 1994, p. 282). And, in fact, a study by a committee organized by the National Academy of Science strongly implies (Assembly, 1982, p. 12) that the government should develop a safe alternative to nitrites.

18   In the meantime, the chemical additive industry doesn't seem very worried that alternatives, such as biopreservatives, will pose a threat to its profits. An industry publication, "Chemical Marketing Reporter," recently reassured its readers by announcing that "around 82.5 million pounds of preservatives, valued at $133 million, were consumed in the US in 1991." The report also stated that "though the trend toward phasing out controversial preservatives like sulfites, nitrates and nitrites continues, natural substitutes remain expensive and often less than effective, making biopreservatives a distant threat" (Tollefson, 1995).

*References
begin on new
page*

References

Assembly of Life Science. (1982). <u>Alternatives to</u>

*Second and
subsequent
lines of entries
are indented
five spaces*

<u>the current use of nitrite in food.</u>

Washington, DC: National Academy Press.

Edlefsen, M., & Brewer, M. S. (n.d.). <u>The</u>   *Use "n.d."
when date is
unavailable.*

<u>national food safety database.</u>

Nitrates/Nitrites. Retrieved April 16, 2006,

from http://www.foodsafety.org/il/il089.html

*Capitalize
only the first
word in
book and
article titles.*

Hunter, B. T. (1972). <u>Fact/book on food additives</u>

<u>and your health.</u> New Canaan, CT: Keats.

International Food Information Council

Foundation. (1997). Nitrite: keeping food

safe. <u>Food Insight.</u> Retrieved April 15, 2006,

from http://ific.org/proactive/newsroom/

release.vtml?id=18036

Jacobson, M. F. (1987). <u>Eater's digest.</u>

Washington, DC: Center for Science in the

Public Interest.

*An online
version
of a
newspaper
article.*

Legator, M., & Daniel, A. (1995). Reproductive

systems can be harmed by toxic exposure.

*Capitalize all
important
words in
newspaper and
periodical titles.*

<u>Galveston County Daily News.</u> Retrieved April

20, 2006, from http://www.utmb.edu/toxics/

newsp.htm#canen   *An online
version of a
magazine
article. Note
that the year
precedes the
month and date
in the
parentheses
following the
author.*

Murphy, K. (1996, May 6). Do food

additives subtract from health?

<u>Business Week,</u> p. 140. Retrieved April

21, 2006, from LexisNexis.

National Cancer Institute (1996, June).

<u>NCI fact sheet.</u> Food additives.

Retrieved April 20, 2006, from

Nitrite   16

http://nisc8a.upenn.edu/pdghtml/6/eng/

600037.html

Tollefson, C. (1995, May 29). Stability
preserved; preservatives; food
additives '95. Chemical Marketing
Reporter 247(22) SR28. April 22, 2006,
from LexisNexis.

A book by two authors. Note use of ampersand between authors' names.

Verrett, J., & Carper, J. (1974). Eating may
be hazardous to your health. New York:
Simon and Schuster.

Warrick, P. (1994, June 8). A frank
discussion. Los Angeles Times,
E1. Retrieved April 20, 2006, from
LexisNexis.

Welford, H. (1973). Sowing the wind; a
report from Ralph Nader's Center for
Study of Responsible Law on food
safety and the chemical harvest. New
York: Bantam.

Winter, R. (1994). A consumer's dictionary
of food additives (Updated 4th ed.).
New York. Crown.

Use "p." or "pp." when citing books or newspapers, but not periodicals. Ramparts is a periodical.

Zwerdling, D. (1971, June). Food pollution.
Ramparts, 9(11), 31-37, 53-54.

A Brief Analysis of Alexander's Use of Sources

Jacob Alexander's **research essay** argues persuasively against eating foods preserved with sodium nitrite even as Alexander acknowledges that the dangers of nitrites haven't been established with absolute certainty. His **balanced, reasonable tone** and his range of **sources** help to establish his credibility. He cites industry and government publications, experts in the field, reference works, news articles, and a variety of other sources. Readers are inclined to trust someone who considers lots of evidence, even evidence that runs counter to his position. We know that at least one reader found his argument convincing: Alexander's writing instructor reports that she hasn't eaten a hot dog since she read his essay.

Here, we will point to some of the specific ways Alexander develops his argument.

- Paragraphs 1–3 capture the reader's attention by **establishing that there is a *problem*,** one that affects almost everyone. Paragraph 1 **introduces the problem** of food additives by quoting an **authority** (a "professor of food and nutrition") and offering a striking piece of information, that people eat their weight in additives each year. Paragraph 2 **develops the problem** by presenting the writer's research questions (how dangerous are additives, and—if they are dangerous—why are they still used?) and offering **evidence** from authorities on both sides. Paragraph 3 **develops the problem further** by presenting frightening **evidence** of deaths due to nitrites.

- Paragraphs 4–10 present the writer's **research** on what nitrites do: how they preserve meat (paragraph 4); how they affect the blood (paragraph 5) and the genes (paragraph 6); and how they may cause cancer in humans (paragraphs 7–10). The writer offers a particularly damning piece of **evidence** in paragraph 7 when he cites the food industry's report that nitrosamines, which form when nitrites and amines combine in the body, cause cancer. The food industry of course profits from preservatives and can be expected to defend nitrites whenever possible, so the admission powerfully supports Alexander's position.

- Paragraphs 11–12 look at the Food and Drug Administration's response, in the 1970s, to public concerns about nitrites and at various experts' current thinking about them. Alexander notes that a bulletin published by a food industry group in the late 1990s celebrates nitrite as a "naturally-derived" substance that may in fact fight cancer—an interesting **counterargument,** but one that seems weak after all the evidence to the contrary. Paragraphs 13–14 present frightening information from current studies that again link nitrites and cancer; the link establishes a **transition** (in paragraph 15) to a discussion of the second part of Alexander's **research question:** why are nitrites still used?

- Paragraphs 16–18 explore and develop this question: Botulism-killing nitrites make lower standards of sanitation possible for meat producers and increase industry profits—but given the dangers, why does the *government* permit their use? The answers: long practice, and regulatory loopholes. Paragraph 19 presents Alexander's **conclusion,** that consumers must be wary. (We like the touch of **wit** in the explanatory footnote to this paragraph.) And paragraph 20—the final paragraph—ends with a chilling **quotation** from a chemical industry publication reassuring its readers that nitrites are here to stay. No summary or further commentary is needed from Alexander; the quotation strikes just the right conclusive note.

CHAPTER ELEVEN

WRITING ESSAY EXAMINATIONS

Do not on any account attempt to write on both sides of the paper at once.
— *W. C. Sellar and R. J. Yeatman*

You never know what is enough unless you know what is more than enough.
— *William Blake*

Why Write Examinations? Examinations as Critical Thinking

Students take essay examinations because, of course, instructors require them. Examinations measure what students have learned. But examinations not only measure learning, they also make it possible for students to convert learning into thinking. An examination can help the student to think about the *whole* of a course, to see the big picture from perhaps a new angle; a challenging and well-constructed question can enable the student to make an imaginative leap that he or she wouldn't otherwise have made. While stressful, taking examinations can be productive, even exciting.

Essay examinations also require writing skills—in a sense, they require all the skills we've discussed in the preceding chapters. In general, successful essay examinations require students to generate ideas quickly, to shape them into paragraphs that contain clear and concise sentences; they require analysis and argument and the effective use of sources. What more is there to be said? We hope the following general advice—some of it perfectly obvious—will be useful. Following our general advice, we have some specific points to make about exams in literature, history and the social sciences, and the physical sciences and math.

Writing Essay Answers

First, some unsurprising suggestions. **Keep up with the reading. Take notes** in the margins of your books and in class. On the night before the exam, **review** the material, and get a decent night's **sleep.**

1. **Scan the entire examination before you begin to write.** Get a sense of the whole and **budget your time.**

2. **Read the exam question or questions carefully.** Make sure you understand what you're being asked to do.

3. **Make notes.** As we illustrate in Chapter 1, making notes can help generate ideas. During an examination, it can help with time management as well.

4. **Turn the question into the beginning of an answer.** For example, you might turn the question, "In what ways is the poetry of Allen Ginsberg influenced by Whitman?" into "Whitman influenced Ginsberg's poetry in at least . . . ways." Doing this will (a) get your pen moving and (b) tell the instructor that you've read the question.

5. **Answer the question.** If you've been asked to *analyze* or to *compare*, don't merely summarize. The instructor wants to know not simply if you have done the reading but if and how you can use it.

6. **Be concrete.** Illustrate your arguments with facts—names, dates, and even quotations if possible.

7. **Leave space for last-minute additions.** Write on every other line, or leave generous margins, or write on every other page of the blue book.

8. **Write legibly.** Pity the poor exam reader.

Now, let's look at some specific types of questions.

Questions on Literature and the Social Sciences

The most common questions can be sorted into five categories:

1. **A passage to explicate.** An explication is a detailed commentary on the meaning of a text. If you are asked to explicate a passage or a

poem, look carefully at the tone (the speaker's attitude toward self, subject, and audience) and at the implications of the words (the connotations or associations), and see if there is a pattern of imagery. For example, religious language ("adore," "saint") in a secular love poem may define the nature of the lover and of the beloved. An explication is not a paraphrase (a putting into other words) but an attempt to show the relations of the parts, and most explications begin with commentary on the first line and go on to the last.

2. **A historical question,** such as "Trace the development of Shakespeare's conception of the tragic hero," or "What are Virginia Woolf's contributions to feminist criticism?" A good essay on a historical question will combine argument and evidence; concrete details will support a compelling thesis. If you are asked to relate a writer or a body of work to an earlier writer or to a period, list the chief characteristics of the earlier writer or the period and then show *specifically* how the material you are discussing is related to these characteristics. And if you can quote some relevant lines from the works, your reader will feel that you know not only titles and stock phrases but also the works themselves.

3. **A critical quotation to be evaluated.** Read the quotation carefully and in your answer take account of *all* of it. If the critic has said, "Eliot in his plays always . . . but in his poems rarely . . . " you will have to write about both the plays and the poems; it will not be enough to talk only about the plays. Watch especially for words like "always," "for the most part," "never"; although the passage may on the whole approach the truth, you may feel that some important qualifications are needed. This is not being picky; thinking involves making subtle distinctions, yielding assent only so far and no further. Again, be sure to give concrete details, supporting your argument with evidence.

4. **A comparison.** For example, a student in a psychology course might be asked to compare Fromm's and Lorenz's explanations of aggression and to discuss the extent to which their theories might help to explain the Arab-Israeli conflict. Notice that you are being called on to compare—not just to summarize—two theories, and that in this case you must also be able to think critically about their relevance to a particular conflict.

5. **A wild question,** such as "What would Dickens think of Stephen King?" or "What would Juliet do if she were in Ophelia's position?" Curiously, a wild question usually produces tame answers: a half

dozen ideas about Dickens or Juliet are neatly applied to King or Ophelia, and the gross incompatibilities are thus revealed. But, as the previous paragraph suggests, it may be necessary to do more than to set up bold and obvious oppositions. The interest in such a question may largely be in the degree to which superficially different figures *resemble* each other in some important ways. And remember that the wildness of the question does not mean that all answers are equally acceptable; as usual, a good answer will be supported by concrete details.

Questions on the Physical Sciences and Mathematics

As we note above, examinations measure the student's ability to convert learning into thinking, and although the answer to an examination question in the physical sciences usually requires a mathematical computation, a few sentences may be useful in such examinations to help document your process of thought.

1. **The general plan:** For instance, if the examination question is "What is the time required for an object to fall from the orbit of the moon to the earth?" the statement of your plan might be: "The time required for an object to fall from the orbit of the moon to the earth can be obtained by integration from Newton's law of motion, taking account of the increasing gravitational force as the object approaches the earth." Making your plan explicit is useful in clarifying your thought: Is the plan a complete one leading to the desired answer? Do I know what I need to know to implement the plan? The statement of plan is useful also in communicating with the instructor. Your plan of solution, although valid, may be a surprise to the instructor (who may have expected a solution to the problem posed above starting from Kepler's laws without any integration). When this is so, the instructor will need your explanation to become oriented to your plan and to assess its merits. Then if you botch the subsequent computation or can't remember how the gravitational force varies with the distance, you will still have demonstrated that you have some comprehension of the problem.

2. **Assumptions or simplifications:** For the same reason, it may also be useful to explain assumptions or simplifications: "I assume the body is released with zero velocity and accordingly set $b=0$," or "The

third term is negligible and I drop it." If you make an incorrect assumption, but your procedure is logical and consistent, you may at least receive some credit for what you have done.

3. **The results:** Finally, the results of your computation should be summarized or interpreted in words to answer the question asked. "The object will fall to the earth in five days." (The correct answer, for those who are curious.) Or, if you arrive at the end of your computation and of the examination hour and find you have a preposterous result, you can still exit gracefully (and increase your partial credit) with an explanation: "The answer of 53 days is clearly erroneous since the fall time of an object from the moon's orbit must be less than the seven days required for the moon to travel a quarter orbit."

PART THREE

A
WRITER'S
HANDBOOK

CHAPTER TWELVE

PUNCTUATING SENTENCES

Speakers can raise or lower the volume or pitch of their voices; they can speak a phrase slowly and distinctly and then (making a parenthetical remark, perhaps) quicken the pace. They can wave their arms, pound a table, or pause, meaningfully. But writers, physically isolated from their audience, can do none of these things. Nevertheless, they can embody some of the tones and gestures of speech—in the patterns of their written sentences, and in the dots, hooks, and lines of punctuation that clarify those patterns.

Punctuation clarifies, first of all, by removing or reducing ambiguity. Consider this headline from a story in a newspaper:

SQUAD HELPS DOG BITE VICTIM

Of course, there is no real ambiguity here—only a laugh—because the stated meaning is so clearly absurd, and on second reading we supply the necessary hyphen in *dog-bite*. But other ill-punctuated sentences may be troublesome rather than entertaining. Take the following sentence:

He arrived late for the rehearsal didn't end until midnight.

Almost surely you stumbled in the middle of the sentence, thinking that it was about someone arriving tardily at a rehearsal, and then, since what followed made no sense, you probably went back and mentally added the comma (by pausing) at the necessary place:

He arrived late, for the rehearsal didn't end until midnight.

Punctuation helps to keep your reader on the right path. And the path is your train of thought. If your punctuation is faulty, you unintentionally point the reader off your path and toward dead-end streets and quagmires.

Even when punctuation is not the key to meaning, it usually helps you get your meaning across neatly. Consider the following sentence:

> There are two kinds of feminism—one is the growing struggle of women to understand and change the shape of their lives and the other is a narrow ideology whose adherents are anxious to clear away whatever does not conform to their view.

The sentence is clear enough, but by changing the punctuation it can be sharpened. Because a dash usually indicates an abrupt interruption—it usually precedes a sort of afterthought—a colon would be better. The colon, usually the signal of an amplification of what precedes it, here would suggest that the two classifications are not impromptu thoughts but carefully considered ones. Second, and more important, in the original version the two classifications are run together without any intervening punctuation, but since the point is that the two are utterly different, it is advisable to separate them by inserting a comma or semicolon, indicating a pause. A comma before "and the other" would do, but probably a semicolon (without the "and") is preferable because it is a heavier pause, thereby making the separation clearer. Here is the sentence, revised:

> There are two kinds of feminism: one is the growing struggle of women to understand and change the shape of their lives; the other is a narrow ideology whose adherents are anxious to clear away whatever does not conform to their view.

The right punctuation enables the reader to move easily through the sentence.

Although punctuation helps a reader to move through a sentence, it must be admitted that some of the rules of punctuation do not contribute to meaning or greatly facilitate reading. For example, in American usage a period never comes immediately after quotation marks; it precedes quotation marks, thus:

> "If you put the period inside the closing quotation mark," the writing instructor said, "I will give you an A."

If you put the period after the closing quotation mark, the meaning remains the same, but you are also informing your reader that you don't know the conventions of American usage—conventions all writers in the United States are expected to adhere to. A pattern of such errors will diminish your authority as a writer: Your reader, noticing that you don't know where to put the period in relation to the quotation mark, may well begin to wonder what else you don't know. Conversely, demonstrating that you know the rules will help to gain your reader's confidence and establish your authority as a writer.

A Word on Computer Grammar and Punctuation Checks

Word-processing programs include a tool that can check grammar and punctuation. At your request, the program will flag sentences that look faulty and offer suggestions for correcting mistakes. These programs can be very helpful: They can draw your attention to sentence fragments, to problems with plurals and possessives, even to passive verbs. But they don't catch everything, and they don't always know how to fix the problems they identify.

Our advice: Use the tool if you have it, but don't let it do your editing for you. Check the program's suggestions against your own knowledge and the advice offered in this book.

Three Common Errors: Fragments, Comma Splices, and Run-on Sentences

Fragments and How to Correct Them

A **fragment** is a part of a sentence set off as if it were a complete sentence:

Because I didn't care.

Being an accident.

Later in the week.

For several reasons.

My oldest sister.

Fragments are common in speech, but they are used sparingly in writing, usually for emphasis. A fragment used carelessly in writing often looks like an afterthought—usually because it *was* an afterthought—that is, an explanation or other addition that belongs to the previous sentence.

With appropriate punctuation (and sometimes with no punctuation at all) a fragment can usually be connected to the previous sentence:

Incorrect

Many nineteenth-century horror stories have been made into films. Such as *Dracula* and *Frankenstein*.

Correct

Many nineteenth-century horror stories have been made into films, such as *Dracula* and *Frankenstein*.

Incorrect

Many schools are putting renewed emphasis on writing. Because SAT scores have declined for ten years.

Correct

Many schools are putting renewed emphasis on writing because SAT scores have declined for ten years.

Incorrect

She decided to wear rope sandals. Being a strict vegetarian.

Correct

Being a strict vegetarian, she wore only rope sandals.
She wore only rope sandals because she was a strict vegetarian.

Incorrect

A fragment often looks like an afterthought. Perhaps because it *was* an afterthought.

Correct

A fragment often looks like an afterthought—perhaps because it *was* an afterthought.

Incorrect

He hoped to get credit for two summer courses. Batik and Hang-Gliding.

Correct

He hoped to get credit for two summer courses: Batik and Hang-Gliding.

Notice in these examples that, depending upon the relationship between the two parts, the fragment and the preceding statement can be joined by a comma, dash, or colon, or by no punctuation at all.

Notice also that unintentional fragments often follow subordinating conjunctions, such as *because* and *although*. Subordinating conjunctions introduce a subordinate (dependent) clause; such a clause cannot stand as a sentence. Here is a list of the most common subordinating conjunctions:

after	though
although	unless
because	until
before	when
if	where
provided	whereas
since	while

Fragments also commonly occur when the writer, as in the third example, mistakenly uses *being* as a main verb.

How to Correct Comma Splices and Run-on Sentences

An error known as a **comma splice** or **comma fault** results when a comma is mistakenly placed between two independent clauses that are not joined by a coordinating conjunction: *and, or, nor, but, for, yet, so.* If the comma is omitted, the error is called a **run-on sentence.**

Here are some examples of the two errors:

Comma splice (or comma fault)

In the second picture the man leans on the woman's body, he is obviously in pain.

Run-on sentence

In the second picture the man leans on the woman's body he is obviously in pain.

Run-on sentences and comma splices may be corrected in five principal ways:

1. Use a period to create two sentences:

   In the second picture the man leans on the woman's body. He is obviously in pain.

2. Use a semicolon:

   In the second picture the man leans on the woman's body; he is obviously in pain.

3. Use a comma and a coordinating conjunction (*and, or, nor, but, for, yet, so*):

   In the second picture the man leans on the woman's body, and he is obviously in pain.

4. Make one of the clauses dependent (subordinate). Use a subordinating conjunction such as *after, although, because, before, if, provided, since, though, unless, until, when, where, whereas, while:*

   In the second picture the man leans on the woman's body because he is in pain.

5. Reduce one of the independent clauses to a phrase, or even to a single word:

   In the second picture the man, obviously in pain, leans on the woman's body.

Run-on sentences and comma splices are especially common in sentences containing transitional words or phrases such as the following:

also	however
besides	indeed
consequently	in fact
for example	nevertheless
furthermore	therefore
hence	whereas

When these words join independent clauses, the clauses cannot be linked by a comma:

Incorrect

She argued from faulty premises, however the conclusions happened to be correct.

Here are five correct revisions, following the five rules we have just given. (In the first two revisions we place "however" after rather than before "the conclusions" because we prefer the increase in emphasis, but the grammatical point is the same.)

Correct

1. She argued from faulty premises. The conclusions, however, happened to be correct. [Two sentences]

2. She argued from faulty premises; the conclusions, however, happened to be correct. [Semicolon]

3. She argued from faulty premises, but the conclusions happened to be correct. [Coordinating conjunction]

4. Although she argued from faulty premises, the conclusions happened to be correct. [Subordinating conjunction]

5. She argued from faulty premises to correct conclusions. [Reduction of an independent clause to a phrase]

The following sentence contains a comma splice:

The husband is not pleased, in fact, he is embarrassed.

How might it be repaired?

The Period

Periods are used to mark the ends of sentences (or intentional sentence fragments) other than questions and exclamations:

A sentence normally ends with a period.
She said, "I'll pass."
Yes.
Once more, with feeling.

But a sentence within a sentence is punctuated according to the needs of the longer sentence. Notice, in the following example, that a period is *not* used after "pass":

She said, "I'll pass," but she said it without conviction.

Periods are used with abbreviations of titles and terms of reference:

Dr. Mr. Mrs. Ms. i.e. e.g. etc.
p., pp. (for "page" and "pages")

But when the capitalized initial letters of the words naming an organization are used in place of the full name, the periods are commonly omitted:

CBS CORE IBM NBA UCLA UNICEF USAF

Periods are also used to separate chapter from verse in the Bible:

Genesis 3.2   Mark 6.10

For further details on references to the Bible, see page 261.

The Question Mark

Use a question mark after a direct question:

Did Bacon write Shakespeare's plays?

Do not use a question mark after an indirect question, or after a polite request:

He asked if Bacon wrote Shakespeare's plays.

Would you please explain what the support for Bacon is really all about.

The Colon

The colon has four uses:

- To introduce a list or series of examples
- To introduce an amplification or explanation of what precedes the colon
- To introduce a quotation (though a quotation can be introduced by other means)
- To indicate time

Now let's look at each of those four uses.

1. The colon may introduce a list or series:

Students are required to take one of the following sciences: biology, chemistry, geology, physics.

2. The colon may introduce an explanation. It is almost equivalent to *namely*, or *that is*. What is on one side of the colon more or less equals what is on the other side. The material on either side of the colon can stand as a separate sentence:

She explained her fondness for wrestling: she did it to shock her parents.

The forces which in China created a central government were absent in Japan: farming had to be on a small scale, there was no need for extensive canal works, and a standing army was not required to protect the country from foreign invaders.

Many of the best of the Civil War photographs must be read as the fossils of earlier events: The caissons with their mud-encrusted wheels, the dead on the field, the empty landscapes, all speak of deeds already past.

—*John Szarkowski*

Notice in the last example that the writer uses a capital letter after the colon; the usage is acceptable when a complete sentence follows the colon, as long as that style is followed consistently throughout a paper.

3. The colon, like the comma, may be used to introduce a quotation; it is more formal than the comma, setting off the quotation to a greater degree.

The black sculptor Ed Wilson tells his students: "Malcolm X is my brother, Martin Luther King is my brother, Eldridge Cleaver is my brother! But Michelangelo is my grandfather!"

—*Albert E. Elsen*

4. A colon is used to separate the hour from the minutes when the time is given in figures:

9:15   12:00

5. Colons (like semicolons) go outside of closing quotation marks if they are not part of the quotation:

"There is no such thing as a free lunch": the truth of these words is confirmed every day.

The Semicolon

There are four main uses of the semicolon. Sheridan Baker (in *The Practical Stylist*) summed them up in this admirable formula: "Use a semicolon where you could also use a period, unless desperate." Correctly used, the semicolon can add precision to your writing; it can also help you out of some tight corners.

1. You may use a semicolon instead of a period between closely related independent clauses not joined by a coordinating conjunction:

All happy families resemble one another; every unhappy family is unhappy in its own fashion.

—*Leo Tolstoy*

The demands that men and women make on marriage will never be fully met; they cannot be.

—*Jessie Bernard*

In our fractured culture, we cannot agree on morals; we cannot even agree that moral matters should come before literary ones when there is a conflict between them.

—*Flannery O'Connor*

When a cat washes its face it does not move its paw; it moves its face.

In each of the examples the independent clauses might have been written as sentences separated by periods; the semicolon pulls the statements together, emphasizing their relationship. Alternatively, the statements might have been linked by coordinating conjunctions (*and, or, nor, but, for, yet, so*). For example:

The demands made upon marriage will never be fully met for they cannot be.

When a cat washes its face it does not move its paw but it moves its face.

The sentences as originally written, using semicolons, have more bite.

2. You *must* use a semicolon (rather than a comma) if you use a *conjunctive adverb* to connect independent clauses. (A conjunctive adverb is a transitional word such as *also, consequently, furthermore, however, moreover, nevertheless, therefore.*)

His hair was black and wavy; however, it was false.

We don't like to see our depressed relative cry; nevertheless, tears can provide a healthy emotional outlet.

She said "I do"; moreover, she repeated the words.

Take note of the following three points:

- A comma goes after the conjunctive adverb.
- Semicolons (like colons) go outside of closing quotation marks if they are not part of the quotation.
- A conjunctive adverb requires a semicolon to join independent clauses. A comma produces a comma splice:

Incorrect

His hair was black and wavy, however, it was false.

3. You may use a semicolon to separate a series of phrases with internal punctuation:

He had a car, which he hadn't paid for; a wife, whom he didn't love; and a father, who was unemployed.

4. Use a semicolon between independent clauses linked by coordinating conjunctions if the sentence would otherwise be difficult to read, because it is long and complex or because it contains internal punctuation:

In the greatest age of painting, the nude inspired the greatest works; and even when it ceased to be a compulsive subject it held its position as an academic exercise and a demonstration of mastery.

(Often it is preferable to break such sentences up, or to recast them.)

The Comma

The comma (from the Greek word meaning "to cut") indicates a relatively slight pause within a sentence. If after checking the rules you are still uncertain of whether or not to use a comma in a given sentence, read the sentence aloud and see if it sounds better with or without a pause; you can then add or omit the comma. A women's shoe store in New York has a sign on the door:

NO MEN PLEASE.

If the proprietors would read the sign aloud, they might want to change it to

NO MEN, PLEASE

When you are typing, always follow a comma with a space.

For your reference, here is a guide to the following pages, which summarize the correct uses of the comma:

1. with independent clauses, page 254
2. with introductory subordinate clauses or long phrases, pages 254–255
3. with tacked-on subordinate phrases or long clauses, page 255

1. Independent clauses (unless short) joined by a coordinating conjunction (*and, or, nor, but, for, yet, so*) take a comma before the conjunction:

> Most students see at least a few football games, and many go to every game of the season.

> Most students seem to have an intuitive sense of when to use a comma, but in fact the "intuition" is the result of long training.

If the introductory independent clause is short, the comma is usually omitted:

> She dieted but she continued to gain weight.

2. An introductory subordinate clause or long phrase is usually followed by a comma:

> Having revised his manuscript for the third time, he went to bed.

> In order to demonstrate her point, the instructor stood on her head.

If the introductory subordinate clause or phrase is short, say four words or fewer, the comma may be omitted, provided no ambiguity results from the omission:

> Having left he soon forgot.

But compare this last example with the following:

> Having left, the instructor soon forgot.

If the comma is omitted, the sentence is misread. Where are commas needed in the following sentences?

Instead of discussing the book she wrote a summary.

When Shakespeare wrote comedies were already popular.

While he ate his poodle would sit by the table.

As we age small things become killers.

3. A subordinate clause or long modifying phrase tacked on as an afterthought is usually preceded by a comma:

I have decided not to be nostalgic about the 1950s, despite the hoopla over Elvis.

Buster Keaton fell down a flight of stairs without busting, thereby gaining his nickname from Harry Houdini.

By the time he retired, Hank Aaron had 755 home runs, breaking Babe Ruth's record by 41.

With afterthoughts, the comma may be omitted if there is a clear sequence of cause and effect, signaled by such words as *because, for,* and *so.* Compare the following examples:

In 1601 Shakespeare wrote *Hamlet*, probably his best-known play.

In 1601 Shakespeare wrote *Hamlet* because revenge tragedy was in demand.

4. A pair of commas can serve as a pair of unobtrusive parentheses. Be sure not to omit the second comma:

Doctors, I think, have an insufficient knowledge of acupuncture.

The earliest known paintings of Christ, dating from the third century, are found in the catacombs outside of Rome.

Medicare and Medicaid, the chief sources of federal support for patients in nursing homes, are frequently confused.

Under this heading we can include a conjunctive adverb (a transitional adverb such as *also, besides, consequently, however, likewise, nevertheless, therefore*) inserted within a sentence. These transitional words are set off between a pair of commas:

Her hair, however, was stringy.

If one of these words begins a sentence, the comma after it is optional. Notice, however, that the presence of such a word as "however" is not always a safeguard against a run-on sentence or comma splice; if the word occurs between two independent clauses and it goes with the second clause, you need a semicolon before it and a comma after it:

His hair was black and wavy; however, it was false.

(See the discussion of comma splices on pages 247–249.)

5. Use a comma to set off a nonrestrictive modifier. A nonrestrictive modifier, as the following examples will make clear, is a sort of parenthetical addition; it gives supplementary information about the subject, but it can be omitted without changing the subject. A restrictive modifier, however, is not supplementary but essential; if a restrictive modifier is omitted, the subject becomes more general. In Dorothy Parker's celebrated poem,

Men seldom make passes
At girls who wear glasses,

"who wear glasses" is a restrictive modifier, narrowing or restricting the subject down from "girls" to a particular group of girls, those who wear glasses. That is, the subject is *not* "girls" but the narrower or more limited group, "girls who were glasses."

Here is a *non*restrictive modifier:

For the majority of immigrants, who have no knowledge of English, language is the chief problem.

Now here is a restrictive modifier:

For the majority of immigrants who have no knowledge of English, language is the chief problem.

These sentences say different things. The first version says—in addition to its obvious message that language is the chief problem—that the majority of immigrants have no knowledge of English. The second version makes no such assertion; it talks not about the majority of immigrants but only about a more restricted group—the majority of those immigrants who have no knowledge of English.

Now look at another example:

Shakespeare's shortest tragedy, *Macbeth*, is one of his greatest plays.

In this sentence, *"Macbeth"* is *non*restrictive because the subject is already as restricted as possible; Shakespeare can have written only one "shortest tragedy." That is, *"Macbeth"* is merely an explanatory equivalent of "Shakespeare's shortest tragedy" and it is therefore enclosed in commas. (A noun or noun phrase serving as an explanatory equivalent to another, and in the same syntactical relation to other elements in the sentence, is said to be in apposition.) But compare

Shakespeare's tragedy *Macbeth* is one of his greatest plays.

with the misleadingly punctuated sentence,

Shakespeare's tragedy, *Macbeth*, is one of his greatest plays.

The first of these is restrictive, narrowing or restricting the subject "tragedy" down to one particular tragedy, and so it rightly does not separate the modifier from the subject by a comma. The second, punctuated so that it is nonrestrictive, falsely implies that *Macbeth* is Shakespeare's only tragedy.

Here is an example of a nonrestrictive modifier correctly punctuated:

Women, who constitute 51.3 percent of the population and 53 percent of the electorate, constitute only 15.4 percent of the House of Representatives and 14 percent of the Senate.

In the next two examples, the first illustrates the correct use of commas after a nonrestrictive appositive, and the second illustrates the correct omission of commas after a restrictive appositive:

Hong Yee Chiu, a Chinese-American physicist, abbreviated the compound adjective *quasi-stellar* to *quasar*.

The Chinese-American physicist Hong Yee Chiu abbreviated the compound adjective *quasi-stellar* to *quasar*.

6. Words, phrases, and clauses in series take a comma after each item except the last. The comma between the last two items may be omitted if there is no ambiguity:

Photography is a matter of eyes, intuition, and intellect.

She wrote plays, poems, and stories.

He wrote plays, sang songs, and danced jigs.

She wrote a wise, witty, humane book.

But adjectives in a series may cause difficulty. The next two examples correctly omit the commas:

a funny silent film

a famous French professor

In each of these last two examples, the adjective immediately before the noun forms with the noun a compound that is modified by the earlier adjective. That is, the adjectives are not a coordinate series (what is funny is not simply a film but a silent film, what is famous is not simply a professor but a French professor) and so commas are not used. Compare:

a famous French professor

a famous, arrogant French professor

In the second example, only "famous" and "arrogant" form a coordinate series. If in doubt, see if you can replace the commas with "and"; if you can, the commas are correct. In the example given, you could insert "and" between "famous" and "arrogant," but not between "arrogant" and "French."

Commas are not needed if all the members of the series are connected by conjunctions:

He ate steak for breakfast and lunch and supper.

7. Use a comma to set off direct discourse:

"It's a total failure," she said.

She said, "It's a total failure."

But do not use a comma for indirect discourse:

She said that it is a total failure.

She said it is a total failure.

8. Use a comma to set off "yes" and "no":

No, I will turn in my essay tomorrow.

9. Use a comma to set off words of address:

Look Bill, you should turn in your essay today.

10. Use a comma to separate a geographical location within another geographical location:

She was born in Brooklyn, New York, in 1895.

Another way of putting it is to say that a comma is used after each unit of an address, except that a comma is *not* used between the name of the state and the zip code.

11. Use a comma to set off the year from the month or day:

He was born on June 10, 1980, at Morristown Memorial Hospital.

No comma is needed if you use the form "10 June 1980."

12. Note the position of the comma when used with other punctuation: If a comma is required with parenthetic material, it follows the second parenthesis:

Because Japan was secure from invasion (even the Mongols were beaten back), its history is unusually self-contained.

The only time a comma may precede a parenthesis is when parentheses surround a digit or letter used to enumerate a series:

Questions usually fall into one of three categories: (1) true-false, (2) multiple choice, (3) essay.

A comma always goes inside closing quotation marks unless the quotation is followed by a parenthesis:

"Sayonara," he said.

"Sayonara" (Japanese for "goodbye"), he said.

The Dash

The dash—more specifically, the em-dash—indicates an abrupt break or pause. Your computer will probably insert the dash automatically if you type two hyphens without hitting the space bar before, between, or after. (If your computer does not automatically inset the em-dash, you will need to locate it on your program's list of special characters.)

1. The words within dashes function as parenthetic material (material that is not essential). However, by setting it within dashes—an emphatic form of punctuation—the writer gives the material more emphasis than it would get within parentheses:

The bathroom—that private place—has rarely been the subject of scholarly study.

The Great Wall of China forms a continuous line over 1400 miles long—the distance from New York to Kansas City—running from Peking to the edge of the mountains of Central Asia.

Note: If the material between two dashes is deleted, the remaining words still form a grammatical sentence.

2. A dash can serve, somewhat like a colon, as a pause before a series. It is more casual than a colon:

The earliest Shinto holy places were natural objects—trees, boulders, mountains, islands.

Each of the brothers had his distinct comic style—Groucho's double-talk, Chico's artfully stupid malapropisms, Harpo's horseplay.

—*Gerald Mast*

A dash is never used next to a comma, and it is used before a period only to indicate that the sentence is interrupted.

Why, they couldn't hit an elephant at this dist—.

—*General John Sedgewick, (last words)*

Overuse of the dash—even only a little overuse—gives writing an unpleasantly agitated—even explosive—quality.

Parentheses

Let's begin with a caution: Avoid using parentheses to explain pronouns:

In his speech he (Hamlet) says . . .
If "he" needs to be explained by "Hamlet," omit the "he" and just say "Hamlet."

1. Use parentheses for subordinate material: What is enclosed in parentheses functions as a casual aside, less essential than similar material set off in commas, less vigorously spoken than similar material set off in dashes:

While guest curator for the Whitney (he has since returned to the Denver Art Museum), Feder assembled a magnificent collection of masks, totems, paintings, clothing, and beadwork.

Another caution: Avoid an abundance of these interruptions, and avoid a long parenthesis within a sentence (you are now reading a simple example of this annoying but common habit of writers who have trouble sticking to the point) because the reader will lose track of the main sentence.

2. Use parentheses to enclose digits or letters in a list that is given in running text:

The exhibition included (1) decorative screens, (2) ceramics, (3) ink paintings, (4) kimonos.

3. Do not confuse parentheses with square brackets. The latter are used around material you add to a quotation (see p. 190).

4. For the use of parentheses in documentation, see Chapter 14, "Documenting Sources."

5. Note the position of other punctuation with a parenthesis. The example under rule 2 is the rare exception to the rule that within a sentence, punctuation other than quotation marks never immediately precedes an opening parenthesis. Note also that in the example under rule 1, the comma *follows* the closing parenthesis:

While guest curator for the Whitney (he has since returned to the Denver Art Museum), Feder assembled a magnificent collection of masks, totems, paintings, clothing, and beadwork.

If an entire sentence is in parentheses, put the final punctuation (period, question mark, or exclamation mark) inside the closing parenthesis.

Italics

In typewritten material *underlining* is the equivalent of *italic* type:

This sentence is printed in italic type.

This sentence is understood to be printed in italic type.

1. Underline or italicize the name of a plane, ship, train, movie, radio or television program, record album, musical work, statue, painting, play, pamphlet, or book. Do not underline or italicize names of sacred works such as the Bible, the Koran, and Acts of the Apostles, or political documents such as the Magna Carta and the

Declaration of Independence. Notice that when you write about a newspaper or periodical whose title begins with the article "the," the convention is to give the article in lower case roman letters. You do not italicize it or underline it; it is not treated as part of the title; for example, the *New Yorker.*

2. Use italics only sparingly for emphasis. Sometimes, however, this method of indicating your tone of voice is exactly right:

> In 1911 Jacques Henri Lartigue was not merely as unprejudiced as a child; he *was* a child.
>
> —*John Szarkowski*

3. Use italics for foreign words that have not become a part of the English language:

> Acupuncture aims to affect the *ch'i,* a sort of vital spirit that circulates through the bodily organs.

But:

> He ate a pizza.
>
> She behaved like a prima donna.
>
> Avoid clichés.

4. You may use italics in place of quotation marks to indicate that you are providing a clarification or definition.

> Honolulu means *safe harbor.*

5. You may also use italics to identify a word or term to which you wish to call special attention:

> Claude Lévi-Strauss tells us that one of the great purposes of art is that of *miniaturization.* He points out that most works of art are miniatures, being smaller (and therefore more easily understood) than the objects they represent.

Capital Letters

Certain obvious conventions—the use of a capital for the first word in a sentence, for names (of days of the week, holidays, months, people, countries), and for words derived from names (such as pro-French)—need not be discussed here.

1. Titles of works in English are usually given according to the following formula. Use a capital for the first letter of the first word, for the first letter of the last word, and for the first letter of all other words that are not articles, conjunctions, or prepositions:

The Merchant of Venice

A Midsummer Night's Dream

Up and Out

"The Short Happy Life of Francis Macomber"

The *Oakland Bee*

2. Use a capital for a quoted sentence within a sentence, but not for a quoted phrase (unless it is at the beginning of your sentence) and not for indirect discourse:

He said, "You can even fool some of the people all of the time."

He said you can fool some people "all of the time."

He said that you can even fool some of the people all of the time.

3. Use a capital for a rank or title preceding a proper name or for a title substituting for a proper name:

She said she was Dr. Perez.

He told President Bush that the Vice President was away.

But:

Why would anyone wish to be president?

Washington was the first president.

4. Use a capital when the noun designating a family relationship is used as a substitute for a proper noun:

If Mother is busy, ask Tim.

But:

Because my mother was busy, I asked Tim.

5. Formal geographical locations (but not mere points on the compass) are capitalized:

North America

Southeast Asia

In the Southwest, rain sometimes evaporates before touching the ground.

Is Texas part of the South?

The North has its share of racism.

But:

The wind came from the south.

Texas is bordered on the north by Arkansas, Oklahoma, and New Mexico.

Do *not* capitalize the names of the seasons:

spring   summer   winter   fall

The Hyphen

The hyphen has three uses, all drawing on the etymology of the word *hyphen*, which comes from the Greek for "in one," "together."

1. Use a hyphen to attach certain prefixes to root words. *All-*, *pro-*, *ex-*, and *self-* are the most common of these (*all-powerful, ex-wife, pro-labor, self-made*), but note that even these prefixes are not always followed by a hyphen. If in doubt, check a dictionary. Prefixes before proper names are always followed by a hyphen:

anti-Semite   pro-NATO   un-American

Prefixes ending in *i* are hyphenated before a word beginning with *i*:

anti-intellectual   semi-intelligible

A hyphen is normally used to break up a triple consonant resulting from the addition of a prefix:

ill-lit

2. Use a hyphen to tie compound adjectives into a single visual unit:

out-of-date theory

twenty-three books

a no-smoking area

eighteenth- and nineteenth-century novels

The sea-tossed raft was a common nineteenth-century symbol of the human tragic condition.

But if a compound modifier follows the modified term, it is usually not hyphenated:

The theory was out of date.

3. Use a hyphen to join some compound nouns:

Scholar-teacher   philosopher-poet

Note: **Use an en dash, which is shorter than an em dash (see p. 259) but longer than a hyphen, to indicate a span of dates or page numbers.** (The en dash is located on your program's list of special characters.)

1957–1959
pp. 162–68

The Apostrophe

Use an apostrophe to indicate the possessive, to indicate a contraction, and to form certain unusual plurals.

1. The most common way to indicate the possessive of a singular noun is to add an apostrophe and then an -*s:*

a dog's life   a week's work

a mouse's tail   Keats's poems   Marx's doctrines

But some authorities suggest that for a proper noun of more than one syllable that ends in -*s* or another sibilant (-*cks*, -*x*, -*z*), it is better to add only an apostrophe:

Sophocles' plays   Chavez' ideas

When in doubt, say the name aloud and notice if you are adding an -*s.* If you are adding an -*s* when you say it, add an apostrophe and an -*s* when you write it. Our own strong preference, however, is to add an apostrophe and an *s* to all proper nouns:

Jones's book   Kansas's highways

Possessive pronouns, such as *his, hers, its, theirs, ours,* do not take an apostrophe:

> The cat shed its fur.
>
> The book is hers, not his or ours.
>
> The book is theirs.

(*Exception:* Indefinite pronouns take an apostrophe, as in "one's hopes" and "others' opinions.")

For plurals ending in -*s,* add only an apostrophe to indicate the possessive:

> the boys' father   the Smiths' house   the Joneses' car

If the plural does not end in -*s,* add an apostrophe and an -*s:*

> women's clothing   mice's eyes

Don't try to form the possessive of the title of a work (for example, of a play, a book, or a film): Write "the imagery in *The Merchant of Venice*" rather than "*The Merchant of Venice*'s imagery." Using an apostrophe gets you into the problem of whether or not to italicize the *s;* similarly, if you use an apostrophe for a work normally enclosed in quotation marks (for instance, a short story), you can't put the apostrophe and the -*s* after the quotation marks, but you can't put it inside either.

2. Use an apostrophe to indicate the omitted letters or numbers in contractions:

> She won't.
>
> It's time to go.
>
> the class of '05

3. Until recently an apostrophe was used to make plurals of words that do not usually have a plural, and (this is optional) to make the plurals of digits and letters:

> Her speech was full of if's and and's and but's.
>
> Ph.D.'s don't know everything.
>
> Mind your p's and q's. I got two A's and two B's.

He makes his 4's in two ways.

the 1920's

This use of the apostrophe is no longer standard, but it remains acceptable.

Abbreviations

In general, avoid abbreviations except in footnotes and except for certain common ones listed below. And don't use an ampersand (&) unless it appears in material you are quoting, or in a title. Abundant use of abbreviations makes an essay sound like a series of newspaper headlines. Usually, for example, *United States* is better than *U.S.*, except when an adjective: the U.S. army.

1. Abbreviations, with the first letter capitalized, are used before a name:

Dr. Bellini   Ms. Smith   St. Thomas

But:

The doctor took her temperature and eighty dollars.

2. Degrees that follow a name are abbreviated:

B.A.   D.D.S   M.D.   Ph.D.

3. Other acceptable abbreviations include:

A.D.   B.C.   A.M.   P.M.   e.g.   i.e.

(By the way, *e.g.* means *for example; i.e.* means *that is;* the two ought not to be confused. See pages 278 and 282.)

4. The name of an agency or institution. For instance, the Congress of Racial Equality, International Business Machines, and Southern Methodist University may be abbreviated by using the initial letters, capitalized and usually without periods (CORE, IBM, SMU). It is advisable to give the name in full when first mentioning it (not everyone knows that AARP means American Association of Retired Persons, for instance), and to use the abbreviation in subsequent references.

Numbers

1. Write numbers out if you can do so in fewer than three words: If you cannot, use figures:

sixteen   seventy-two   ten thousand   one-sixth

10,200 10,200,000

There are 336 dimples on a golf ball.

But write out round millions and billions, to avoid a string of zeros:

a hundred and ten million

For large round numbers you can also use a combination of figures and words:

The cockroach is about 250 million years old.

However, if a number begins a sentence, note that it should always be written out:

Two hundred and fifty million years ago the cockroach first appeared on earth.

2. Use figures in dates, addresses, decimals, percentages, page numbers, and hours followed by A.M. or P.M.:

February 29, 1900   .06 percent   6 percent   8:16 A.M.

But hours unmodified by minutes are usually written out, followed by *o'clock:*

Executions in England regularly took place at eight o'clock.

3. Use an apostrophe to indicate omitted figures:

class of '98

the '90s (but: the nineties)

4. Use an en dash to indicate a span:

1975–79

10–20

In giving inclusive numbers, give the second number in full for the numbers up through ninety-nine (2–5, 8–11, 28–34). For larger numbers, give only the last two digits of the second number (101–06; 112–14) unless the full number is necessary (198–202).

5. Dates can be given with the month first, followed by numerals, a comma, and the year:

February 10, 1999

or they can be given with the day first, then the month and then the year (without a comma after the day or month):

10 February 1999

6. BC follows the year, but AD precedes it:

10 BC
AD 200

The abbreviations BC and AD are falling out of favor, and are being replaced with BCE ("before the common era") and CE ("common era"). Both abbreviations follow the year.

7. Roman numerals are less used than formerly. Capital roman numerals were used to indicate a volume number, but volume numbers are now commonly given in arabic numerals. Capital roman numerals are still used, however, for the names of individuals in a series (Elizabeth II) and for the primary divisions of an outline; lowercase roman numerals are used for the pages in the front matter (table of contents, foreword, preface, etc.) of a book. The old custom of citing acts and scenes of a play in roman numerals and lines in arabic numerals (II.iv.17–25) is still preferred by many instructors, but the use of arabic numerals throughout (2.4.17–25) is gaining acceptance.

CHAPTER THIRTEEN

USING THE RIGHT WORD

Some things are said or written and some are not. More precisely, anything can be said or written, but only some things are acceptable to the ears and minds of readers. "She don't know nothing about it" has been said and will be said again, but readers who encounter such a sentence will probably judge the speaker as an uneducated person with little of interest to say—and immediately tune out.

Although such a double negative is not acceptable today, it used to be: Chaucer's courteous Knight "never spoke no baseness," and Shakespeare's courtly Mercutio, in *Romeo and Juliet*, "will not budge for no man." But things have changed; what was acceptable in the Middle Ages and the Renaissance (for example, emptying chamber pots into the gutter) would not be acceptable now. And some of what was once unacceptable has become acceptable. At the beginning of the twentieth century, grammarians suggested that one cannot use *drive* in speaking of a car; one drives (forces into motion) an ox, or even a person ("He drove her to distraction"), but not a machine. A century of usage, however, has erased all objections.

This chapter presents a list of expressions that, although commonly used, set many teeth on edge. Several decades from now some of these expressions may be as acceptable as "drive a car"; but we are writing for today, and we might as well try to hold the attention of today's readers by following today's taste in language.

A Note on Idioms

An idiom (from a Greek word meaning "peculiar") is a fixed group of words, peculiar to a given language. Thus in English we say, "I took a walk," but Germans "make a walk," Spaniards "give a walk," and

Japanese "do a walk." (If we think the German, Spanish, and Japanese expressions are odd, we might well ask ourselves where it is that we take a walk to.) If a visitor from Argentina says, in English, that she "gave a walk," she is using *un*idiomatic English, just as anyone who says he knows a poem "at heart" instead of "by heart" is using unidiomatic English.

Probably most unidiomatic expressions use the wrong preposition, as in the following examples:

Unidiomatic	Idiomatic
comply to	comply with
superior with	superior to

Sometimes while we write, or even while we speak, we are unsure of the idiom and we pause to try an alternative—"parallel with?" "parallel to?"—and we don't know which sounds more natural, more idiomatic. At such moments, more often than not, either is acceptable, but if you are in doubt, check a dictionary. (*The American Heritage Dictionary* has notes on usage following the definitions of hundreds of its words.)

In any case, if you are a native speaker of English, when you read your draft you will probably detect unidiomatic expressions such as *superior with;* that is, you will hear something that sounds odd, and so you will change it to something that sounds familiar, idiomatic—here, *superior to.* If any unidiomatic expressions remain in your essay, the trouble may be that an effort to write impressively has led you to use unfamiliar language. A reader who sees such unidiomatic language may sense that you are straining for an effect. Try rewriting the passage in your own voice.

If English is not your first language and you are not yet fluent in it, plan to spend extra time revising and editing your work. Check prepositional phrases with special care. In addition to using a college edition of an English language dictionary, consult reference works designed with the international or bilingual student in mind. One compact book our students find particularly useful is Michael Swan's *Practical English Usage,* published by Oxford University Press. But don't neglect another invaluable resource: students who are native speakers. They will usually be able to tell you whether or not a phrase "sounds right," though they may not know why.

DILBERT reprinted by permission of United Feature Syndicate, Inc.

A Writer's Glossary

a, an Use *a* before words beginning with a consonant ("a book") or with a vowel sounded as a consonant ("a one-way ticket," "a university"). Use *an* before words beginning with a vowel ("an egg") including those beginning with a silent *h* ("an egg," "an hour"). If an initial *h* is pronounced, *a* is normal ("a history course") but if the accent is not on the first syllable, *an* is acceptable, as in "*an* historian."

above Try to avoid writing *for the above reasons, in view of the above*, or *as above*. These expressions sound unpleasantly legalistic. Substitute *for these reasons*, or *therefore*, or some such expression or word.

academics Only two meanings of this noun are widely accepted: (1) "members of an institution of higher learning," and (2) "persons who are academic in background or outlook." Avoid using it to mean "academic subjects," as in "Students should pay attention not only to academics but also to recreation." *Revised:* "Students should pay attention not only to their courses but also to recreation."

accept, except *Accept* means "to receive with consent." *Except* means "to exclude" or "excluding."

affect, effect *Affect* is usually a verb, meaning (1) "to influence, to produce an effect, to impress," or (2) "to pretend, to put on," as in "He affected an English accent." Psychologists use it as a noun for "feeling" ("The patient experienced no affect"). *Effect*, as a verb, means "to bring about" ("The workers effected the rescue in less than an hour"). As a noun, *effect* means "result" ("The effect was negligible").

African American Both forms are acceptable to denote an American of African ancestry. In recent years these words have been preferred to *black*.

aggravate To worsen, to increase for the worse, as in "Smoking aggravated the irritation." Although it is widely used to mean "annoy" ("He aggravated me"), many readers are annoyed by such a use.

all ready, already *All ready* means "everything is ready." *Already* means "by this time."

all right, alright The first of these is the preferable spelling; for some readers it is the only acceptable spelling.

all together, altogether *All together* means that members of a group act or are gathered together ("They voted all together"); *altogether* is an adverb meaning "entirely," "wholly" ("This is altogether unnecessary").

allusion, reference, illusion An *allusion* is an implied or indirect reference. "As Lincoln says" is a *reference* to Lincoln, but "As a great man has said," along with a phrase quoted from the Gettysburg Address, constitutes an *allusion* to Lincoln. *Allusion* has nothing to do with *illusion* (a deception). Note the spelling (especially the second *i*) in "disillusioned" (left without illusions, disenchanted).

almost See *most.*

a lot Two words (not *alot*).

ambiguous, ambivalent *Ambiguous* refers to things that are unclear; *ambivalent* refers to people who are uncertain. One could say that the reasons for Hamlet's inaction are ambiguous; his famous soliloquy, which begins with the question, "to be, or not to be," suggests his ambivalence.

among, between See *between.*

amount, number *Amount* refers to bulk or quantity: "A small amount of gas was still in the tank." Use *number*, not *amount*, to refer to separate (countable) units: "He did not know the number of gallons that the tank held." Similarly, "A large number of people heard the lecture" (not "a large amount of people"). Note also "an amount of money" but "a number of dollars."

analyzation Unacceptable; use *analysis.*

and etc. Because *etc.* is an abbreviation for *et cetera* ("and others"), the *and* in *and etc.* is redundant. (See also the entry on *et cetera.*)

and/or Acceptable, but a legalism and unpleasant-sounding. Often *or* by itself will do, as in "students who know Latin or Italian." When *or* is not enough ("Scripts for the second season of *The Sopranos* were written by Todd Kessler and/or David Chase") it is better to recast ("Scripts for the second season of *The Sopranos* were written by Todd Kessler or David Chase, or both").

ante, anti   *Ante* means "before" (*antebellum,* "before the Civil War"); *anti* means "against" (*antivivisectionist*). Hyphenate *anti* before capitals (*anti-Semitism*) and before *i* (*anti-intellectual*).

anxious   Best reserved for uses that suggest anxiety ("He was anxious before the examination"), though some authorities now accept it in the sense of "eager" ("He was anxious to serve the community").

anybody   One word ("Do you know anybody here?"). If two words (*any body*), you mean any corpse ("Several people died in the fire, but the police cannot identify any body").

any more, anymore   *Any more* is used as an adjective: "I don't want any more meat" (here *any more* says something about meat). *Anymore* (one word) is used as an adverb: "I don't eat meat anymore" (here *anymore* says something about eating).

anyone   One word ("Why would anyone think that?"), unless you mean "any one thing," as in "Here are three books; you may take any one." *Anyone* is an indefinite singular pronoun meaning *any person:* "If anyone has a clue, he or she should call the police." In an astounding advertisement, the writer moved from *anyone* (singular) to *their* (third person plural) to *your* (second person): "Anyone who thinks a Yonex racquet has improved their game, please raise your hand."

area of   Like *field of* and *topic of* ("the field of literature," "the topic of politics"), *area of* can usually be deleted. "The area of marketing" equals "marketing."

around   Avoid using *around* in place of *about:* "He wrote it in about three hours." See also *centers on.*

as, like   *As* is a conjunction; use it in forming comparisons, to introduce clauses. (A clause has a subject and a verb.)

You can learn to write, as you can learn to swim.

Huck speaks the truth as he sees it.

Like is a preposition; use it to introduce prepositional phrases:

He looks like me.

Like Hamlet, Laertes has lost a father.

She thinks like a lawyer.

A short rule: use *like* when it introduces a noun *not* followed by a verb: "Nothing grabs people like *People.*"

Writers who are fearful of incorrectly using *like* resort to cumbersome evasions: "He eats in the same manner that a pig eats." But there's nothing wrong with "He eats like a pig."

Asian, Oriental   *Asian* as a noun and as an adjective is the preferred word. *Oriental* (from *oriens*, "rising sun," "east") is in disfavor because it implies a Eurocentric view—that is, that things "oriental" are east of the European colonial powers who invented the term. Similarly, **Near East, Middle East,** and **Far East** are terms that are based on a Eurocentric view. No brief substitute has been agreed on for *Near East* and *Middle East*, but *East Asia* is now regarded as preferable to *Far East.*

as of now   Best deleted, or replaced by *now.* Not "As of now I don't smoke" but "Now I don't smoke" or "I don't smoke now" or "I don't smoke."

aspect   Literally, "a view from a particular point," but it has come to mean *topic*, as in "Several aspects should be considered." Try to get a sharper word; for example, "Several problems should be considered," or "Several consequences should be considered."

as such   Often meaningless, as in "Tragedy as such evokes pity."

as to   Usually *about* is preferable. Not "I know nothing as to the charges," but "I know nothing about the charges."

bad, badly   *Bad* used to be only an adjective ("a bad movie"), and *badly* was an adverb ("she sings badly"). In "I felt bad," *bad* describes the subject, not the verb. (Compare "I felt happy," or "I felt good about getting a raise." After verbs of appearing, such as "feel," "look," "seem," "taste," an adjective, not an adverb, is used. If you are in doubt, substitute a word for *bad*, for instance *sad*, and see what you say. Since you would say "I feel sad about his failure," you can say "I feel bad. . . .") But "badly" is acceptable and even preferred by many. Note, however, this distinction: "This meat smells bad" (an adjective describing the meat), and "Because I have a stuffed nose I smell badly" (an adverb describing my ability to smell something).

being   Do not use *being* as a main verb, as in "The trouble being that his reflexes were too slow." The result is a sentence fragment. See pages 245–247.

being that, being as   A sentence such as "Being that she was a stranger . . ." sounds like an awkward translation from the Latin. Use *because.*

beside, besides   *Beside* means "at the side of." Because *besides* can mean either "in addition to" or "other than," it is ambiguous, as in "Something besides TB caused his death." It is best, then, to use *in addition to* or *other than*, depending on what you mean.

between   Only English teachers who have had a course in Middle English are likely to know that *between* comes from *by twain*. And only English teachers and editors are likely to object to its use (and to call for *among*) when more than two are concerned, as in "among the three of us." Note, too, that even conservative usage accepts *between* in reference to more than two when the items are at the moment paired: "Negotiations *between* Israel and Egypt, Syria, and Lebanon seem stalled." *Between*, a preposition, takes an object ("between you and me"): not "between you and I."

biannually, bimonthly, biweekly   Every two years, every two months, every two weeks (*not* twice a year, etc.). Twice a year is *semi-annually*, i.e., "half yearly." Because *biannually*, *bimonthly*, and *biweekly* are commonly misunderstood, it is best to avoid them and to say "every two. . . ."

Black, black   Although one sometimes sees the word capitalized when it refers to race, most publishers use a lowercase letter, making it consistent with *white*, which is never capitalized. See also *African American*.

can, may   When schoolchildren asked "Can I leave the room?" their teachers used to correct them thus: "You *can* leave the room if you have legs, but you *may not* leave the room until you receive permission." In short, *can* indicates physical possibility, *may* indicates permission. But because "you may not" and "why mayn't I?" sound not merely polite but stiff, *can* is usually preferred except in formal contexts.

capital, capitol   A *capital* is a city that is a center of government. *Capital* can also mean wealth ("It takes capital to start a business"). A *capitol* is a building in which legislators meet. Notice the distinction in the following sentence: "Washington, D.C., is the nation's capital; the capitol ought to have a gold dome."

centers on, centers around   Use *centers on*, because *center* refers to a point, not to a movement around.

Chicana, Chicano   A Mexican American (female or male, respectively; the male plural, *Chicanos*, is used for a group consisting of males and females). Although the term sometimes was felt to be derogatory, today it usually implies ethnic pride.

collective nouns   A collective noun, singular in form, names a collection of individuals. Examples: *audience, band, committee, crowd, jury, majority, minority, team.* When you are thinking chiefly of the whole as a unit, use a singular verb (and a singular pronoun, if any): "The majority rules"; "The jury is announcing its verdict." But when you are thinking of the individuals, use a plural verb (and pronoun, if any): "The majority are lawyers"; "The jury are divided and they probably cannot agree." If the plural sounds odd, you can usually rewrite: "The jurors are divided and they probably cannot agree."

compare, contrast   To *compare* is to note likenesses or differences: "Compare a motorcycle with a bicycle." To *contrast* is to emphasize differences.

complement, compliment   *Complement* as a noun means "that which completes"; as a verb, "to fill out, to complete." *Compliment* as a noun is an expression of praise; as a verb it means "to offer praise."

comprise   To include, contain, consist of: "The university comprises two colleges and a medical school" (not "is comprised of"). Conservative authorities hold that "to be comprised of" is always incorrect, and they reject the form one often hears: "Two colleges and a medical school comprise the university." Here the word should be *compose*, not *comprise*.

concept   Should often be deleted. For "The concept of the sales tax is regressive" write "The sales tax is regressive."

contact   Because it is vague, avoid using *contact* as a verb. *Not* "I contacted him" but "I spoke with him" or "I wrote to him," or whatever.

continual, continuous   Conservative authorities hold that *continuous* means "uninterrupted," as in "It rained continuously for six hours"; *continually* means "repeated often, recurring at short intervals," as in "For a year he continually wrote letters to her."

contrast, compare   See *compare.*

could have, could of   See *of.*

criteria   Plural of *criterion;* hence it is always incorrect to speak of "a criteria," or to say "The criteria is . . ." Correct: "The criterion is simple"; "the criteria are unfair."

data   Plural of *datum.* Although some social scientists speak of "this data," "these data" is preferable: "These data are puzzling." Because the singular, *datum,* is rare and sounds odd, it is best to substitute *fact* or *figure* for *datum.*

different from Prefer it to *different than,* unless you are convinced that in a specific sentence *different from* sounds terribly wrong, as in "These two books are more different than I had expected." (In this example, "more," not "different," governs "than." But this sentence, though correct, is awkward and therefore it should be revised: "These two books differ more than I had expected.")

dilemma A situation requiring a choice between equally undesirable alternatives; not every difficulty or plight or predicament is a *dilemma.* Not "Her dilemma was that she had nowhere to go," but "Her dilemma was whether to go out or to stay home: one was frightening, the other was embarrassing." And note the spelling (two *m*'s, no *n*).

disinterested Though the word is often used to mean "indifferent," "unconcerned," "uninterested," reserve it to mean "impartial": "A judge should be disinterested."

due to Some people, holding that *due to* cannot modify a verb (as in "He failed due to illness"), tolerate it only when it modifies a noun or pronoun ("His failure was due to illness"). They also insist that it cannot begin a sentence ("Due to illness, he failed"). In fact, however, daily usage accepts both. But because it almost always sounds stiff, try to substitute *because of,* or *through.*

due to the fact that Wordy for *because.*

each Although many authorities hold that *each,* as a subject, is singular, even when followed by "them" ("Each of them is satisfactory"), some authorities accept and even favor the plural ("Each of them are satisfactory"). But it is usually better to avoid the awkwardness by substituting *all* for *each:* "All of them are satisfactory." When *each* refers to a plural subject, the verb must be plural: "They each have a book"; "We each are trying." *Each* cannot be made into a possessive; you cannot say "Each's opinion is acceptable."

effect See *affect.*

e.g. Abbreviation for *exempli gratia,* Latin for "for example." It is thus different from *i.e.* (an abbreviation for *id est,* Latin for "that is"). "E.g." (not italicized) introduces an example: "common pets (e.g., cats, dogs, and birds) have few diseases that can be transmitted to humans." "I.e." (also not italicized) introduces a definition: "Pets (i.e., animals kept for companionship) cost Americans billions of dollars annually." Because these two abbreviations of Latin words are often confused, it may be preferable to avoid them and use their English equivalents.

either . . . or, neither . . . nor   If the subjects are singular, use a singular verb: "Either the boy or the girl is lying." If one of the subjects joined by *or* or *nor* is plural, most grammarians say that the verb agrees with the nearer subject, thus: "A tree or two shrubs are enough," or "Two shrubs or a tree is enough." But because the singular verb in the second of these sentences may sound odd, follow the first construction; that is, put the plural subject nearer to the verb and use a plural verb. Another point about *either . . . or:* In this construction, "either" serves as advance notice that two equal possibilities are in the offing. Beware of putting "either" too soon, as in "Either he is a genius or a lunatic." Better: "He is either a genius or a lunatic."

enthuse   Objectionable to many readers. For "He enthused," say "He was enthusiastic." Use *enthuse* only in the sense of "to be excessively enthusiastic," "to gush."

et cetera, etc.   Latin for "and other things"; if you mean "and other people," you need *et al.*, short for *et alii*. Because *etc.* is vague, its use is usually inadvisable. Not "He studied mathematics, etc." but "He studied mathematics, history, economics, and French." Or, if the list is long, cut it by saying something a little more informative than *etc.*—for example, "He studied mathematics, history, and other liberal arts subjects." Even *and so forth* or *and so on* is preferable to *etc.* Confine *etc.* (and most other abbreviations, including *et al.*) to footnotes, and even in footnotes try to avoid it.

Eurocentric language   Language focused on Europe—for instance, the word *Hispanic* when used to refer not to persons from Spain but persons from Mexico and Central and South America, who may in fact have little or no Spanish heritage. (The Latin name for Spain was *Hispania*.) Similarly, the terms *Near East* and *Far East* represent a European point of view (near to, and far from Europe), objectionable to many persons not of European heritage. See *Asian* and *Hispanic*.

everybody, everyone   These take a singular verb ("Everybody is here"), and a pronoun referring to them is usually singular ("Everybody thinks his problems are suitable topics of conversation"), but use a plural pronoun if the singular would seem unnatural ("Everybody was there, weren't they?"). To avoid the sexism of "Everybody thinks his problems . . ." revise to "All people think their problems. . . ."

examples, instances See *instances.*

except See *accept.*

exists Often unnecessary and a sign of wordiness. Not "The problem that *exists* here is" but "The problem here is."

expound Usually pretentious for *explain* or *say.* To *expound* is to give a methodical explanation of theological matters.

facet Literally "little face," especially one of the surfaces of a gem. Don't use it (and don't use *aspect* or *factor* either) to mean "part" or "topic." It is most acceptable when, close to its literal meaning, it suggests a new appearance, as when a gem is turned: "Another *facet* appears when we see this law from the taxpayer's point of view."

the fact that Usually wordy. "Because of the fact that boys played female roles in Elizabethan drama" can be reduced to "Because boys played female roles in Elizabethan drama."

factor Strictly speaking, a *factor* helps to produce a result. Although *factor* is often used in the sense of "point" ("Another factor to be studied is . . ."), such use is often wordy. "The possibility of plagiarism is a factor that must be considered" simply adds up to "The possibility of plagiarism must be considered." *Factor* is almost never the precise word: "the factors behind Gatsby's actions" are, more precisely, "Gatsby's motives."

famous, notorious See *notorious.*

Far East See *Asian.*

farther, further Some purists claim that *farther* always refers to distance and *further* to time ("The gymnasium is farther than the library"; "Let us think further about this").

fatalistic, pessimistic *Fatalistic* means "characterized by the belief that all events are predetermined and therefore inevitable"; *pessimistic,* "characterized by the belief that the world is evil," or, less gloomily, "expecting the worst."

fewer, less See *less.*

field of See *area of.*

firstly, secondly Acceptable, but it is better to use *first, second.*

former, latter These words are acceptable, but they are often annoying because they force the reader to reread earlier material in order to locate what *the former* and *the latter* refer to. The expressions are legitimately used in order to avoid repeating lengthy terms, but if you are talking about an easily repeated subject—say, Lincoln and Grant—don't hesitate to replace *the former* and *the latter* with their names. The repetition will clarify rather than bore.

good, well   *Good* is an adjective ("a good book"). *Well* is usually an adverb ("She writes well"). Standard English does not accept "She writes good." But Standard English requires *good* after verbs of appearing, such as *seems, looks, sounds, tastes*: "it looks good," "it sounds good." *Well* can also be an adjective meaning *healthy:* "I am well."

graduate, graduate from   Use *from* if you name the institution or if you use a substitute word as in "She graduated from high school"; if the institution (or substitute) is not named, *from* is omitted: "She graduated in 1983." The use of the passive ("She was graduated from high school") is acceptable but sounds fussy to many.

he or she, his or her   These expressions are awkward, but the implicit male chauvinism in the generic use of the male pronoun ("A citizen should exercise his right to vote") may be more offensive than the awkwardness of *he or she* and *his or her*. Moreover, sometimes the male pronoun, when used for males and females, is ludicrous, as in "The more violence a youngster sees on television, regardless of his age or sex, the more aggressive he is likely to be." Do what you can to avoid the dilemma. Sometimes you can use the plural *their:* "Students are expected to hand in their papers on Monday" (instead of "The student is expected to hand in his or her paper on Monday"). Or eliminate the possessive: "The student must hand in a paper on Monday." See *man;* see also "Avoiding Sexist Language," pages 81–83.

Hispanic, Latina, Latino   A person who traces his or her origin to a Spanish-speaking country is a *Hispanic.* (Hispania was the Latin name for Spain.) But some people object to the term when applied to persons in the Western Hemisphere, arguing that it overemphasizes the European influence on ethnic identity and neglects the indigenous and black heritages. Many who object to *Hispanic* prefer to call a person of Latin-American descent a *Latina* (the feminine form) or a *Latino* (the masculine form), partly because these words are themselves Latin-American words. (The male plural, *Latinos,* commonly is used for a group consisting of males and females.) But many people object that these words too obscure the unique cultural heritages of, say, Mexican Americans, Cuban Americans, and Puerto Ricans.

hopefully   Commonly used to mean "I hope" or "It is hoped" (*"Hopefully*, the rain will stop soon"), but it is best to avoid what some consider a dangling modifier. After all, the rain itself is not hopeful. If you mean "I hope the rain will stop soon," say exactly that. Notice, too, that *hopefully* is often evasive. If the president of the college says, "Hopefully tuition will not rise next year," don't think that you have heard a promise to fight against an increase; you only have heard someone evade making a promise. In short, confine *hopefully* to its adverbial use, meaning "in a hopeful manner": "Hopefully he uttered a prayer."

however   Independent clauses (for instance, "He tried" and "He failed") should not be linked with a *however* preceded by a comma. Incorrect: "He tried, however he failed." What is required is a period ("He tried. However, he failed") or a semicolon before *however* ("He tried; however, he failed").

the idea that   Usually dull and wordy. Not "The idea that we grow old is frightening," but "That we grow old is frightening," or (probably better) "Growing old is frightening."

identify   When used in the psychological sense, "to associate oneself closely with a person or an institution," it is preferable to include a reflexive pronoun, thus: "He identified himself with Hamlet," *not* "He identified with Hamlet."

i.e.   Latin for *id est*, "that is." The English words are preferable to the Latin abbreviation. On the distinction between *i.e.* and *e.g.*, see *e.g.*

immanent, imminent   *Immanent*, "remaining within, intrinsic"; *imminent*, "likely to occur soon, impending."

imply, infer   The writer or speaker *implies* (suggests); the perceiver *infers* (draws a conclusion): "Karl Marx implied that . . . but his modern disciples infer from his writings that. . . ." Although *infer* is widely used for *imply*, preserve the distinction.

incidence, incident   The *incidence* is the extent or frequency of an occurrence: "The incidence of violent crime in Tokyo is very low." The plural, *incidences*, is rarely used: "The incidences of crime and of fire in Tokyo. . . ." An *incident* is one occurrence: "The incident happened yesterday." The plural is *incidents:* "The two incidents happened simultaneously."

individual   Avoid using the word to mean only "person": "He was a generous individual." But it is precise when it implicitly makes a contrast with a group: "In a money-mad society, he was a generous individual"; "Although the faculty did not take a stand on this issue, faculty members as individuals spoke out."

instances Instead of *in many instances* use *often.* Strictly speaking an *instance* is not an object or incident in itself but one offered as an example. Thus "another instance of his failure to do his duty" (not "In three instances he failed to do his duty").

irregardless Unacceptable; use *regardless.*

it is Usually this expression needlessly delays the subject: "It is unlikely that many students will attend the lecture" could just as well be "Few students are likely to attend the lecture."

its, it's The first is a possessive pronoun ("The flock lost its leader"); the second is a contraction of *it is* ("It's a wise father that knows his child."). You'll have no trouble if you remember that the possessive pronoun *its*, like other possessive pronouns such as *our, his, their,* does *not* use an apostrophe.

kind of Singular, as in "That kind of movie bothers me." (*Not:* "Those kind of movies bother me.") If, however, you are really talking about more than one kind, use *kinds* and be sure that the demonstrative pronoun and the verb are plural: "Those kinds of movies bother me." Notice also that the phrase is *kind of,* not *kind of a.* Not "What *kind of a* car does she drive?" but "What *kind of* car does she drive?"

Latina, Latino See *Hispanic.*

latter See *former.*

lay, lie *To lay* means "to put, to set, to cause to rest." It takes an object: "May I lay the coats on the table?" The past tense and the participle are *laid:* "I laid the coats on the table"; "I have laid the coats on the table." *To lie* means "to recline," and it does not take an object: "When I am tired I lie down." The past tense is *lay,* the participle is *lain:* "Yesterday I lay down"; "I have lain down hundreds of times without wishing to get up."

lend, loan The usual verb is *lend:* "Lend me a pen." The past tense and the participle are both *lent. Loan* is a noun: "This isn't a gift, it's a loan." But, curiously, *loan* as a verb is acceptable in past forms: "I loaned him my bicycle." In its present form ("I often loan money") it is used chiefly by bankers.

less, fewer *Less* (as an adjective) refers to bulk amounts (also called mass nouns): less milk, less money, less time. *Fewer* refers to separate (countable) items: fewer glasses of milk, fewer dollars, fewer hours.

lifestyle, life-style, life style All three forms are acceptable, but because many readers regard the expression as imprecise, try to find a substitute such as *values.*

like, as See *as.*

literally It means "to the letter," "exactly as stated," and "strictly in accord with the primary meaning; not metaphorically." It is not a mere intensive. "He was literally dead" means that he was a corpse; if he was merely exhausted, *literally* won't do. You cannot be "literally stewed" (except by cannibals), "literally tickled pink," or "literally walking on air."

loose, lose *Loose* is an adjective ("The nail is loose"); *lose* is a verb ("Don't lose the nail").

the majority of Usually a wordy way of saying *most.* Of course if you mean "a bare majority," say so; otherwise *most* will usually do. Certainly "The majority of the basement is used for a cafeteria" should be changed to "Most of the basement is used for a cafeteria." *Majority* can take either a singular verb or a plural verb. When *majority* refers to a collection—for example, a group acting as a body—the verb is singular, as in "The majority has withdrawn its support from the mayor." But when *majority* refers to members of a group acting as individuals, as in "The majority of voters in this district vote Republican," a plural verb (here, "vote") is usually preferred. If either construction sounds odd, use "most," with a plural verb: "Most voters in this district vote Republican."

man, mankind The use of these words in reference to males and females sometimes is ludicrous, as in "Man, being a mammal, breast-feeds his young." But even when not ludicrous the practice is sexist, as in "man's brain" and "the greatness of mankind." Consider using such words as *human being, person, humanity, humankind, people.* Similarly, for "manmade," *artificial* or *synthetic* may do. See also "Avoiding Sexist Language," pages 81–83.

may, can See *can.*

me The right word in such expressions as "between you and me" and "They gave it to John and me." It is the object of verbs and of prepositions. In fact, *me* rather than *I* is the usual form after any verb, including the verb *to be;* "It is me" is nothing to be ashamed of. See the entry on *myself.*

medium, media *Medium* is singular, *media* is plural: "TV is the medium to which most children are most exposed. Other media include film, radio, and publishing." It follows, then, that *mass media* takes a plural verb: "The mass media exert an enormous influence."

Middle East See *Asian*.

might of, might have; must of, must have *Might of* and *must of* are colloquial for *might have* and *must have*. In writing, use the *have* form: "He might have cheated; in fact, he must have cheated."

more Avoid writing a false (incomplete) comparison such as: "His essay includes several anecdotes, making it more enjoyable." Delete "more" unless there really is a comparison with another essay. On false comparisons see also the entry on *other*.

most, almost Although it is acceptable in speech to say "most everyone" and "most anybody," it is preferable in writing to use "almost everyone," "almost anybody." But of course: "Most students passed."

myself *Myself* is often mistakenly used for *I* or *me*, as in "They praised Tony and myself," or "Professor Chen and myself examined the dead rat." In the first example, *me* is the word to use; after all, if Tony hadn't been there the sentence would say, "They praised me." (No one would say, "They praised myself.") Similarly, in the second example if Professor Chen were not involved, the sentence would run, "I examined the dead rat," so what is needed here is simply "Professor Chen and I examined. . . ."

In general, use *myself* only when (1) it refers to the subject of the sentence ("I look out for myself"; "I washed myself") or (2) when it is an intensive: ("I myself saw the break-in"; "I myself have not experienced racism").

nature You can usually delete *the nature of*, as in "The nature of my contribution is not political but psychological."

Near East See *Asian*.

needless to say The reader may well wonder why you go on to say it. Of course this expression is used to let readers know that they are probably familiar with what comes next, but usually *of course* will better serve as this sign.

Negro Capitalized, whether a noun or an adjective, though *white* is not. In recent years *Negro* has been replaced by *black* or *African American*.

neither . . . nor See *either . . . or*.

nobody, no one, none *Nobody* and *no one* are singular, requiring a singular verb ("Nobody believes this," "No one knows"); but they can be referred to by a plural pronoun: "Nobody believes this, do they?" "No one knows, do they?" *None*, though it comes from *no one*, almost always requires a plural verb when it refers to people ("Of the ten people present, none are students") and a singular verb when it refers to things ("Of the five assigned books, none is worth reading").

not only . . . but also Keep in mind these two points: (1) many readers object to the omission of "also" in such a sentence as "She not only brought up two children but practiced law"—it's preferable to write "She not only brought up two children but also practiced law"—and (2) all readers dislike a faulty parallel, as in "She not only is bringing up two children but practices law." ("Is bringing up" needs to be paralleled with "is also practicing.")

notorious Widely and unfavorably known; not merely famous, but famous for some discreditable trait or deed.

not . . . un- Such an expression as "not unfamiliar" is useful only if it conveys something different from the affirmative. Compare the frostiness of "I am not unfamiliar with your methods" with "I am familiar with your methods." If the negative has no evident advantage, use the affirmative.

number, amount See *amount*.

a number of Requires a plural verb: "A number of women are presidents of corporations." But when *number* is preceded by *the* it requires a singular verb: "The number of women who are presidents is small." (The plural noun after *number* of course may require a plural verb, as in "women are," but the subject of the sentence is *the number*, which itself remains singular; hence its verb is singular, as in "is small.")

of Be careful not to use *of* when *have* is required. Not "He might of died in the woods," but "He might have died in the woods." Note that what we often hear as "would've" or "should've" or "must've" or "could've" is "would have" or "should have" or "must have" or "could have," *not* "would of," etc.

off of Use *off* or *from*: "Take if off the table"; "He jumped from the bridge."

often-times Use *often* instead.

old-fashioned, old-fashion Only the first is acceptable.

one British usage accepts the shift from *one* to *he* in "One begins to die the moment he is born," but American usage prefers "One begins to die the moment one is born." A shift from *one* to *you* ("One begins to die the moment you are born") is unacceptable. As a pronoun, *one* can be useful in impersonal statements such as the sentence about dying, at the beginning of this entry, where it means "a person," but don't use it as a disguise for yourself ("One objects to Smith's argument"). Try to avoid *one;* one *one* usually leads to another, resulting in a sentence that, in James Thurber's words, "sounds like a trombone solo" ("If one takes oneself too seriously, one begins to . . ."). See also *you.*

one of Takes a plural noun, and if this is followed by a clause, the preferred verb is plural: "one of those students who are," "one of those who feel." Thus, in such a sentence as "One of the coaches who have resigned is now seeking reinstatement," notice that "have" is correct; the antecedent of "who" (the subject of the verb) is "coaches," which is plural. Coaches have resigned, though "one . . . is seeking reinstatement." But in such an expression as "one out of a hundred," the following verb may be singular or plural ("One out of a hundred is," "One out of a hundred are").

only Be careful where you put it. The classic textbook example points out that in the sentence "I hit him in the eye," *only* can be inserted in seven places (beginning in front of "I" and ending after "eye") with at least six different meanings. Try to put it just before the expression it qualifies. Thus, not "Presidential aides are only responsible to one person," but "Presidential aides are responsible to only one person" (or "to one person only").

oral, verbal See *verbal.*

Oriental See *Asian.*

other Often necessary in comparisons. "No American president served as many terms as Franklin Roosevelt" absurdly implies that Roosevelt was not an American president. The sentence should be revised to "No other American president served as many terms as Franklin Roosevelt."

per Usually it sounds needlessly technical ("twice per hour") or disturbingly impersonal ("as per your request"). Preferable: "twice an hour," "according to your request," or "as you requested."

per cent, percent, percentage The first two of these are interchangeable; both mean "per hundred," "out of a hundred," as in "Ninety per cent (or percent) of the students were white." *Per cent* and *percent* are always accompanied by a number (written out, or in figures). It is usually better to write out *per cent* or *percent* than to use a per cent sign (12%), except in technical or statistical papers. *Percentage* means "a proportion or share in relation to the whole," as in "A very large percentage of the student body is white." Many authorities insist that *percentage* is never preceded by a number. Do not use percentage to mean "a few," as in "Only a percentage of students attended the lecture"; a percentage can be as large as 99.99. It is usually said that with *per cent*, *percent*, and *percentage*, whether the verb is singular or plural depends on the number of the noun that follows the word, thus: "Ninety percent of their books are paperbacks"; "Fifty percent of their library is worthless"; "A large percentage of their books are worthless." But some readers (including the authors of this book) prefer a singular verb after *percentage* unless the resulting sentence is as grotesque as this one: "A large percentage of the students is unmarried." Still, rather than say a "percentage . . . are," we would recast the sentence: "A large percentage of the student body is unmarried," or "Many (or "Most," or whatever) of the students are unmarried."

per se Latin for "by itself." Usually sounds legalistic or pedantic, as in "Meter per se has an effect."

pessimistic See *fatalistic.*

phenomenon, phenomena The plural is *phenomena;* thus, "these phenomena" but "this phenomenon."

plus Unattractive and imprecise as a noun meaning "asset" or "advantage" ("When he applied for the job, his appearance was a plus"), and equally unattractive as a substitute for *moreover* ("The examination was easy, plus I had studied") or as a substitute for *and* ("I studied the introduction plus the first chapter").

politics Preferably singular ("Ethnic politics has been a strong force for a century") but a plural verb is acceptable.

precede, proceed To *precede* is to go before or ahead ("*X* precedes *Y*"). To *proceed* is to go forward ("The spelling lesson proceeded smoothly").

prejudice, prejudiced *Prejudice* is a noun: "It is impossible to live entirely without prejudice." But use the past participle *prejudiced* as an adjective: "They were prejudiced against me from the start."

preventative, preventive Both are acceptable but the second form is now used by writers on medicine ("preventive medicine"); *preventative* therefore has come to seem amateurish.

principal, principle *Principal* is (1) an adjective meaning "main," "chief," "most important" ("The principal arguments against IQ testing are three"), and (2) a noun meaning "the chief person" ("Ms. Murphy was the principal of Jefferson High") or "the chief thing" ("She had so much money she could live on the interest and not touch the principal"). *Principle* is always a noun meaning "rule" or "fundamental truth" ("It was against his principles to eat meat").

prior to Pretentious for *before*.

protagonist Literally, the first actor, and, by extension, the chief actor. It is odd, therefore, to speak of "the protagonists" in a single literary work or occurrence. Note also that the prefix is *proto*, "first," not *pro*, "for"; it does *not* mean one who strives for something.

quite Usually a word to delete, along with *definitely, pretty, rather,* and *very*. *Quite* used to mean "completely" ("I quite understand") but it has come also to mean "to a considerable degree," and so it is ambiguous as well as vague.

quotation, quote Quotation is a noun, quote is a verb. "I will quote Churchill" is fine, but not "these quotes from Churchill." (In fact, "quote" as a noun is gaining acceptance, but you should avoid this usage because it offends many readers.) And remember, you may *quote* one of Hamlet's speeches, but Hamlet does not *quote* them; he says them.

rather Avoid use with strong adjectives. "Rather intelligent" makes sense, but "rather tremendous" does not. "Rather brilliant" probably means "bright"; "rather terrifying" probably means "frightening," "rather unique" probably means "unusual." Get the right adjective, not *rather* and the wrong adjective.

the reason . . . is because Usually *because* is enough (not "The reason they fail is because they don't study," but simply "They fail because they don't study"). Similarly, *the reason why* can usually be reduced to *why*. Notice, too, that because *reason* is a noun, it cannot neatly govern a *because* clause: not "The reason for his absence is because he was sick," but "The reason for his absence was illness."

rebut, refute To rebut is to argue against, but not necessarily successfully. If you mean "to disprove," use *disprove* or *refute*.

in regard to, with regard to Often wordy for *about, concerning,* or *on*, and sometimes even these words are unnecessary. Compare: "She knew a great deal in regard to jazz"; "She knew a great deal about jazz." Compare: "Hemingway's story is often misunderstood with regard to Robert Wilson's treatment of Margot Macomber"; "In

Hemingway's story, Robert Wilson's treatment of Margot Macomber is often misunderstood."

relate to   Usually a vague expression, best avoided, as in "I can relate to Hedda Gabler." Does it mean "respond favorably to," "identify myself with," "interact with" (and how can a reader "interact with" a character in a play?). Use *relate to* only in the sense of "have connection with" (as in "How does your answer relate to my question?"); even in such a sentence a more exact expression is preferable.

repel, repulse   Both verbs mean "to drive back," but only *repel* can mean "to cause distaste," "to disgust," as in "His obscenities repelled the audience."

respectfully, respectively   *Respectfully* means "with respect, showing respect" ("Japanese students and teachers bow respectfully to each other"). *Respectively* means "each in turn" ("Professors Arnott, Bahktian, and Cisneros teach, respectively, chemistry, business, and biology").

sarcasm   Heavy, malicious sneering ("Oh you're really a great friend, aren't you?" addressed to someone who won't lend the speaker ten dollars). If the apparent praise, which really communicates dispraise, is at all clever, conveying, say, a delicate mockery or wryness, it is irony, not sarcasm.

seem   Properly it suggests a suspicion that appearances may be deceptive: "He seems honest (but . . .)." Don't say "The book seems to lack focus" if you believe it does lack focus.

semiannually, semimonthly, semiweekly   See *biannually*.

sexist language   Language that is not gender-neutral. For example, the use of *he* with reference to females as well as to males ("When a legislator votes, he takes account of his constituency"), like the use of *man* for all human beings ("Man is a rational animal"), is now widely perceived as sexist. See the entries on *he or she; man, mankind;* and *s/he*.

shall, will, should, would   The old principle held that in the first person *shall* is the future indicative of *to be* and *should* the conditional ("I shall go," "We should like to be asked"); and that *will* and *would* are the forms for the second and third persons. When the forms are reversed ("I will go," "Government of the people . . . shall not perish from the earth"), determination is expressed. But today almost nobody adheres to these principles. Indeed, *shall* (except in questions) sounds stilted to many ears.

s/he This relatively new gender-free pronoun ("As soon as the student receives the forms, s/he should fill them out") is sometimes used in place of *he or she* or *she or he*, which are used to avoid the sexism implied when the male pronoun "he" is used to stand for women as well as men ("As soon as the student receives the forms, he should fill them out"). Other, less noticeable and therefore better ways of avoiding sexist writing are suggested under *he or she*. See also "Avoiding Sexist Language," pages 81–83.

simplistic Means "falsely simplified by ignoring complications." Do not confuse it with *simplified*, whose meanings include "reduced to essentials" and "clarified."

since, because Traditional objections to *since*, in the sense of "because," have all but vanished. Note, however, that when *since* is ambiguous and may also refer to time ("Since he joined the navy, she found another boyfriend") it is better to say *because* or *after*, depending on which you mean.

situation Overused, vague, and often unnecessary. "His situation was that he was unemployed" adds up to "He was unemployed." And "an emergency situation" is probably an emergency.

split infinitives The infinitive is the verb form that merely names the action, without indicating when or by whom performed ("walk," rather than "walked" or "I walk"). Grammarians, however, developed the idea that the infinitive was "to walk," and they held that one should not separate or split the two words: "to quickly walk." But almost all authorities today accept this usuage. Notice, however, that often the inserted word can be deleted ("to really understand" is "to understand"), and that if many words are inserted between *to* and the verb, the reader may get lost ("to quickly and in the remaining few pages before examining the next question conclude").

stanza See *verse*.

subjunctive For the use of the subjunctive with conditions contrary to fact (for instance, "If I were you"), see the entry on *was, were*. The subjunctive is also used in *that* clauses followed by verbs demanding, requesting, or recommending: "She asked that the students be prepared to take a test." But because this last sort of sentence sounds stiff, it is better to use an alternative construction, such as "She asked the students to prepare for a test."

than, then *Than* is used chiefly in making comparisons ("German is harder than French"), but also after "rather," "other," and "else"

("I'd rather take French than German"; "He thinks of nothing other than sex"). *Then* commonly indicates time ("She took German then, but now she takes French"; "Until then, I'll save you a seat"), but it may also mean "in that case" ("It's agreed, then, that we'll all go"), or "on the other hand" ("Then again, she may find German easy"). The simplest guide: Use *than* after comparisons and after "rather," "other," "else"; otherwise use *then*.

that, which, who   Many pages have been written on these words; opinions differ, but you will offend no one if you observe the following principles. (1) Use *that* in restrictive (that is, limiting) clauses: "The rocking chair that creaks is on the porch." (2) Use *which* in nonrestrictive (in effect, parenthetic) clauses: "The rocking chair, which creaks, is on the porch." (See pages 256–257.) The difference between these two sentences is this: In the first, one rocking chair is singled out from several—the one that creaks; in the second, the fact that the rocking chair creaks is simply tossed in and is not added for the purpose of identifying the one chair out of several. (3) Use *who* for people, in restrictive and in nonrestrictive clauses: "The women who were playing poker ignored the men"; "The women, who were playing poker, ignored the men." But note that often *that*, *which*, and *who* can be omitted: "The creaky rocking chair is on the porch"; "The women playing poker ignored the men." "The women, playing poker, ignored the men." In general, omit these words if the sentence remains clear.

their, there, they're   The first is a possessive pronoun: "Chaplin and Keaton made their first films before sound tracks were developed." The second, *there*, sometimes refers to a place ("Go there," "Do you live there?"), and sometimes is what is known in grammar as an introductory expletive ("There are no solutions to this problem"). The third, *they're*, is a contraction of "they are" ("They're going to stay for dinner").

this   Often refers vaguely to "what I have been saying." Does it refer to the previous sentence, the previous paragraph, the previous page? Try to modify it by being specific: "This last point"; "This clue gave the police all they needed."

thusly   Unacceptable; *thus* is an adverb and needs no adverbial ending.

till, until   Both are acceptable, but *until* is preferable because *till*—though common in speech—looks literary in print. The following are *not* acceptable: *til*, *'til*, *'till*.

to, too, two *To* is toward; *too* is either "also" ("She's a lawyer, too") or "excessively" ("It's too hot"); *two* is one more than one ("It's two feet long").

topic of See *area of.*

toward, towards Both are standard English; *toward* is more common in the United States, *towards* in Great Britain.

type Often colloquial (and unacceptable in most writing) for *type of*, as in "this type teacher." But *type of* is not especially pleasing either. Better to write "this kind of teacher." And avoid using *type* as a suffix: "essay-type examinations" are essay examinations; "natural-type ice cream" is natural ice cream. Sneaky manufacturers make "Italian-type cheese," implying that their domestic cheese is imported and at the same time protecting themselves against charges of misrepresentation.

unique The only one of its kind. Someone or something therefore cannot be "rather unique" or "very unique" or "somewhat unique." Instead of saying "rather unique," say *rare*, or *unusual*, or *extraordinary*, or whatever seems to be the best word.

US, United States Generally, *United States* is preferable to *US*, except when used as an adjective (*US Air Force*).

usage Don't use *usage* where *use* will do, as in "Here Vonnegut completes his usage of dark images." *Usage* properly implies a customary practice that has created a standard: "Usage has eroded the difference between *shall* and *will*."

use of The use of *use of* is usually unnecessary. "Through the use of setting he conveys a sense of foreboding" may be reduced to "The setting conveys . . ." or "His setting conveys. . . ."

utilize, utilization Often inflated for *use* and *using*, as in "The infirmary has noted that it is sophomores who have most utilized the counseling service." But when one means "find an effective use for," *utilize* may be the best word, as in (here we borrow from *The American Heritage Dictionary*), "The teachers were unable to utilize the new computers," where *use* might wrongly suggest that the teachers could not operate the computers.

verbal Often used where *oral* would be more exact. *Verbal* simply means "expressed in words," and thus a *verbal agreement* may be either written or spoken. If you mean spoken, call it an *oral agreement*.

verse, stanza A *verse* is a single line of a poem; a *stanza* is a group of lines, commonly bound by a rhyme scheme. But in speaking or writing about songs, usage sanctions *verse* for *stanza*, as in "Second verse, same as the first."

viable A term from physiology, meaning "capable of living" (for example, referring to a fetus at a stage of its development). Now pretentiously used and overused, especially by politicians and journalists, to mean "workable," as in "a viable presidency." Avoid it.

was, were Use the subjunctive form—*were* (rather than *was*)—in expressing a wish ("I wish I were younger") and in "if-clauses" that are contrary to fact ("If I were rich," "If I were you . . .").

we If you mean *I*, say *I*. Not "The first fairy tale we heard" but "the first fairy tale I heard." (But of course *we* is appropriate in some statements: "We have all heard fairy tales"; "If we look closely at the evidence, we can probably agree that. . . .") The rule: Don't use *we* as a disguise for *I*. See pages 95–96.

well See *good.*

well known, widely known Athletes, performers, politicians, and such folk are not really *well known* except perhaps by a few of their friends and their relatives; use *widely known* if you mean they are known (however slightly) to many people.

which Often can be deleted. "Students are required to fill out scholarship applications which are lengthy" can be written "Students are required to fill out lengthy scholarship applications." Another example: "*The Tempest*, which is Shakespeare's last play, was written in 1611"; "*The Tempest*, Shakespeare's last play, was written in 1611," or "Shakespeare wrote his last play, *The Tempest*, in 1611." For the distinction between *which* and *that*, see also the entry on *that*.

while Best used in a temporal sense, meaning "during the time": "While I was speaking, I suddenly realized that I didn't know what I was talking about." While it is not wrong to use *while* in a nontemporal sense, meaning "although" (as at the beginning of this sentence), it is better to use *although* in order to avoid any ambiguity. Note the ambiguity in: "While he was fond of movies he chiefly saw westerns." Does it mean "Although he was fond of movies," or does it mean "During the time when he was fond of movies"? Another point: Do not use *while* if you mean *and*; "First-year students take English 1-2, while sophomores take English 10-11" (substitute *and* for *while*).

who, whom Strictly speaking, *who* must be used for subjects, even when they look like objects: "He guessed who would be chosen." (Here *who* is the subject of the clause "who would be chosen.") *Whom* must be used for the objects of a verb, verbal (gerund, participle), or preposition: "Whom did she choose?"; "Whom do you want me to choose?"; "To whom did he show it?" We may feel stuffy in writing "Whom did she choose?" or "Whom are you talking about?" but to use *who* is certain to annoy some reader. Often you can avoid the dilemma by rewriting: "Who was chosen?"; "Who is the topic of conversation?" See also the entry on *that*.

whoever, whomever The second of these is the objective form. It is often incorrectly used as the subject of a clause. Incorrect: "Open the class to whomever wants to take it." The object of "to" is not "whomever" but is the entire clause—"whoever wants to take it"— and of course "whoever" is the subject of "wants."

who's, whose The first is a contraction of *who is* ("Who's on first?"). The second is a possessive pronoun: "Whose book is it?" "I know whose it is."

will, would See *shall* and also *would*.

would "I would think that" is a wordy version of "I think that." (On the mistaken use of *would of* for *would have*, see also the entry on *of*.)

you In relatively informal writing, *you* is ordinarily preferable to the somewhat stiff *one*: "If you are addicted to cigarettes, you may find it helpful to join Smokenders." (Compare: "If one is addicted to cigarettes, one may. . . .") But because the direct address of *you* may sometimes descend into nagging, it is usually better to write: "Cigarette addicts may find it helpful. . . ." Certainly a writer (you?) should not assume that the reader is guilty of vices ("You should not molest children") unless the essay is clearly aimed at an audience that admits to these vices, say a pamphlet directed to child molesters who are seeking help. Thus, it is acceptable to say, "If you are a poor speller," but it is not acceptable to say, to the general reader, "You should improve your spelling"; the reader's spelling may not need improvement. And avoid *you* when the word cannot possibly apply to the reader: "A hundred years ago you were faced with many diseases that now have been eradicated." Something like "A hundred years ago people were faced . . ." is preferable.

your, you're The first is a possessive pronoun ("your book"); the second is a contraction of *you are* ("You're mistaken").

CHAPTER FOURTEEN

DOCUMENTING SOURCES

Documentation

One purpose of documentation is to enable your readers to retrace your steps, to find your source and to read what you read—whether you read it in the library, on the Internet, or in your local newspaper. To make this possible, you must give your readers enough information to locate and identify each source you cite. For books, this information generally includes the following:

- Author
- Title
- Publisher
- Date and place of publication
- Page numbers

Electronic sources require this information (at minimum):

- Site address
- Date on which you accessed the information

The way this information is presented varies from discipline to discipline: Sociologists, for example, present the date of publication more prominently than do historians; engineers usually list their sources by number at the end of a research work and in order of their appearance in the text; and literary critics list sources alphabetically by authors' names. In the following pages we discuss in detail two of the most widely used systems of documentation: the Modern Language Association (MLA) and the American Psychological Association (APA). At the end of this chapter we provide information on where you can obtain guidance on other systems of documentation.

MLA Format

Citationɟ Within the Text

Brief parenthetic citations within the body of the essay are made clear by a list of your sources, entitled Works Cited, appended to the essay. Thus, an item in your list of works cited will clarify such a sentence in your essay as

```
According to Angeline Goreau, Aphra Behn in her nov-
els continually contradicts "the personal politics
she had defended from the outset of her career as a
writer" (252).
```

This citation means that the words inside the quotation marks appear on page 252 of a source written by Goreau, which will be listed in Works Cited. More often than not the parenthetic citation appears at the end of a sentence, as in the example just given, but it can appear elsewhere in the sentence. Its position will depend in part on your ear, and in part on the requirement that you point clearly to the place where your source's idea ends and your point begins. (In the following example, the idea that follows the parenthetic citation is not Gardiner's, but the writer's own.)

```
Judith Kegan Gardiner, on the other hand, acknowl-
edges that Behn's work "displays its conflicts with
patriarchal authority" (215), conflicts that appear
most notably in the third volume of Love Letters.
```

Seven points must be made about these examples:

1. Quotation marks: The closing quotation mark appears after the last word of the quotation, *not* after the parenthetic citation. Since the citation is not part of the quotation, the citation is not included within the quotation marks.

2. Omission of words (ellipsis): If the quoted words are merely a phrase, as in the example above, you do not need to indicate (by an ellipsis—three spaced periods) that you are omitting material before or after the quotation. But if the quotation is longer than a phrase and is not a complete sentence, you must use an ellipsis to indicate that you are omitting material. If you omit material from the middle of a sentence, indicate the omission with an ellipsis. If you omit material from the end of the sentence, indicate the omission with an ellipsis followed by a period, the sentence period. If you omit a whole sentence, the sentence period comes first, followed by an ellipsis. If you omit material from the middle of one sentence to the end of another, the sentence period *follows* the ellipsis. If the ellipsis is followed by a parenthetical citation, the sentence period follows the parenthesis. (For more on ellipses, see page 190.)

3. Addition of words: On occasion, you'll need to add a word or two to a quotation in order to clarify its meaning. If you must make such an addition—and such additions should be kept to a minimum because they're distracting—enclose the word or words in square brackets, *not* parentheses. If the quotation contains a misspelling or other error, transcribe it as it appears in the source, and insert the word *sic* (Latin for "thus," as in "thus the word appears in the source; it's not *my* error") in italics and in square brackets:

```
Smith writes, "Jane Austin [sic] led an uneventful

life."
```

4. Punctuation with parenthetic citations: Look again at the examples of citations from Goreau and Gardiner given a moment ago. Notice that if you follow a quotation with a parenthetic citation, any necessary period, semicolon, or comma *follows* the parenthetic citation. In the first example (citing page 252 in Goreau), a period follows the citation; in the second (citing page 215 in Gardiner), a comma. In the next example, notice that the comma follows the citation.

```
Johnson insists that "these poems can be interpreted

as Tory propaganda" (72), but his brief analysis is

not persuasive.
```

If, however, the quotation itself uses a question mark or an exclamation mark, this mark of punctuation appears *within* the closing quotation mark; even so, a period follows the parenthetic citation.

```
Jenkins-Smith is the only one to suggest doubt: "How

can we accept such a superficial reading of these

works?" (178). He therefore rejects the entire

argument.
```

5. Two or more titles by one author: If your list of Works Cited includes more than one work by an author, you will have to give additional information (either in your comment or within the parenthetic citation) in order to indicate *which* of the titles you are referring to. We will go further into this on page 301.

6. Long (or "block") quotations: We have been talking about short quotations, which are not set off but are embedded within your own sentences. Long quotations, usually defined as more than three lines of poetry or four lines of prose, are indented ten spaces from the left, as in the example below.

```
Janet Todd explains Behn's reverence for the Stuart

monarchy:

          She was a passionate supporter of both

          Charles II and James II as not simply

          rulers but as sacred majesties, god-kings

          on earth, whose private failings in no way

          detracted from their high office. . . . For

          her, royalty was not patriarchal anachro-

          nism as it would be for liberated women

          writers a hundred years on, but a mystical

          state. (73)
```

In introducing a long quotation, keep in mind that a reader will have trouble reading a sentence that consists of a lead-in, a long quotation, and then a continuation of your own sentence. It's better to have a short lead-in ("Janet Todd explains Behn's reverence for the Stuart monarchy"), and then set off a long quotation that is a complete sentence or group of sentences and therefore ends with a period. To set off a quotation, begin on a new line, double-space and indent ten spaces (or one inch) from the left margin, and do *not* enclose the quotation within quotation marks. Put a period at the end of the quotation (since the quotation is a complete sentence or group of sentences and is not embedded within a longer sentence of your own), hit the space bar twice, and then, on the same line, give the citation in parentheses. Do *not* put a period after the parenthetic citation that follows a long quotation.

7. Citing a summary or a paraphrase: Even if you don't quote a source directly but use its point in a paraphrase or a summary, you will give a citation:

```
Goreau notes (89-90) that Behn participated in pub-

lic life and in politics not only as a writer: In the

1660s she went to Antwerp as a spy for Charles II.
```

The basic point, then, is that the system of in-text citation gives the documentation parenthetically. Notice that in all but one of the previous examples the author's name is given in the student's text (rather than within the parenthetic citation). But there are several other ways of giving the citation, and we shall now look at them.

Author and Page Number in Parenthetic Citation

```
Heroines who explore their own individuality (with

varying degrees of success and failure) abound in

Chopin's work (Shinn 358).
```

It doesn't matter whether you summarize (as in this example) or quote directly; the parenthetic citation means that your source is page 358 of a work by Shinn, listed in Works Cited, at the end of your essay.

Title and Page Number in Parentheses   If, as we mentioned earlier, your list of Works Cited includes two or more titles by an author, you cannot in the text simply give a name and a page reference; the reader would not know to which of the titles you are referring. Let's assume that Works Cited includes two items by Larzer Ziff. In a sentence in your essay you might specify one title, saying something like, "For example, Larzer Ziff, in *The American 1890's*, claims. . . ." If, however, you do not mention the title in your lead-in, you will have to give the title (in a shortened form) in the parenthetic citation:

```
Larzer Ziff, for example, claims that the novel

"rejected the family as the automatic equivalent of

feminine self-fulfillment" (American 175).
```

Notice in this example that *American* is a short title for Ziff's book *The American 1890's: Life and Times of a Lost Generation*. The full title is given in Works Cited, as is the title of another work by Ziff, but the short title in the parenthetic citation is enough to direct the reader to page 175 of the correct source named in Works Cited.

Notice also that when a short title and a page reference are given in parentheses, a comma is *not* used after the title.

Author, Title, and Page Number in Parentheses We have just seen that if Works Cited includes two or more works by an author, and if in your lead-in you do not specify which work you are at the moment making use of, you will have to give the title as well as the page number in parentheses. Similarly, if for some reason you do not in your lead-in mention the name of the author, you will have to add this bit of information to the parenthetic citation, thus:

```
At least one critic has claimed that the novel

"rejected the family as the automatic equivalent of

feminine self-fulfillment" (Ziff, American 175).
```

Notice, again, that a comma does *not* separate the title from the page reference; but notice, too, that a comma *does* separate the author's name from the title. (Don't ask us why; ask the Modern Language Association. Or just obey orders.)

A Government Document or a Work of Corporate Authorship Treat the issuing body as the author. Thus, you will probably write something like this:

```
In Food Resources Today, the Commission on Food

Control, concludes that there is no danger (36-37).
```

A Work by Two or Three Authors If a work is by *two or three authors*, give their names, either in the parenthetic citation (the first example below) or in a lead-in (the second example):

```
Where the two other siblings strive compulsively

either to correct or create problems, the sibling in

the middle passively escapes from her painful family

situation by withdrawing into herself (Seixas and

Youcha 48-49).
```

or

> Barnet, Bellanca, and Stubbs suggest that the most
> efficient way to learn about your library's online
> resources is to consult a reference librarian (365).

If there are more than *three authors*, give the last name of the first author, followed by "et al." (an abbreviation for *et alii*, Latin for "and others"):

> Gardner et al. found that . . .

or

> Sometimes even higher levels are found (Gardner et
> al. 83).

Parenthetic Citation of an Indirect Source (Citation of Material That Itself Was Quoted or Summarized in Your Source)

Suppose you are reading a book by Jones, and she quotes Smith, and you wish to use Smith's material. Your citation will be to Jones—the source you are using—but of course you cannot attribute Smith's words to Jones. You will have to make it clear that you are quoting not Jones but Smith, and so your parenthetic citation will look like this:

> (qtd. in Jones 84–85)

Parenthetic Citation of Two or More Works

A semicolon, followed by a space, is used to separate two sources:

> Some scholars have speculated that Poe died of
> rabies, not alcoholism (Walk 44; Hayward 173).

A Work in More Than One Volume

This is a bit tricky.

1. If you have used only one volume, in Works Cited you will specify the volume, and so in your parenthetic in-text citation you will need to give only a page number—as most of our examples illustrate.

2. If you have used more than one volume, your parenthetic citation will have to specify the volume as well as the page:

> Landsdale points out that nitrite combines with
> hemoglobin to form a pigment which cannot carry
> oxygen (2: 370).

The reference is to page 370 of volume 2 of a work by Landsdale.

3. If, however, you are citing not a page but an entire volume—let's say volume 2—your parenthetic citation would be

```
(vol. 2)
```

Or, if you did not name the author in your lead-in, it would be

```
(Landsdale, vol. 2)
```

Notice also some other points:

- When citing a volume and page, the volume number, like the page number, is given in arabic (not roman) numerals.
- The volume number is followed by a colon, then a space, then the page number.
- Abbreviations such as "vol." and "p." and "pp." are *not* used, except when citing a volume number without a page number, as illustrated in the last two examples.

An Anonymous Work   For an anonymous work, give the title in your lead-in, or give it in a shortened form in your parenthetic citation:

```
Official Guide to Food Standards includes a statis-

tical table on nitrates (362).
```

or

```
A statistical table on nitrites is available

(Official Guide 362).
```

But double-check to make sure that the work is truly anonymous. Some encyclopedias, for example, give the authors' names quietly. If initials follow the article, these are the initials of the author's name. Check the alphabetic list of authors given at the front or back of the encyclopedia.

A Literary Work   Because classic works of literature are widely available, and your readers may have at hand editions different from the one that you have read, you can help them locate the material (if they wish to check it) by giving information—for instance, a chapter number—in addition to a page reference. The following forms are customary.

1. A novel. In parentheses give the page number of the edition you specify in Works Cited, followed by a semicolon, a space, and the relevant additional helpful information, such as the chapter number, or the book number (some novels are divided into "books," which themselves are then divided into chapters).

```
Chopin in The Awakening describes the Pontelliers'

house as "charming" (69; ch. 17).
```

or

```
George Eliot characterizes Glegg effectively when in

The Mill on the Floss she says that his "ordinary

tone" was one of "sharp questioning" (235; bk 3,

ch. 4).
```

2. A play. Most instructors want the act, scene, and (if the lines are numbered) line numbers, rather than a page reference, thus:

```
The Ghost, in his first encounter with Hamlet,

speaks of "Murder most foul" (1.5.28).
```

This reference is to line 28 in the fifth scene of the first act.

If you are quoting a few words within a sentence of your own, immediately after closing the brief quotation give the citation (enclosed within parentheses), and, if your sentence ends with the quotation, put the period after the closing parenthesis.

```
That Macbeth fully understands that killing Duncan

is not a manly act but a villainous one is clear

from his words to Lady Macbeth: "I dare do all that

may become a man" (1.7.46). Moreover, even though he

goes on to kill Duncan, he does not go on to deceive

himself into thinking that his act was noble.
```

If, however, your sentence continues beyond the citation, after the parenthetic citation put whatever punctuation may be necessary (for instance, a comma may be needed), complete your sentence, and end it with a period.

```
This is clear from his words, "I dare do all that
does become a man" (1.7.46), and he never loses his
awareness of true manliness.
```

3. A poem. Preferences vary, and you can't go wrong in citing the page, but for a poem longer than, say, a sonnet (fourteen lines), most instructors find it useful if students cite the line numbers, in parentheses, after the quotations. In your first use, preface the numerals with "line" or "lines" (not in quotation marks, of course); in subsequent citations simply give the numerals. For very long poems that are divided into books, such as Homer's *Odyssey*, give the page, a semicolon, a space, the book number, and the line number(s). The following example refers to page 327 of a title listed in Works Cited; it goes on to indicate that the passage occurs in the ninth book of the poem, lines 130 to 135.

```
(327; 9.130-35)
```

Long quotations (more than three lines of poetry) are indented ten spaces. As we explained on page 299, if you give a long quotation, try to give one that can correctly be concluded with a period. After the period, hit the space bar three times, and then, on the same line, give the citation in parentheses. As good an example as any of the absurdity and yet the pathos of T. S. Eliot's Prufrock are these line from near the end of the poem:

```
Shall I part my hair behind? Do I dare to eat a peach?

I shall wear white flannel trousers, and walk upon

the beach.

I have heard the mermaids singing, each to each.

I do not think that they will sing to me. (122-25)
```

Notice that the period here is given at the end of the quotation, *not* after the parenthetic citation of lines 122–25.

A Personal Interview Probably you won't need a parenthetic citation, because you'll say something like

```
Cyril Jackson, in an interview, said . . .
```

or

```
According to Cyril Jackson . . .
```

and when your readers turn to Works Cited, they will see that Jackson is listed, along with the date of the interview. But if you do not mention the source's name in the lead-in, you will have to provide it within parentheses:

```
It has been estimated that chemical additives earn

the drug companies well over five hundred million

dollars annually (Jackson).
```

Lectures   If you use in your research essay a distinctive phrase, idea, or piece of information from a class lecture or discussion, you'll want to give the speaker credit for it. If you give a signal phrase such as "In a lecture at NYU, Jones said," the parenthetic citation should include only the date of the lecture; if you don't give a signal phrase, then include the speaker's name, followed by a comma, followed by the date:

```
The Museum world today, is "now parts of show biz"

(Orlofsky, Sept. 20, 2004).
```

The entry for the lecture on the Works Cited list will contain the title of the lecture—if there is one—and the place it was given.

Electronic Sources   Follow the format for print sources. In some cases, page numbers will be available; in others, paragraphs will be numbered; in still others; no number at all will be given. Use what you have, indicating the author's name or the title of the source where necessary, as determined by context. When giving paragraph numbers, use the abbreviation "par." (Use a comma to separate the abbreviation from the author's name or title.)

```
One lawyer argued that Monica Lewinsky was nowhere

near the White House that day (Hedges, pars. 2-3).
```

A Note on Footnotes in an Essay Using Parenthetic Citations

There are two reasons for using footnotes in an essay that chiefly uses parenthetic citations.

1. In a research paper you will of course draw on many sources, but in other kinds of papers you may be using only one source, and yet

within the paper you may often want to specify a reference to a page or
(for poetry) a line number, or (for a play) to an act, scene, and line number. In such a case, to append a page headed Work Cited, with a single
title, is silly; it is better to use a single footnote when you first allude to
the source. Such a note can run something like this

    [1]All references are to Mary Shelley, Frankenstein,

    afterword by Harold Bloom (New York: Signet, 1965).

2. Footnotes can also be used in another way in an essay that documents sources by giving parenthetic citations. If you want to include some
material that might seem intrusive in the body of the essay, you may rele-
gate it to a footnote. For example, in a footnote you might translate a
quotation given in a foreign language, or in a footnote you might write
a paragraph—a sort of mini-essay—in which you offer an amplification
of some point. By putting the amplification in a footnote you are signaling
to the reader that it is dispensable; it is, so to speak, thrown in as something extra, something relevant but not essential to your argument.

A raised arabic numeral indicates in the body of your text that
you are adding a footnote at this point. (The "insert" function of your
word-processing program will insert both the raised numeral and the
text of your footnote in the appropriate places in your essay; simply click
"insert" at the point in the text where you want the footnote to appear,
and follow the program's instructions.)

    Joachim Jeremias's The Parables of Jesus is probably

    the best example of this sort of book.[1]

Usually the number is put at the end of a sentence, immediately after
the period, but put it earlier if clarity requires you to do so.

    Helen Cam[1] as well as many lesser historians held

    this view.

The List of Works Cited

Your parenthetic documentation consists of references that become
meaningful when the reader consults a list entitled Works Cited,
given at the end of your essay. We present sample entries below, but
see also the list of Works Cited at the end of the documented
essay presented in Chapter 10, "Writing the Research Essay"
(pp. 216–217).

The list of Works Cited continues the pagination of the essay; if the last page of text is 10, then the list begins on page 11. Your last name and the page number will appear in the upper-right corner, half an inch from the top of the sheet. Next, type "Works Cited," centered, one inch from the top, then double-space and type the first entry. Here are the governing conventions.

Alphabetic Order

1. Arrange the list alphabetically by author, with the author's last name first.

2. List an anonymous work alphabetically under the first word of the title, or under the second word if the first word is *A*, *An*, or *The*, or a foreign equivalent.

3. If your list includes two or more works by one author, the work whose title comes earlier in the alphabet precedes the work whose title comes later in the alphabet.

Form on the Page

1. Begin each entry flush with the left margin. If an entry runs to more than one line, indent five spaces for each succeeding line of the entry.

2. Double-space each entry, and double-space between entries.

From here on, things get complicated. We will focus on four categories:

- Books (pp. 308–315)
- Articles in journals and newspapers, and interviews and lectures. (pp. 318–319)
- Films, television and radio programs (pp. 317–318)
- Electronic sources (pp. 320–323).

The forms for books are as follows.

Author's Name   Note that the last name is given first, but otherwise the name is given as on the title page. Do not substitute initials for names written out on the title page. (Books by more than one author are treated later in this discussion, p. 311.)

If your list includes two or more works by an author, the author's name is not repeated for the second title but is represented by three hyphens followed by a period and two spaces. When you give two or more works by the same author, the sequence is determined by the alphabetic order of the titles, as in the example below, listing two books by Blassingame, where *Black* precedes *Slave*.

> Bishop, Robert. <u>American Folk Sculpture</u>. New York:
>
> Dutton, 1974.
>
> Blassingame, John W. <u>Black New Orleans, 1860–1880</u>.
>
> Chicago: U of Chicago P, 1973.
>
> ---. <u>The Slave Community: Plantation Life in the</u>
>
> <u>Antebellum South</u>. Rev. ed. New York: Oxford
>
> UP, 1979.
>
> Danto, Arthur. <u>Embodied Meanings</u>. New York: Farrar,
>
> 1994.

We have already discussed the treatment of an anonymous work; in a few moments we will discuss books by more than one author, government documents, and works of corporate authorship.

Title of Book Take the title from the title page, not from the cover or the spine, but disregard any unusual typography—for instance, the use of only capital letters, or the use of & for *and*. Italicize or underline the title and subtitle. (The MLA recommends underlining rather than italicizing in texts submitted in courses or for publication because underlining may be more visible to readers.) If you choose to underline the title, use one continuous underline, but do not underline the period that concludes this part of the entry.) Example:

> <u>Frankenstein: Or, The Modern Prometheus</u>.

A peculiarity: Italicizing is used to indicate the title of a book, but if a title of a book itself includes the title of a book (for instance, a book about Mary Shelley's *Frankenstein* might include the title of her novel in its own title), the title-within-the-title is neither italicized nor underlined. Thus the title would be given as (if italicized)

> *The Endurance of* Frankenstein

If it were underlined, it would be

> <u>The Endurance of</u> Frankenstein

Place of Publication, Publisher, and Date For the place of publication, give the name of the city (you can usually find it either on the title page or on the copyright page, which is the reverse of the title page). If several cities are listed, give only the first. If the city is not likely to be widely known, or if it may be confused with another city of the same name (for instance, Cambridge, Massachusetts, and Cambridge, England), add the abbreviated name of the state or country (Cambridge, MA, or Cambridge, Eng.).

The name of the publisher is shortened. Usually the first word is enough (Random House becomes Random; Little, Brown and Co. becomes Little), but if the first word is a first name, such as in Alfred A. Knopf, the surname (Knopf) is used instead. University presses are abbreviated thus: Yale UP, U of Chicago P, State U of New York P.

The date of publication of a book is given when known; if no date appears on the book, write "n.d." to indicate "no date," (without the quotation marks).

Here are sample entries, illustrating the points we have covered thus far:

Douglas, Ann. The Feminization of American Culture.

New York: Knopf, 1977.

Early, Gerald. One Nation Under a Groove: Motown

and American Culture. Hopewell, NJ: Echo,

1995.

Feitlowitz, Marguerite. A Lexicon of Terror:

Argentina and the Legacies of Torture. New

York: Oxford UP, 1998.

Frye, Northrop. Fables of Identity: Studies in

Poetic Mythology. New York: Harcourt, 1963.

---. Fools of Time: Studies in Shakespearian

Tragedy. Toronto: U of Toronto P, 1967.

Kennedy, Paul. Preparing for the Twenty-First

Century. New York: Random, 1993.

Notice that a period follows the author's name, and another period follows the title. If a subtitle is given, as it is for Feitlowitz's book, it is separated from the title by a colon and a space. A colon follows the place of publication, a comma follows the publisher, and a period follows the date.

A Book by More Than One Author   A book written by *two or three authors* is alphabetized under the last name of the first author named on the title page. The names of other authors are given after the first author's name (with last name first) in the normal order, *first name first.*

> Majors, Richard, and Janet Mancini Billson. <u>Cool</u>
>
>   <u>Pose: The Dilemmas of Black Manhood in</u>
>
>   <u>America</u>. Lexington, MA: Lexington, 1992.

Notice that a comma is put after the first name of the first author, separating it from the names that follow.

If there are *more than three authors*, give the name of only the first, and then add "et al." (Latin for "and others"), without the quotation marks.

> Belenky, Mary Field, et al. <u>Women's Ways of</u>
>
>   <u>Knowing: The Development of the Self, Voice,</u>
>
>   <u>and Mind</u>. New York: Basic Books, 1986.

Government Documents   If the writer is not known, treat the government and the agency as the author. Most federal national documents are issued by the Government Printing Office in Washington (abbreviated to GPO).

> U.S. Congress. Office of Technology Assessment.
>
>   <u>Computerized Manufacturing Automation</u>
>
>   <u>Employment, Education and the Workplace</u>.
>
>   Washington: GPO, 1984.

Works of Corporate Authorship   Begin the citation with the corporate author, even if the same body is also the publisher, as in the first example:

American Psychiatric Association. Psychiatric

Glossary. Washington: American Psychiatric

Association, 1984.

Carnegie Council on Policy Studies in Higher

Education. Giving Youth a Better Chance:

Options for Education, Work, and Service. San

Francisco: Jossey, 1980.

Republished Work   After the title, give the date of original publication (it can usually be found on the copyright page of the reprint you are using), then a period, and then the place, publisher, and date of the edition you are using. The example indicates that Rourke's book was originally published in 1931 and that the student is using the Doubleday reprint of 1953.

Rourke, Constance. American Humor. 1931. Garden

City, NY: Doubleday, 1953.

A Book in Several Volumes

Friedel, Frank. *Franklin D. Roosevelt*. 4 vols.

Boston: Little, 1973.

If you have used more than one volume, in your essay you will (as we explained on pages 302–303) indicate a reference to, say, page 250 of volume 3 thus: (3: 250).

If, however, you have used only one volume of the set—let's say volume 3—in your entry in Works Cited write, after the period following the date, "Vol. 3," as in the next entry:

Friedel, Frank. Franklin D. Roosevelt. 4 vols.

Boston: Little, 1973. Vol. 3.

In this case, the parenthetic citation in the text will be to the page only, not to the volume and page, since a reader will understand that the page reference must be to this volume. But notice that in Works Cited, even though you say you used only volume 3, you also give the total number of volumes.

One Book with a Separate Title in a Set of Volumes   Sometimes a set of volumes with a title makes use also of a separate title for each book in the set. If you are listing such a book, use the following form:

> Churchill, Winston. The Age of Revolution. Vol. 3
>
>   of A History of the English-Speaking Peoples.
>
> New York: Dodd, 1957.

A Book with an Author and an Editor

> Churchill, Winston, and Franklin D. Roosevelt. The
>
>   Complete Correspondence. 3 vols. Ed. Warren F.
>
>   Kimball. Princeton, NJ: Princeton UP, 1985.
>
> Shakespeare, William. The Sonnets. Ed. William
>
>   Burto. New York: NAL, 1965.

If you are making use of the editor's introduction or other editorial material, rather than of the author's work, list the book under the name of the editor, rather than of the author, following the form given below for an introduction, foreword, or afterword.

A Revised Edition of a Book

> Hall, James. Dictionary of Subjects and Symbols in
>
>   Art. 2nd ed. New York: Harper, 1979.

A Translated Book

> Allende, Isabel. The Stories of Eva Luna. Trans.
>
>   Margaret Sayens Peden. New York: Atheneum,
>
>   1991.

But if you are discussing the translation itself, as opposed to the book, list the work under the translator's name:

> MacAdam, Alfred, trans. Family Portrait with Fidel:
>
>   A Memoir. By Carlos Franqui. New York: Random,
>
>   1984.

An Introduction, Foreword, or Afterword

```
Wolff, Cynthia Griffin. Introduction. The House Of

    Mirth. By Edith Wharton. New York: Penguin,

    1985. vii-xxvi.
```

Usually a book with an introduction or some such comparable material is listed under the name of the author of the book (here Wharton), rather than under the name of the writer of the introduction (here Wolff), but if you are referring to the apparatus rather than to the book itself, use the form just given. The words *Introduction*, *Preface*, *Foreword*, and *Afterword* are neither enclosed within quotation marks nor underlined.

A Book with an Editor but No Author   Anthologies of literature fit this description, but here we have in mind a book of essays written by various people but collected by an editor (or editors), whose name appears on the collection.

```
Baldick, Chris, ed. The Oxford Book of Gothic

    Tales. New York: Oxford UP, 1993.
```

A Work in a Volume of Works by One Author   The following entry indicates that a short work by Susan Sontag—an essay called "The Aesthetics of Science"—appears in a book by Sontag entitled *Styles of Radical Will*. Notice that the inclusive page numbers of the short work are cited—not merely page numbers that you may happen to refer to, but the page numbers of the entire piece.

```
Sontag, Susan. "The Aesthetics of Science." In

    Styles of Radical Will. New York: Farrar,

    1969. 3-34.
```

A Work in a Collection of Works by Several Authors   There are several possibilities here. Let's assume, for a start, that you have made use of one work in an anthology. In Works Cited, begin with the author (last name first) and title of the work you are citing, not with the name of the anthologist or the title of the anthology. Here is an entry for Coleridge's poem "Kubla Khan," found on pages 501–3 in the second volume of a two-volume anthology edited by David Damrosch and several others.

```
Coleridge, Samuel Taylor. "Kubla Khan." The Longman

    Anthology of British Literature. Ed. David

    Damrosch et al. 2 vols. New York: Longman,

    1999. 2: 501-3.
```

Now let's assume that during the course of your essay you refer to several works rather than to only one work in this anthology. You can, of course, list each work in the form just given. Or you can have an entry in Works Cited for Damrosch's anthology, under Damrosch's name, and then in each entry for a work in the anthology you can eliminate some of the data by simply referring to Damrosch, thus:

```
Coleridge, Samuel Taylor. "Kubla Khan." Damrosch 2:

    501-3.
```

Again, this requires that you also list Damrosch's volume, thus:

```
Damrosch, David, et al., eds. The Longman Anthology

    of British Literature. 2 vols. New York:

    Longman, 1999.
```

The advantage of listing the anthology separately is that if you are using a dozen works from the anthology, you can shorten the dozen entries in Works Cited merely by adding one entry, that of the anthology itself. Notice, of course, that in the body of the essay you would still refer to Coleridge and to your other eleven authors, not to the editor of the anthology—but the entries in Works Cited will guide the reader to the book you have used.

A Book Review

```
Vendler, Helen. Rev. of Essays on Style. Ed. Roger

    Fowler. Essays in Criticism 16 (1966): 457-63.
```

If the review has a title, give it between the period following the reviewer's name and "Rev."

If a review is anonymous, list it under the first word of the title, or under the second word if the first word is *A*, *An*, or *The*. If an anonymous review has no title, begin the entry with "Rev. of" and then give the title of the work reviewed; alphabetize the entry under the title of the work reviewed.

An Article or Essay—Not a Reprint—in a Collection A book may consist of a collection (edited by one or more persons) of new essays by several authors. Here is a reference to one essay in such a book. (The essay, by Smith, occupies pages 178–94 in a collection edited by Lubiano.)

> Smith, David Lionel. "What Is Black Culture?" The
>
> House That Race Built. Ed. Wahneema Lubiano.
>
> New York: Vintage, 1998. 178-94.

An Article or Essay Reprinted in a Collection The previous example (Smith's essay in Lubiano's collection) was for an essay written for a collection. But some collections reprint earlier material—for example, essays from journals, or chapters from books. The following example cites an essay that was originally printed in a book called *The Cinema of Alfred Hitchcock*. This essay has been reprinted in a later collection of essays on Hitchcock, edited by Arthur J. LaValley, and it was LaValley's collection that the student used.

> Bogdanovich, Peter. "Interviews with Alfred
>
> Hitchcock." The Cinema of Alfred Hitchcock.
>
> New York: Museum of Modern Art, 1963. 15-18.
>
> Rpt. in Focus on Hitchcock. Ed. Albert J.
>
> LaValley. Englewood Cliffs, NJ: Prentice,
>
> 1972. 28-31.

The student has read Bogdanovich's essay or chapter, but not in Bogdanovich's book, where it occupied pages 15–18. The student actually read the essay on pages 28–31 in a collection of writings on Hitchcock, edited by LaValley. Details of the original publication—title, date, page numbers, and so forth—were found in LaValley's collection. Almost all editors will include this information, either on the copyright page or at the foot of the reprinted essay, but sometimes they do not give the original page numbers. In such a case, you need not give the original numbers in the entry.

Notice that the entry begins with the author and the title of the work you are citing (here, Bogdanovich's interviews), not with the name of the editor of the collection or the title of the collection. In the following example, the student used an essay by Arthur Sewell; the

essay was originally on pages 53–56 in a book by Sewell entitled
Character and Society in Shakespeare, but the student encountered the
piece on pages 36–38 in a collection of essays, edited by Leonard Dean,
on Shakespeare's *Julius Caesar*. Here is how the entry should run:

> Sewell, Arthur. "The Moral Dilemma in Tragedy:
>
> Brutus." Character and Society in Shakespeare.
>
> Oxford: Clarendon, 1951. 53–56. Rpt. in
>
> Twentieth Century Interpretations of Julius
>
> Caesar. Ed. Leonard F. Dean. Englewood Cliffs,
>
> NJ: Prentice, 1968. 36–38.

**An Encyclopedia or Other Alphabetically Arranged Reference
Work**   The publisher, place of publication, volume number, and page
number do *not* have to be given. For such works, list only the edition
(if it is given) and the date.

For a *signed* article, begin with the author's last name. (If the article
is signed with initials, check the volume for a list of abbreviations—it is
usually near the front, but it may be at the rear—which will say what
the initials stand for, and use the following form.)

> Messer, Thomas. "Picasso." Encyclopedia Americana.
>
> 1998 ed.

For an *unsigned article*, begin with the title of the article.

> "Automation." The Business Reference Book. 1977 ed.
>
> "Picasso, Pablo (Ruiz y)." Encyclopaedia
>
> Britannica: Macropaedia. 1985 ed.

A Film   Begin with the director's name (last name first), followed by
"dir." Next give the title of the film, underlined, then a period, two
spaces, the form of the recording (e.g., "videocasette," "DVD") the
name of the distributor, the date, and a period.

> Coppola, Sophia, dir. Lost in Translation. DVD.
>
> Focus Features, 2003.

A Television or Radio Program

Sixty Minutes. CBS. 31 Jan. 2001.

An Article in a Scholarly Journal   The title of the article is enclosed within quotation marks, and the title of the journal is underlined to indicate italics.

Some journals are paginated consecutively—the pagination of the second issue begins where the first issue leaves off; but other journals begin each issue with page 1. The forms of the citations differ slightly. Let's look first at an article in a *journal that is paginated consecutively:*

Julie Nelson Christoph. "Reconceiving Ethos in

Relation to the Personal: Strategies of

Placement in Pioneer Women's Writing."

College English 64 (2002): 660-79.

Christoph's article occupies pages 660–79 of volume 64, which was published in 2002. (Note that the volume number is followed by a space, and then by the year, in parentheses, and then by a colon, a space, and the page numbers of the entire article.) Because the journal is paginated consecutively, the issue number does *not* need to be specified.

For a *journal that begins each issue with page 1* (there will be four page 1's each year if such a journal is a quarterly), the issue number must be given. After the volume number, type a period and (without hitting the space bar) the issue number, as in the next example.

Spillers, Hortense J. "Martin Luther King and the

Style of the Black Sermon." The Black Scholar

3.1 (1971): 14-27.

Spillers's article appeared in the first issue of volume 3 of *The Black Scholar*.

An Article in a Weekly, Biweekly, or Monthly Publication   The date and page numbers are given, but volume numbers and issue numbers are usually omitted for these publications. The following example is for an article in a weekly publication:

Malcolm, Janet. "Gertrude Stein's War." New Yorker

2 June 2003: 58-81.

An Article in a Newspaper   Because a newspaper usually consists of several sections, a section number or a capital letter may precede the page number. The example indicates that an article begins on page 1 of section 1 and is continued on a later page.

```
Bennet, James. "Judge Cites Possible Breaches of
     Ethics Guidelines by Starr." New York Times 8
     Aug. 1998. sec. 1: 1.
```

An Interview   The citation gives the name of the person you interviewed, the form of the interview ("personal," "telephone," "e-mail"), and the date.

```
Curley, Michael. Personal interview. 7 Nov. 2005.
```

A Lecture   In addition to the date of the lecture and the name of the speaker, the citation should include the title of the presentation (if there is one) and the place it was given. If there is no title, use a descriptive word or phrase such as "class lecture," but do not use quotation marks. If the lecture was sponsored by a particular organization or group, give that information before the date.

```
Cahill, Patricia A. Class lecture on Othello. Emory
     Univ. 20 Sept. 2006.
McNamara, Eileen. "Truth and Ethics in Writing."
     The Writers Writing for a Living Lecture.
     Wellesley College Writing Program, Wellesley,
     MA. 10 Feb. 1999.
```

Portable Database Sources   Material obtained from a portable database, such as a CD-ROM, magnetic tape, or diskette, is treated like print material, but with one important difference: You must specify the physical form of the source. This information comes after the underlined title of the source, and before the city of publication.

```
Database of African-American Poetry, 1760-1900.
     CD-ROM. Alexandria, VA: Chadwyck-Healy, 1995.
```

Gates, Henry Louis, and Kwame Anthony Appiah, eds.

Encarta Africana. CD-ROM. Redmond, WA:

Microsoft, 1999.

If the database is periodically published and updated, then some additional information is required. You must include the original date of publication of the material you're using, as well as the date of publication for the database. And if the source of the information is not also the distributor (the MLA publishes the CD-ROM version of the MLA International Bibliography, for example, but SilverPlatter distributes it), you must include the distributor's (or vendor's) name as well.

Odygaard, Floyd D. P. "California's Collodion

Artist: The Images of William Dunniway."

Military Images 1995 16.5: 14–19.

America: History and Life on Disc. CD-ROM.

ABC-Clio. Winter 1997–98.

Online Sources Online sources are treated like books and articles, with four major (and many minor) exceptions:

- The **Internet address,** or URL (uniform resource locator), of the source is given in angle brackets at the end of the entry.
- The **date accessed**—the date on which *you* found the source—is included in the citation.
- **Page numbers** are included in the citation *only* if the source is paginated. (This is often the case with full-text online versions of books and journal articles, in which case the pagination follows that of the print source.)
- Sometime paragraphs are numbered; the citation gives **paragraph numbers** when the sources provide them.

    The basic format for an online source is the same as that of a print source, given in the following order:

- Author
- Title
- Publication information (including date of original publication, if applicable)

- Page or paragraph numbers if available.

Additional information—as much as is applicable and available—is then given in the following order:

- Name of database, project, periodical, or site (underlined)
- Number of volume, issue, or version
- Date on which document was published in electronic source
- Name of site sponsor (if applicable)
- Date *you* consulted the material
- Internet address (or URL) in angle brackets. *Note:* The MLA suggests giving the address of the site's search page *instead of the URL* if the URL is very long and would be difficult to transcribe.

Again, keep in mind that one purpose of documentation is to enable your readers to retrace your steps. It may also be useful to keep in mind that like the Internet itself, guidelines for citing electronic sources are continually evolving. Our guidelines are based on the format given in the sixth edition of the *MLA Handbook for Writers of Research Papers* (2003).

Here are some examples:

1. Novel:

Jewett, Sarah Orne. The Country of the Pointed Firs.

1910. Bartleby Archive. Columbia U. 6 Nov.

2005. <http://www.bartleby.com/125/1.html>.

2. Journal article:

Fluck, Winfried. "'The American Romance' and the

Changing Functions of the Imaginary." New

Literary History 27.3 (1996): 415-57.

Project Muse. JHU. 1 Apr. 2006.

<http://muse:jhu.edu:80/journals/

new_literary_history/v27/27.3fluck.html>.

3. Journal article retrieved from database:

Picker, John M. "The Victorian Aura of the Recorded

Voice." New Literary History 32.3

(2001):769-86. JSTOR. 11 Nov. 03 <http://
80-muse.jhu.edu.ezp2.harvard.edu/journals/new_
literary_history/v032/32.3picker.html>.

4. Magazine article (from a print source):

Murphy, K. "Do Food Additives Subtract from
Health?" Business Week 21 Apr. 2006: 140.
LexisNexis. 12 Nov. 2003 http://
80-web.lexisnexis.com.ezp2.harvard.edu/
universe/form/academic/s_guidednews.html

5. Article in online periodical (no print source):

Green, Laura. "Sexual Harassment Law: Relax and Try
to Enjoy It." Salon 3 March 1998. 20 Oct.
2005. <http://archive.salon.com/mwt/feature/
1998/03/cov_03featurea.html>.

6. Review retrieved from a database:

Sadovi, Carlos. "Working Class Hero." Rev. of
Shutter Island, by Dennis Lehane. Chicago
Sun-Times. 25 Apr. 03. LexisNexis. 11 Nov. 05
<http://80-web.lexis-nexis.com.ezp2.
harvard.edu/universe/form/academic/
s_guidednews.html>

7. Article in reference work:

"Chopin, Kate." Encyclopaedia Britannica. 2003.
Encyclopaedia Britannica Online. 11 Nov. 2003
<http://www.search.eb.com/eb/article?eu=84515>.

Reuben, Paul P. "Chapter 6: Late Nineteenth Century

1890-1910--Kate Chopin (1851-1904)." <u>PAL:</u>

<u>Perspectives in American Literature--</u>

<u>A Research and Reference Guide</u>. 20 March 2006.

<http://www.csustan.edu/english/reuben/pal/cha

p6/chopin.html>.

8. Personal Web site:

Mendelsson, Jonathan. Homepage. 8 Jan. 1999.

<http://www.mit.edu./~jrmendel/index.html>.

9. E-mail:

Clineff, Kimberly. "Re: Margaret Mead's pho-

tographs." E-mail to author. 4 May 2003.

10. Posting to a discussion list:

Searls, Damion. "Re: Fiction Inspired by Woolf."

VWOOL@Flists.acs.ohio-state.edu. Online post-

ing. 30 Oct. 1998.

Although we have covered the most common sources, it is entirely possible that you will come across a source that does not fit any of the categories that we have discussed. For several hundred pages of explanation of these matters, covering the proper way to cite all sorts of troublesome sources, see Joseph Gibaldi, *MLA Handbook for Writers of Research Papers,* 6th ed. (New York: Modern Language Association of America, 2003).

Note: On pages 203–217 we reprint a student's research essay in MLA format.

APA Format

The MLA style is used chiefly by writers in the humanities. Writers in the social sciences and in business, education, and psychology commonly use a style developed by the American Psychological Association.

In the following pages we give the chief principles of the APA style, but for full details the reader should consult the fifth edition of the *Publication Manual of the American Psychological Association* (2001).

A paper using the format prescribed by the American Psychological Association will contain brief parenthetical citations within the text and will end with a page headed "References," which lists all of the author's sources. This list of sources begins on a separate page, continuing the pagination of the last page of the essay itself. Thus, if the text of the essay ends on page 8, the first page of references is page 9.

Here are some general guidelines for formatting both the citations within the text and the list of references at the end of the essay.

Citations Within the Text

The APA style emphasizes the date of publication; the date appears not only in the list of references at the end of the paper but also within the paper itself, when you give a brief parenthetic citation of a source that you have quoted or summarized or in any other way used. Here is an example:

```
Statistics for church attendance are highly unreli-

able (Catherton, 1991, p. 17).
```

Note that unlike the MLA, the APA uses commas to separate elements inside the parenthetic citation, and that a "p." precedes the page number. The parenthetic citation may appear at the end of the sentence, or after the clause that contains the references, or after the author's name—whichever placement makes things clearest for the reader. In the example below, the date of publication appears immediately after the author's name; the page reference is given at the end of the sentence:

```
According to Catherton (1991), statistics for church

attendance are highly unreliable (p. 17).
```

The title of Catherton's book or article will be given in the list entitled References. By turning to the list, the reader will learn in what publication Catherton made this point.

A Summary of an Entire Work

```
Catherton (1991) concluded the opposite.
```

    or

```
Similar views are easily found (Catherton, 1991;

Brinnin and Abse, 1992).
```

A Reference to a Page or Pages

```
Catherton (1991, p. 107) argues that "church attendance

is increasing but religious faith is decreasing."
```

A Reference to an Author Represented by More Than One Work Published in a Given Year in the References

As we explain in discussing the form of the material in references, if you list two or more works that an author published in the same year, the works are listed in alphabetic order, by the first letter of the title. The first work is labeled *a*, the second *b*, and so on. Here is a reference to the second work that Catherton published in 1997:

```
Boston is "a typical large Northern city" so far as

church attendance goes (Catherton, 1997b).
```

The List of References
Form on the Page

1. Begin each entry flush with the left margin, but if an entry runs to more than one line, indent five spaces for each succeeding line of the entry.
2. Double-space each entry, and double-space between entries.

Alphabetic Order

1. Arrange the list **alphabetically by author.**

2. Give the **author's last name first,** then the initial *only* of the first and of the middle name (if any).

3. If there is more than one author: Name all of the authors, again inverting the name (last name first) and giving only initials for first and middle names. (But do not invert the editor's name when the entry begins with the name of an author who has written an article in an edited book. See the example on page 328, illustrating a work in a collection of essays.) When there are two or more authors, use an ampersand (&) before the name of the last author. When there are more than six authors, the seventh and all additional authors are indicated with "et al." Here is an example of an article in the seventh volume of a journal called *Journal of Experimental Social Psychology:*

Berscheid, E., Hatfield, E., & Bohrnstett, G.

(1971). Physical attractiveness and dating

choice: A test of the matching hypothesis.

Journal of Experimental Social Psychology 7,

173–89.

4. If there is more than one work by an author: List the works in the order of publication, the earliest first. If two works by an author were published in the same year, give them in alphabetic order by the first letter of the title, disregarding *A*, *An*, or *The*, and their foreign equivalents. Designate the first work as "a," the second as "b." Repeat the author's name at the start of each entry.

If the author of a work or works is also the coauthor of other works listed, list the single-author entries first, arranged by date. Following these, list the multiple-author entries, in a sequence determined alphabetically by the second author's name. Thus, in the example below, notice that the works Bem wrote unassisted are listed first, arranged by date, and when two works appear in the same year they are arranged alphabetically by title. These single-author works are followed by the multiple-author works, with the work written with Lenney preceding the work written with Martyna and Watson.

Bem, S. L. (1974). The measurement of psychological

androgyny. Journal of Consulting and Clinical

Psychology, 42, 155–62.

Bem, S. L. (1981a). The BSRI and gender schema the-

ory: A reply to Spence and Helmreich.

Psychological Review, 88, 369–71.

Bem, S. L. (1981b). Gender schema theory: A cogni-

tive account of sex typing. Psychological

Review, 88, 354–64.

Bem, S. L., & Lenney, E. (1976). Sex-typing and the

avoidance of cross-sex behavior. Journal of

Personality and Social Psychology, 33, 48–54.

Bem, S. L., Martyna, W., & Watson, C. (1976). Sex-
   typing and androgyny: Further exploration of
   the expressive domain. Journal of Personality
   and Social Psychology, 34, 1016-23.

Form of Title

1. In references to books, capitalize only the first letter of the first word of the title (and of the subtitle, if any) and capitalize proper nouns. Italicize the complete title and type a period after it.

2. In references to articles in periodicals or in edited books, capitalize only the first letter of the first word of the article's title (and subtitle, if any), and all proper nouns. Do not put the title within quotation marks. Type a period after the title of the article. For the title of the journal, and the volume and page numbers, see the next instruction.

3. In references to periodicals, capitalize all important words, as you would usually do. (Note that the rule for the titles of periodicals differs from the rule for books and articles.) Give the volume number in arabic numerals, and underline it. Do *not* use *vol.* before the number, and do not use *p.* or *pp.* before the page numbers.

Sample References
A Book by One Author

Lancaster, R. M. (2003). The trouble with nature:
   Sex in science and popular culture. Berkeley:
   University of California Press.

A Book by More Than One Author

Spence, J. T., & Helmreich, R. L. (1978).
   Masculinity and femininity. Austin: University
   of Texas Press.

A Collection of Essays

Bhabha, H. K. (Ed.). (1990). Nation and narration.
   London: Routledge.

A Work in a Collection of Essays

Rogers, B. (1985). The Atlantic alliance. In W. P.

    Bundy (Ed.). <u>The nuclear controversy</u> (pp.

    41-52). New York: New American Library.

Government Documents If the writer is not known, treat the government and the agency as the author. Most federal documents are issued by the Government Printing Office in Washington.

U.S. Congress. Office of Technology Assessment

    (1984). <u>Computerized manufacturing automation:</u>

    <u>Employment, education, and the workplace.</u>

    Washington, DC: U.S. Government Printing

    Office.

An Article in a Journal That Paginates Each Issue Separately

Swinton, E. (1993, Winter). New wine in old casks:

    Sino-Japanese and Russo-Japanese war prints.

    <u>Asian Art</u>, 27-49.

The publication is issued four times a year, each issue containing a page 27. It is necessary, therefore, to tell the reader that this article appears in the winter issue.

An Article in a Journal with Continuous Pagination

Herdt, G. (1991). Representations of homosexuality.

    <u>Journal of the History of Sexuality</u>, 1,

    481-504.

An Article from a Monthly or Weekly Magazine

Chelminsky, R. (2003, April). The Curse of Count

    Dracula. <u>Smithsonian</u>, p. 110.

An Article in a Newspaper

```
Perry, T. (1993, 16 February). Election to give

    Latinos new political clout in San Diego. Los

    Angeles Times, sec. A, p. 3.
```

Note: If no author is given, simply begin with the article title, followed by the date in parentheses.

A Book Review

```
Bayme, S. (1993). Tradition or modernity? [Review

    of Neil Gillman, Sacred fragments: Recovering

    theology for the modern Jew. Judaism, 42,

    106-13.
```

Bayme is the reviewer, not the author of the book. The book under review is called *Sacred fragments: Recovering theology for the modern Jew*, but the review, published in volume 42 of a journal called *Judaism*, had its own title, "Tradition or Modernity?"

Electronic Sources References to electronic sources generally follow the format for printed sources and include the following information:

- Author
- Year of publication (in parentheses)
- Title (and edition, if applicable)

The retrieval statement is given next. This includes the following:

- Date retrieved
- Name and/or the address of the source

(Note that the period does *not* come at the end of an Internet address.)

The examples below follow guidelines set forth in the fifth edition of the *Publication Manual of the American Psychological Association* (2001).

1. Professional or government site:

Edlefsen, M., & Brewer, M. S. (no date).

Nitrates/nitrites. Retrieved April 16, 2006,

from The National Food Safety Database:

http://www.foodsafety.org/il/il089.htm

National Cancer Institute (1996, June). NCI fact

sheet. Food additives. Retrieved April 20,

2006, from http://nisc8a.upenn.edu/pdg_html/

6/eng/600037.html

2. Encyclopedia article:

Muckraker (journ.). (1994-1998). In Britannica

Online. Retrieved January 2, 2005, from

http://www.eb.com:180cgibin/g?DocF=index/

mu/ckr.html

3. Newspaper article:

Legator, M., & Daniel, A. (1995). Reproductive

systems can be harmed by toxic exposure.

Galveston County Daily News. Retrieved

April 20, 2006, from http://www.utmb.

edu/toxics/newsp.htm#canen

Warrick, P. (1994, June 8). A frank discussion.

Los Angeles Times, E1. Retrieved

April 20, 2006, from LexisNexis.

4. Journal article:

Tollefson, C. (1995, May 29). Stability preserved;

preservatives; food additives '95. Chemical

Marketing Reporter 247(22) SR28. Retrieved

April 22, 2006, from LexisNexis.

5. Book:

Riis, J. (1890). How the other half lives. New

York: Charles Scribner's Sons [Electronic

Version]. David Phillips. Retrieved September

14, 2005, from http://www.cis.edu/amstud/

inforev/riis/ch#3/html

A Note on Other Systems of Documentation

The MLA style is commonly used in the humanities, and the APA style is commonly used in the social sciences. The documentation system detailed in *The Chicago Manual of Style*, 15th edition (Chicago University of Chicago Press, 2003) is used by some social scientists and by many historians. But many other disciplines use their own styles. The following handbooks discuss the systems used in some other disciplines.

Biology and Other Sciences

Council of Biology Editors, Style Manual Committee. *Scientific Style and Format: CBE Style Manual for Authors, Editors, and Publishers in the Biological Sciences.* 6th ed. New York: Cambridge University Press, 1994.

Style Manual Committee, Council of Science Editors *The CSE Manual for Authors, Editors, and Publishers.* 7th ed. New York: Cambridge University Press, 2006.

Chemistry

American Chemical Society. *ACS Style Guide: A Manual for Authors and Editors.* 2nd ed. Washington, DC: American Chemical Society, 1997.

Geology

U.S. Geological Survey. *Suggestions to Authors of the Reports of the United States Geological Survey.* 8th ed. Washington, DC: GPO, Department of the Interior, 1997.

Law

The Bluebook: A Uniform System of Citation. 18th ed. Cambridge, MA: Harvard Law Review Association, 2005.

Medicine

American Medical Association. *Manual of Style.* 9th ed. Acton, MA: Publishing Sciences Group, 1997.

Physics

American Institute of Physics. *Style Manual for Guidance in the Preparation of Papers.* 4th ed. New York: American Institute of Physics, 1990–1997.

CHAPTER FIFTEEN

PREPARING THE MANUSCRIPT

> I love being a writer. What I can't stand is
> the paperwork.
>
> —*Peter De Vries*

Basic Manuscript Form

When you submit a piece of writing to your instructor or to anyone else, make sure it looks good. You want to convey the impression that you care about what you've written, that you've invested yourself and your time in it, that the details matter to you.

Much of what follows is ordinary academic procedure. Unless your instructor specifies something different, you can adopt these principles as a guide.

1. Print your essay on $8\frac{1}{2}$-by-11-inch paper of good weight. Use fresh, plain white paper; don't use the reverse sides of an old draft or lab report; avoid fancy or colored paper.

2. Make sure that the printer has enough ink and that the print is dark and clear. One sure way to irritate your instructor is to turn in an essay with nearly invisible print.

3. Do not use a fancy font. Unless your instructor specifies something else, stick to Times or Courier. And use a reasonable point size: Generally a twelve-point font will do.

4. Print your essay on one side of the paper only. If for some reason you have occasion to submit a handwritten copy, use lined paper and write on every other line in black or dark blue ink.

5. Set the line spacing at "double." The essay (even the heading—see item 6 below) should be double-spaced—not single-spaced, not triple-spaced.

6. In the upper left-hand corner, one inch from the top, put your name, your instructor's name, the course number, and the date. Put your last name before the page number (in the upper right-hand corner) of each subsequent page, so the instructor can easily reassemble your essay if somehow a page gets detached and mixed with other papers.

7. Titles. Use this form for your title: Hit the "enter" (or "return") key *once* after the date and then center the title of your essay. We give instructions for punctuating titles in Chapter 12, but we'll reiterate the most important points here. Capitalize the first letter of the first and last words of your title, the first word after a semicolon or colon if you use either one, and the first letter of all the other words except articles, conjunctions, and prepositions, thus:

`Two Kinds of Symbols in `To Kill a Mockingbird

Notice that your own title is neither underlined nor enclosed in quotation marks. (If, as here, your title includes material that would normally be italicized or in quotation marks, that material continues to be so written.) If the title runs more than one line, double-space between the lines.

8. Begin the essay just below the title. (Again, you'll hit "enter" or "return" only once.) If your instructor prefers a title page, begin the essay on the next page and number it 1. The title page is not numbered.

9. Margins. Except for page numbers, which should appear one-half inch from the top of the page, leave a one-inch margin at top, bottom, and sides of text.

10. Number the pages consecutively, using arabic numerals in the upper right-hand corner, half an inch from the top. Do not put a period or a hyphen after the numeral, and do not precede the numeral with "page" or "p." (Again, if you give the title on a separate sheet, the page that follows it is page 1. Do not number the title page.)

11. Paragraphs. Indent the first word of each paragraph five spaces from the left margin.

12. Proofreading. Check for typographical errors, and check spelling. Use your word processor's spell-check program—but don't rely on it exclusively. This program will flag words that are not in its dictionary and offer suggestions for correcting mistakes. (A misspelled word is of course not in the dictionary and thus flagged.) But a word flagged is not necessarily misspelled; it may simply not be in the program's dictionary. Proper names, for example, regularly get flagged. Keep in mind also that most programs cannot distinguish between homophones (*to, too, two; there, their; alter, altar*), nor can they tell you that you should have written *accept* instead of *except*.

13. Print a copy of your essay for yourself and keep it until the original has been returned. It is a good idea to keep notes and drafts too. They may prove helpful if you are asked to revise a page, substantiate a point, or supply a source you omitted.

14. Fasten the pages of your paper with a paper clip in the upper left-hand corner. Stiff binders are unnecessary; indeed, they are a nuisance to the instructor, adding bulk and making it awkward to write annotations.

1"

Your Name

Your Instructor's Name — *Font is Courier*

Double space

Writing 127

April 1, 2006

— Capitalize main words in title

Formatting Your Essays: The Right

Center title

Way to Do It

Print your essay on 8 1/2-by-11-inch paper of good weight, and make sure that the printer has enough ink and that the print is dark and clear. Do not use a fancy font. Unless your instructor specifies something else, stick to Times or Courier. And use a reasonable point size: generally a 12-point font will do. The essay (even the heading) should be double-spaced--not single-spaced, not triple-spaced--and it should be printed on one side of the paper only.

5 spaces, or tab

In the upper left-hand corner, one inch from the top, put your name, your instructor's name, the course number, and the date, all on separate lines. Put your last name before the page number (in the upper right-hand corner) of

←— 1" —→

each subsequent page, so the instructor can easily reassemble your essay if somehow a page gets detached and mixed with other papers. Hit the "enter" (or "return") key once after the date and then center the title of your essay. Capitalize the first letter of the first and last words of your title, the first word after a semicolon or colon if you use either one, and

1"

the first letter of all the other words except articles, conjunctions, and prepositions. Notice that your own title is neither underlined nor enclosed in quotation marks. If the title runs more than one line, double-space between the lines. Begin the essay just below the title. (Again, you'll hit "enter" or "return" only once.) If your instructor prefers a title page, begin the essay on the next page and number it 1.

Except for page numbers, which should appear one-half inch from the top of the page, leave a one-inch margin at top, bottom, and sides of text. Number the pages consecutively, using arabic numerals in the upper right-hand corner, half an inch from the top. Do not put a period or a hyphen after the numeral, and do not precede the numeral with "page" or "p."

Indent the first word of each paragraph five spaces from the left margin.

Fasten the pages of your paper with a paper clip in the upper left-hand corner. Stiff binders are unnecessary; indeed, they are a nuisance because they add bulk and make essays difficult to annotate. Spell-check your essay and proofread it carefully; make a copy for yourself, and then turn the essay in.

Using Quotations (and Punctuating Them Correctly)

If you are writing about a text, or about an interview, quotations from your material or subject are indispensable. They not only let your readers know what you are talking about, they give your readers the material you are responding to, thus letting them share your responses. But quote sparingly and quote briefly. Use quotations as evidence, not as padding. If the exact wording of the original is crucial, or especially effective, quote it directly, but if it is not, don't bore the reader with material that can be effectively reduced either by summarizing or by cutting. And make sure, by a comment before or after a quotation, that your reader understands why you find the quotation relevant. Don't count on a quotation to make your point for you.

Here are some additional matters to keep in mind, especially as you revise.

1. Identify the speaker or writer of the quotation. Usually this identification precedes the quoted material (e.g., "Smith says . . .") in accordance with the principle of letting readers know where they are going. But occasionally it may follow the quotation, especially if the name will provide a meaningful surprise. For example, in a discussion of a proposed tax reform, you might quote a remark hostile to it and then reveal that the author of the proposal was also the author of the remark.

2. When you introduce a quotation, consider using verbs other than "says." Depending on the context—that is, on the substance of the quotation and its place in your essay—it might be more accurate to say Smith "argues," "adds," "contends," "points out," "admits," or "comments." Or, again with just the right verb, you might introduce the quotation with a transitional phrase: "In another context Smith had observed that . . ." or "To clarify this point Smith refers to . . . ?" or "In an apparent contradiction Smith suggests. . . ." But avoid such inflated words as "opines," "avers," and "is of the opinion that." The point is not to add "elegant variation" (see page 105) to your introduction of someone else's words, but accuracy and grace. A verb often used *in*accurately is "feels." Ralph Smith does not "feel" that "the term *primitive art* has come to be used with at least three distinct meanings." He "points out," "writes," "observes," or "says."

3. Distinguish between short and long quotations and treat each appropriately. Enclose *short quotations*, four (or fewer) lines of typing, within quotation marks:

```
Anne Lindbergh calls the harrowing period of the
kidnapping and murder of her first child the "hour
of lead." "Flying," she wrote, "was freedom and
beauty and escape from crowds."
```

Set off *long quotations* (more than four lines of typing). Do *not* enclose them within quotation marks. To set off a quotation, begin a new line, indent ten spaces from the left margin, and type the quotation double-spaced:

```
The last paragraphs of Five Years of My Life contain

Dreyfus's words when he was finally freed:

          The Government of the Republic gives me

          back my liberty. It is nothing to me with-

          out honor. Beginning with today, I shall

          unremittingly strive for the reparation of

          the frightful judicial error of which I

          am still the victim. I want all France

          to know by a final judgment that I am

          innocent.

But he was never to receive that judgment.
```

Note that long quotations are usually introduced by a sentence ending with a colon (as in the above example) or by an introductory phrase, such as "Dreyfus wrote."

4. Don't try to introduce a long quotation into the middle of one of your own sentences. It is too difficult for the reader to come out of the quotation and to pick up your thread. Instead, introduce the quotation, as we did above, set the quotation off, and then begin a new sentence of your own.

5. An embedded quotation (that is, a quotation embedded into a sentence of your own) must fit grammatically into the sentence of which it is a part. For example, suppose you want to use Othello's line "I have done the state some service."

Incorrect

Near the end of the play Othello says that he "have done the state some service."

Correct

Near the end of the play Othello says that he has "done the state some service."

Correct

Near the end of the play, Othello says, "I have done the state some service."

6. Quote exactly. Check your quotation for accuracy at least twice. If you need to edit a quotation—for example, in order to embed it grammatically, or to inform your reader of a relevant point—observe the following rules:

- Enclose any words that you add or substitute in square brackets—not parentheses.

  "In the summer of 1816 we [Mary Wollstonecraft and Percy Bysshe Shelley] visited Switzerland and became the neighbors of Lord Byron."

  Trotsky became aware that "Stalin would not hesitate a moment to organize an attempt on [his] life."

- Indicate the omission of material with ellipses (three periods, with a space between periods and before and after each period).

  The New York Times called it "the most intensive man-hunt . . . in the country's history."

- If your sentence ends with the omission of the last part of the original sentence, use four periods: one immediately after the last word quoted, and three (spaced) to indicate the omission.

```
The manual says, "If your sentence ends with the

omission of the last part of the original sen-

tence, use four spaced periods. . . ."
```

Notice that if you begin the quotation with the beginning of a sentence (in the example we have just given "If your" is the beginning of a quoted sentence), you do *not* indicate that material preceded the words you are quoting. Similarly, if you end your quotation with the end of the quoted sentence, you give only a single period, not an ellipsis, although of course the material from which you are quoting may have gone on for many more sentences. But if you begin quoting from the middle of a sentence, or end quoting before you reach the end of a sentence in your source, it is customary to indicate the omissions. But even such omissions need not be indicated when the quoted material is obviously incomplete—when, for instance, it is a word or phrase.

7. Use punctuation accurately. There are three important rules to observe:

- Commas and periods go inside the quotation marks:

```
"The land," Nick Thompson observes, "looks after

us."
```

- Semicolons and colons go outside quotation marks:

```
He turned and said, "Learn the names of all these

places"; it sounded like an order.
```

- Question marks, exclamation points, and dashes go inside if they are part of the quotation, outside if they are your own.

```
Amanda ironically says to her daughter, "How old

are you, Laura?"
```

(The question mark is part of the quotation and therefore goes inside the quotation marks.)

```
Did you really tell your brother "no"?
```

8. Use single quotation marks for a quotation within a quotation.

```
The student told the interviewer, "I ran back to the

dorm and I called my boyfriend and I said, 'Listen,

this is just incredible,' and I told him all about

it."
```

9. Enclose titles of short works in quotation marks. Short works include chapters in books, short stories, essays, short poems, songs, lectures, speeches, and unpublished works (even if long).

Underline, or use italic type, for titles of long works. Underline (or italicize) titles of published book-length works: novels, plays, periodicals, collections of essays, anthologies, pamphlets, textbooks, and long poems (such as *Paradise Lost*). Underline (or italicize) also titles of films, compact discs, television programs, ballets, operas, works of art, and the names of planes, ships, and trains. As we note on page 261, the MLA recommends using underlining rather than italics in manuscripts submitted for evaluation or publication because underlining is usually easier to see.

Exception: Titles of sacred works (for example, the New Testament, the Hebrew Bible, Genesis, Acts, the Gospels, the Koran) are neither underlined nor enclosed within quotation marks. To cite a book of the Bible with chapter and verse, give the name of the book, then a space, then an arabic numeral for the chapter, a period, and an arabic numeral (*not* preceded by a space) for the verse, thus: Exodus 20.14–15. Standard abbreviations for the books of the Bible (for example, Chron.) are permissible in footnotes and in parenthetic citations within the text.

10. Use quotation marks to identify a word or term to which you wish to call special attention. (But italics, indicated by underlining, may be used instead of quotation marks.)

```
By "comedy" I mean not only a funny play, but any

play that ends happily.
```

11. Do not use quotation marks to enclose slang or a term that you fear is too casual. Use the term or don't use it, but don't apologize by putting it in quotation marks, as in these examples.

Incorrect
```
Because of "red tape" it took three years.
```

Incorrect

```
At last I was able to "put in my two cents."
```

In both sentences the writers are signaling their uneasiness; in neither is there any cause for uneasiness.

12. Do not use quotation marks to convey sarcasm. The following sentence should be rewritten:

```
These "politicians" are nothing but thieves.
```

Sarcasm, usually a poor form of argument, is best avoided. But of course there are borderline cases when you may want to convey your dissatisfaction with a word used by others.

```
African sculpture has a long continuous tradition,

but this tradition has been jeopardized by the

introduction of "civilization" to Africa.
```

Perhaps the quotation marks here are acceptable, because the writer's distaste has not yet become a sneer and because she is, in effect, quoting. But it is probably better to change "civilization" to "western culture," omitting the quotation marks.

13. Do not enclose the title of your own essay in quotation marks, and do not underline or italicize it.

Corrections in the Final Copy

Extensive revisions should have been made in your drafts, but minor last-minute revisions may be made on the finished copy. Proofreading may catch some typographical errors, and you may notice some small weaknesses.

Read the words in the three triangles.

If you did not find an error in each triangle, look again.

When you proofread your manuscript, you can make corrections with the following proofreading symbols, but of course it is preferable to print a corrected page if possible.

1. *Changes* in wording may be made by crossing through words and rewriting just above them, either on the typewriter or by hand in pen:

```
When I first moved to the United States at the age
                          no
of nine, I had few doubts as to my identity.
```

2. *Additions* should be made above the line, with a caret (^) below the line at the appropriate place:

```
When I first moved to the United States at the
       of
age nine, I had no doubts as to my identity.
   ^
```

3. *Transpositions* of letters may be made thus:

```
When I frist moved to the United States at the age
of nine, I had no doubts as to my identity.
```

4. *Deletions* are indicated by a horizontal line through the word or words to be deleted. Delete a single letter by drawing a vertical or diagonal line through it.

```
When I first moved to the United States at at the
age of nine, I had no doubts as to my identity.
```

5. *Separation* of words accidentally run together is indicated by a vertical line, *closure* by a curved line connecting the things to be closed up.

```
When I first moved to the United States at the age of
nine, I had no dou bts as to my identity.
```

6. *Paragraphing* may be indicated by the paragraph symbol before the word that is to begin the new paragraph.

```
When I first moved to the United States at the age
of nine, I had no doubts as to my identity. ¶Within a
year, however, . . .
```

Last Words

A rich patron once gave money to the painter Chu Ta, asking him to paint a picture of a fish. Three years later, when he still had not received the painting the patron went to Chu Ta's house to ask why the picture was not done. Chu Ta did not answer, but dipped a brush in ink and with a few strokes drew a splendid fish. "If it is so easy," asked the patron, "why didn't you give me the picture three years ago?" Again Chu Ta did not answer. Instead, he opened the door of a large cabinet. Thousands of pictures of fish tumbled out.

Credits

Index

Additional Titles of Interest

Allison, *Bastard Out of Carolina*

Alvarez, *How the Garcia Girls Lost Their Accents*

Augustine, *The Confessions of St. Augustine*

Austen, *Persuasion*

Austen, *Pride and Prejudice*

Austen, *Sense and Sensibility*

Bloom, *Shakespeare: The Invention of the Human*

C. Brontë, *Jane Eyre*

E. Brontë, *Wuthering Heights*

Burke, *Reflections on the Revolution in France*

Cather, *My Ántonia*

Cather, *O Pioneers!*

Cellini, *The Autobiography of Benvenuto Cellini*

Chapman, *Black Voices*

Chesnutt, *The Marrow of Tradition*

Chopin, *The Awakening and Selected Stories*

Conrad, *Heart of Darkness*

Conrad, *Nostromo*

Coraghessan-Boyle, *The Tortilla Curtain*

Defoe, *Robinson Crusoe*

Descartes, *Discourse on Method and The Meditations*

Descartes, *Meditations and Other Metaphysical Writings*

de Tocqueville, *Democracy in America*

Dickens, *Hard Times*

Douglass, *Narrative of the Life of Frederick Douglass*

Dubois, *The Souls of Black Folk*

Equiano, *The Interesting Narrative and Other Writings*

Gore, *Earth in the Balance*

Grossman, *Electronic Republic*

Hawthorne, *The Scarlet Letter*

Hutner, *Immigrant Voices*

Jacobs, *Incidents in the Life of a Slave Girl*

Jen, *Typical American*

M. L. King Jr., *Why We Can't Wait*

Lewis, *Babbitt*

Machiavelli, *The Prince*

Marx, *The Communist Manifesto*

Mill, *On Liberty*

More, *Utopia and Other Essential Writings*

Orwell, *1984*

Paine, *Common Sense*

Plato, *The Republic*

Postman, *Amusing Ourselves to Death*

Rose, *Lives on the Boundary*

Rossiter, *The Federalist Papers*

Rousseau, *The Social Contract*

Shelley, *Frankenstein*

Sinclair, *The Jungle*

Steinbeck, *Of Mice and Men*

Stevenson, *The Strange Case of Dr. Jekyll and Mr. Hyde*

Stoker, *Dracula*

Stowe, *Uncle Tom's Cabin*

Swift, *Gulliver's Travels*

Taulbert, *Once Upon a Time When We Were Colored*

Thoreau, *Walden*

Truth, *The Narrative of Sojourner Truth*

Woolf, *Jacob's Room*

Zola, *Germinal*